THE MYTH OF PRESIDENTIAL REPRESENTATION

In *The Myth of Presidential Representation*, B. Dan Wood evaluates the nature of American presidential representation, examining the strongly embedded belief – held by the country's founders, as well as current American political culture and social science theory – that presidents should represent the community at large. Citizens expect presidents to reflect prevailing public sentiment and compromise in the national interest. Social scientists express these same ideas through theoretical models depicting presidential behavior as driven by centrism and issue stances adhering to the median voter. Yet partisanship seems to be a dominant theme of modern American politics.

Do American presidents adhere to a centrist model of representation, as envisioned by the founders? Or do presidents typically attempt to lead the public toward their own more partisan positions? If so, how successful are they? What are the consequences of centrist versus partisan presidential representation? *The Myth of Presidential Representation* addresses these questions both theoretically and empirically.

B. Dan Wood holds the Cornerstone Fellowship at Texas A&M University. He is the author of *The Politics of Economic Leadership: The Causes and Consequences of Presidential Rhetoric* (2007) and the coauthor of *Bureaucratic Dynamics: The Role of Bureaucracy in a Democracy* (1994), as well as numerous scholarly articles. Professor Wood has served on the editorial boards of the *American Journal of Political Science, Presidential Studies Quarterly, Political Analysis, Political Research Quarterly,* and *American Politics Quarterly* and is a frequent instructor at the European Consortium for Political Research summer methods program at the University of Essex.

To Patricia

The Myth of Presidential Representation

B. Dan Wood

Texas A&M University

CAMBRIDGE
UNIVERSITY PRESS

CAMBRIDGE UNIVERSITY PRESS
Cambridge, New York, Melbourne, Madrid, Cape Town, Singapore, São Paulo, Delhi

Cambridge University Press
32 Avenue of the Americas, New York, NY 10013-2473, USA

www.cambridge.org
Information on this title: www.cambridge.org/9780521133425

First published 2009

Printed in the United States of America

A catalog record for this publication is available from the British Library.

Library of Congress Cataloging in Publication data

Wood, B. Dan.
The myth of presidential representation / B. Dan Wood.
    p.   cm.
Includes bibliographical references and index.
ISBN 978-0-521-11658-9 (hardback) – ISBN 978-0-521-13342-5 (pbk.)
1. Presidents – United States.   2. Representative government and representation –
United States.   3. Political parties – United States.   4. United States – Politics and
government.   I. Title.
JK516.W66   2009
352.2301 – dc22   2009007321

ISBN   978-0-521-11658-9 hardback
ISBN   978-0-521-13342-5 paperback

Contents

Figures and Tables

TABLES

Preface

This book evaluates the nature of modern presidential representation. Presidents since George Washington have often expressed the view that they represent the community at large. Consider, for example, the following remarks by Washington in a letter to the Selectmen of Boston on July 28, 1795: "In every act of my administration, I have sought the happiness of my fellow citizens. My system for the attainment of this object has uniformly been to overlook all personal, local, and partial considerations; to contemplate the United States as one great whole..." (Fitzpatrick 1931). In this letter Washington rejected a role for personal values, local interests, and partisanship in determining presidential behavior and actions. Rather, he believed that presidents should reject these tendencies to reflect the nation as "one great whole."

Modern presidents have commonly expressed similar beliefs about the nature of presidential representation, especially during election seasons and early in their administrations. However, consider the following excerpt from an oral history interview with George W. Bush on November 12, 2008: "I would like to be... remembered as a person who, first and foremost, did not sell his soul in order to accommodate the political process. I came to Washington with a set of values, and I'm leaving with the same set of values. And I darn sure wasn't going to sacrifice those values..." (Koch 2008). In this statement Bush tacitly admitted that his personal values and partisanship drove many of his decisions as president. If this assessment is true for all modern presidents, then we have moved a great distance from George Washington and the founders' vision of presidential representation.

The founders' vision that presidents should represent the community at large is manifest in notes from the constitutional convention, the Federalist Papers, as well as the original institutional design of the presidency. A belief in nonpartisan, centrist presidential representation is also strongly embedded in American political culture and social science theory. Citizens expect presidents to be willing to compromise in the national interest and to respond to public sentiment. Social scientists express these same ideas through theoretical models depicting presidential behavior as driven by centrism and issue stances adhering to the median voter.

Yet little social science research evaluates the validity of these beliefs and theories. Do modern presidents adhere to a centrist model of representation such as the model reflected in Washington's remarks? Or do they primarily represent their own partisan values, as might be suggested by Bush's remarks? Do presidents change their mode of representation while in office, sometimes following a centrist model and at other times a partisan model? If so, under what conditions are presidents centrists versus partisans? Do presidents attempt to lead the public toward their own partisan positions through persuasion? If so, then how successful are they at leading the public toward their own partisan positions? What factors enhance or diminish presidential efforts at partisan persuasion? What are the consequences for presidential support of partisan representation or failed persuasion?

This book addresses all of these research questions, both theoretically and empirically. The centrist model has been the primary paradigm for social scientists seeking to explain electoral representation in the American system. However, this book develops and tests an alternative theoretical model of presidential representation, which posits that presidents respond to the median partisan, rather than the median voter. The theoretical model is developed formally in Chapter 2. Measures of presidential and public liberalism for testing the partisan versus centrist models are described in Chapter 3. The presidential liberalism measure is constructed by coding every unique liberal and conservative sentence spoken publicly by the president across nine issue domains from World War II through the first George W. Bush administration. The partisan model of presidential representation is then evaluated empirically in Chapters 4 through 6.

The "take away" themes from this book are the following: (1) Modern presidents typically behave as partisan rather than centrist representatives. (2) As partisans, modern presidents have consistently adopted a strategy of attempting to persuade those near the political center toward their own positions, rather than altering their own positions toward the median voter. (3) Presidents have not been very successful at partisan persuasion but are more successful during honeymoon periods, periods of high public approval, periods when they have strong institutional allies, and periods when the proportion of persuadable citizens is high. (4) Presidents are punished by the public for their partisanship through declining policy support and lower approval ratings. (5) Nevertheless, presidents are likely to remain partisan representatives due to self-interest and the nature of the two-party electoral system.

This research reported in this book was initiated in the spring of 2004, with various convention papers delivered in 2006 and 2007. As with any project of this duration, there are many to whom I am indebted. My work has always centered on issues of representation and responsiveness for various political institutions. However, George Edwards, my colleague at Texas A&M, piqued my interest in questions of presidential representation and persuasion. The work of Jim Stimson, my former mentor and friend, sparked my interest in how public opinion affects institutional behavior. Some of my earlier work (Flemming and Wood 1997; Wood and Andersson 1998) confirmed his work with Mike MacKuen and Bob Erikson on Congress and the Supreme Court (Erikson, MacKuen, and Stimson 2002; Stimson, MacKuen, and Erikson 1995). However, I was compelled to question their work on dynamic representation by the presidency. Thanks to Jim Stimson for providing the data on public mood that were used in the third through sixth chapters. Jeff Cohen read and commented on various convention papers that later became chapters in this book. Jeff also read the entire manuscript when it neared completion and made various helpful suggestions. I also thank two anonymous reviewers for their insightful suggestions, most of which are implemented in the final manuscript.

I am also indebted to those who provided research assistance to this project. The data on presidential liberalism were initially machine coded. However, machines are fallible, and considerable human effort was required to ensure valid and reliable measures. The bulk of the human effort was supplied by Han Soo Lee and Sarah Kessler, with work also done by Stephen Huss. Note that some of the findings reported in Chapters 3 and 4 are replicated using different statistical methods in the *Journal of Politics* (Wood and Lee 2009). Han Soo's dissertation potentially extends the work reported here through the inclusion of a measure of media liberalism.

In the interest of future research, I encourage further replication, as well as further application of the data. Thus, all of the data on presidential liberalism reported in the empirical chapters are available on my Web site hosted by Texas A&M University. The Web link is currently http://www-polisci.tamu.edu/bdanwood. A Google search for my name should always find the data.

Ed Parsons of Cambridge University Press offered good advice on how to craft the manuscript. Given my strong methodological leanings, he encouraged me to focus on substance, rather than technical matters that might interest those in the political methodology community. Nevertheless, this book contains both math and statistics to accommodate both social scientific and casual audiences. Where it seemed appropriate, technical materials are relegated to footnotes. Casual readers are encouraged to read explanations in the footnotes, but this should not be necessary to follow the major themes of the book. Where footnotes were not appropriate, discussions involving math or statistics are often accompanied by explanations in plain English. I hope that the materials in this book are not so complex as to deter serious readers. If this is so, then Ed deserves some credit. If not, then I apologize in advance for my shortcomings at communication. Ed was also a pleasure to work with as an editor, especially in securing expert reviewers and facilitating the review and editorial process. Thanks also to Jason Przybylski, who is Ed's Editorial Assistant. Peter Katsirubas of Aptara was the project manager who transformed the manuscript into a book. William H. Stoddard did the actual copyediting.

Financially, the work reported in this book was supported by Texas A&M University through a University Faculty Fellowship from 2002 through 2006 and a Cornerstone Fellowship starting in 2007. I am also deeply appreciative of my department and university for their supportive intellectual environment.

Finally, I want to thank those closest to me for their understanding and support for my career and research. My wife, Patricia, has been steadfast in helping me in every possible way. I dedicate the book to her.

CHAPTER 1

The Nature of Presidential Representation

On August 14, 1795, President George Washington signed the Jay Treaty between the United States and Great Britain. This treaty was intended to resolve various economic and foreign policy disputes that remained between the United States and Britain following the Revolutionary War.

The intensity of popular feeling about the Jay Treaty ran very high. Washington's decision to sign the Jay Treaty followed months of bitter conflict about whether the treaty adequately protected American interests and preserved national honor. Indeed, the debate over the Jay Treaty has long been recognized as an important factor in the development of American political parties. Federalists wanted to settle matters with Britain peacefully and regularize economic and political relations. However, Democratic-Republicans, who had gained control of the House of Representatives in the elections of 1792 and 1794, bitterly opposed the treaty for its alleged deference to British interests, hostility to French interests, and failure to achieve war reparations for southern slave owners.

Popular sentiment ran heavily against the treaty at the time Washington signed it. James Madison, a Democratic-Republican, wrote that Virginians were almost unanimously opposed to the treaty in every "town or county" with the exception of perhaps Alexandria. He also reported that in Boston, Portsmouth, New York, and Philadelphia, there had been unanimous "remonstrances" against the treaty. In Charleston, Boston, New York, and Philadelphia, copies of the treaty had been burned, along with effigies of its negotiator, John Jay. The British flag was dragged through the streets in Charleston. Rioters in

Philadelphia broke the windows of British officials. At a town meeting in New York, Alexander Hamilton, the chief architect of the treaty, attempted to give a speech in support of ratification. However, he was "drowned out by hisses and catcalls, the mood of the audience being so ugly and the sentiment so hostile to Hamilton" that he was pelted by stones (Sharp 1993, 119; see also Beschloss 2007, 1–17; Elkins and McKitrick 1993, 420–21).

Washington received numerous petitions warning that ratification of the treaty would mean the breakup of the union. For example, citizens of Clarke County, Kentucky told him that if he signed the treaty "western America is gone forever – lost to the union." Similar resolutions were also passed in North Carolina. A Virginia newspaper declared that accepting the treaty would initiate a petition to the legislature that it secede from the union (Sharp 1993, 119). The more populist and democratically inclined press extolled opponents of the treaty as representative of the republican spirit of the American people (Sharp 1993, 120).

As commissioner of the treaty, Washington himself was subject to various personal attacks. In Virginia, Revolutionary War veterans toasted "A speedy Death to General Washington!" Newspapers of the time published cartoons of the president being marched to a guillotine for favoring the British over the French. Several columnists alleged that Washington had been secretly bribed by the British (Beschloss 2007, 2). The president was also attacked for "signing Jay's Treaty and thus forming a close union with despotic England; being hostile to France; and condemning the Democratic-Republican societies" and for "conducting his administration upon principles incompatible with the spirit of republicanism and on precedents derived from the corrupt government of England" (Sharp 1993, 126).

In the Senate the treaty had been ratified by the barest of margins along strict partisan lines, receiving 20 Federalist votes and opposed by 10 Democratic-Republicans. Given the narrow margin of passage, strong public opposition, and partisan turmoil, Washington could have compromised with the Democratic-Republicans or pursued further negotiations. However, he chose instead to sign the treaty roughly six weeks after it was approved by the Senate. By signing the treaty, he subjected himself to claims of partisanship, a force that he greatly detested. Indeed, partisanship was initially viewed by Washington,

Jefferson, Hamilton, Madison, and virtually all of the founding fathers as the greatest threat to the new republic.

Washington signed the treaty because of what he perceived as a more immediate threat, the rising potential for a new war with Britain. The British had refused to give up their fortifications in western American territories following the Revolutionary War. There was also evidence that the British were arming and provoking the Indians in western territories to attack American interests. The British were also confiscating American goods shipped to the French West Indies and France after war had broken out between Britain and France in 1793. Indeed, British men-of-war had captured almost 250 American ships allegedly engaged in commerce with France, and many American seamen were impressed into British service (Beschloss 2007, 2–3; Elkins and McKitrick 1993, 388–96; Sharp 1993, 114–15). Most Americans viewed the British actions as an arrogant affront to national pride, and there was growing talk of declaring war against Britain. These provocations made it appear likely to Washington that another war with Britain might be imminent.

Washington had serious reservations about the treaty, but he signed it anyway to prevent a potential war. If a new war with Britain was to come, then Washington wanted the nation to be ready (Beschloss 2007, 31; Sharp 1993, 121). War with Britain at this time would have been disastrous to the fledgling American economy and very divisive to the newly established political system. The nation's economy was still reeling from the indebtedness required to fight the Revolutionary War. The new government had little ability to raise taxes and establish a military such as would be required to remove British fortifications or defend American shipping. American commerce was still dependent on the British and would clearly suffer in a war.

Partisan and sectional rivalries also boded poorly for a new war with Britain. Federalists were supportive of better relations. The mercantile interests of the Northeast were dependent on British commerce and wanted to renew economic ties. However, southern states had less to gain from the treaty, which failed to get compensation for British confiscation of slaves during the Revolutionary War. More generally, southerners and Democratic-Republicans were more supportive of an alliance with the French and viewed the treaty as hostile to their interests. Therefore, it was unclear if there was sufficient political unity for the fledgling nation to pursue a new war with Britain. Given these circumstances and growing partisan tumult across the new nation, Washington deemed it better to sign the treaty, rather than leave things unsettled (Elkins and McKitrick 1993, 424).

Washington wanted to settle these issues peacefully and end the partisan tumult. However, partisan opposition did not cease with Washington's signing of the Jay Treaty. After the signing, some of the more radical opponents began calling for Washington's impeachment (Sharp 1993, 123–27). A series of essays appeared in major newspapers charging the House of Representatives to "save the Constitution and rescue liberty" and attacking the president's conduct of his office (Sharp 1993, 126) However, more moderate members of the Democratic-Republican opposition, such as Jefferson and Madison, urged caution in pursuing impeachment due to "the president's long and faithful service to the republic" (Sharp 1993, 127).

Refusing to give up after the president's signing of the treaty, Democratic-Republicans made a final attempt to block its implementation through the House of Representatives (Sharp 1993, 127–33). The Constitution gives the president the authority to negotiate treaties with the advice and consent of the Senate. However, the treaty required $90,000 to implement various requirements for further arbitration. The power of appropriations originates in the House of Representatives, and both chambers must agree to passage. Democratic-Republicans sought to prevent funding the treaty through the 59–47 majority they held in the House.

If the president and the Federalists were to prevail, then it was obviously necessary to persuade the public and House Democratic-Republicans to support funding. Recognizing this, Washington and the Federalists set about the task of changing public opinion. Washington remained the most highly respected leader in the nation, and his reputation was a powerful weapon in this effort. The Federalists organized petition campaigns to support the treaty by taking advantage of Washington's reputation and raising the specter of war with Britain if the appropriations measure failed. They also raised the Democratic-Republicans' threat to impeach the president against them as an issue to mobilize Washington's popular support.

In a series of 38 essays published nationally under the pseudonym "Camillus," Alexander Hamilton and Rufus King vigorously defended the treaty section by section. Contrary to what was claimed by the Democratic-Republicans, they argued, "the treaty made no improper concessions to Great Britain" (Sharp 1993, 121). They also framed the debate over the treaty as a choice between war and peace.

After a nine-month public relations campaign by Washington and the Federalists, public opinion had swung in the other direction toward support of the treaty. As a democratic representative, Washington had used the presidential power of persuasion to move the public toward his own preferences and those of the Federalists. He had also exerted significant political pressure on partisan opponents in the House of Representatives. The appropriations measure passed the House of Representatives on April 30, 1796 by a vote of 56–48. The worst crisis for the new republic to that point was over roughly two years after it began.

THE JAY TREATY CONTROVERSY AND PRESIDENTIAL REPRESENTATION

The events surrounding the signing and funding of the Jay Treaty pose some interesting theoretical questions about the nature of presidential representation in the early American republic. Was the president through this period representing the community at large? Was the president behaving more as a partisan, representing Federalist over Democratic-Republican interests? Or was the president doing both, and acting as a statesman who perceived the Federalist stance on the Jay treaty to be more consistent with national interests?

A Centrist Interpretation of the Jay Treaty Controversy

It is clear from Washington's writings and speeches that he viewed the presidency as representing the community at large, rather than narrow partisan interests. He had stated this view in his third annual address on October 25, 1791:

> It is desirable on all occasions to unite with a steady and firm adherence to constitutional and necessary acts of Government the fullest evidence of a disposition as far as may be practicable to consult the wishes of every part of the community and to lay the foundations of the public administration in the affections of the people. (Richardson 1907)

Washington despised the idea of political parties formed in such a way as to pit one group of citizens against another. In his farewell address to the nation he made this clear:

> They [political parties] serve to organize faction, to give it an artificial and extraordinary force; to put, in the place of the delegated will of the nation, the will of a party, often a small but artful and enterprising minority of the community; and, according to the alternate triumphs of different parties, to make the public administration the mirror of the ill-concerted and incongruous projects of faction, rather than the organ of consistent and wholesome plans digested by common counsels, and modified by mutual interests. (Richardson 1907)

As noted in the Preface, Washington's views on presidential representation also showed clearly in a letter of July 28, 1795 to the Selectmen of Boston during the campaign to fund the Jay Treaty. He wrote,

> In every act of my administration, I have sought the happiness of my fellow citizens. My system for the attainment of this object has uniformly been to overlook all personal, local, and partial considerations; to contemplate the United States as one great whole; to confide that sudden impressions, when erroneous, would lead to candid reflection; and to consult only the substantial and permanent interests of our country. (Fitzpatrick 1931)

Washington's publicly expressed views on presidential representation suggest that he believed presidents should first and foremost reflect the nation as a whole while remaining oblivious to the passions inspired by partisan divisions. His writings allude to consulting "the wishes of every part of the community," administering with "the affections of the people," pursuing "the will of the nation," and actions driven by "the happiness of my fellow citizens." These phrases imply that he believed that presidents should seek whenever possible to satisfy a centrist majority beyond partisan considerations.

However, Washington also saw a national interest apart from public sentiment that might at times require divergence from public opinion. In other words, Washington viewed himself as a caretaker of the public good, catering to the popular will whenever possible, but deviating when he perceived the nation would be better served by doing so.

When deviating from the popular will, the president also found it appropriate to persuade the public to support his conception of the national interest.

This nonpartisan centrist view of presidential representation is consistent with sentiments expressed by other founding fathers. For example, Thomas Jefferson stated in a letter of March 13, 1789 from Paris,

> I am not a Federalist, because I never submitted the whole system of my opinions to the creed of any party of men whatever in religion, in philosophy, in politics, or in anything else where I was capable of thinking for myself. Such an addiction is the last degradation of a free and moral agent. If I could not go to heaven but with a party, I would not go there at all. (Lipscomb and Bergh 1904a, 300)

In discussing the evils of partisanship, James Madison in Federalist 10 defined faction as "a number of citizens, whether amounting to a minority or majority of the whole, who are united and actuated by some common impulse of passion, or of interest, adverse to the rights of other citizens, or to the permanent and aggregate interests of the community." Thus, Madison's early view was that partisanship, whether reflected through "a minority or majority of the whole," generally runs counter to the interests of the nation at large, or what he termed the "aggregate interests of the community."

Similarly, Alexander Hamilton, discussing the presidency in Federalist 71, stated that

> The republican principle demands that the deliberate sense of the community should govern the conduct of those to whom they intrust the management of their affairs; but it does not require an unqualified complaisance to every sudden breeze of passion, or to every transient impulse which the people may receive from the arts of men, who flatter their prejudices to betray their interests.

Hamilton's view of presidential representation expressed through this statement seems perfectly consistent with Washington's behavior during the Jay Treaty crisis. In signing the treaty, Washington acted in what he perceived to be the nation's best interest, regardless of popular sentiment or partisan interests. However, he also understood the importance of public sentiment to presidential success. Therefore,

Washington conducted a successful campaign to persuade the public toward his own position.

The antipartisan centrist view of presidential representation is also reflected in the original design of the presidency as an institution. By embedding the presidency in a single elected official, the Constitution focused accountability on one individual who presumably would represent the community at large above the political fray. The presidency was designed as the only elected institution in the United States that had the entire nation as a constituency. As such, once in office, presidents should feel obligated to put the aggregate community above partisan considerations.

Another aspect of the original design of the presidency suggesting a nonpartisan interpretation comes from noting that there was no provision in the original Constitution for partisan elections. Article Two stated that the U.S. Electoral College would elect both the president and the vice president in a single election; the person with a majority would become president and the runner-up would become vice president. Through these provisions, it was expected simply that persons of good faith and integrity would be put forward to represent the larger interests of the community.

However, problems with this nonpartisan electoral system arose as political parties began to emerge. The first problem occurred in the election of 1796, when the nation chose a president and vice president from different political parties. Washington's former vice president, John Adams, became president, with the Democratic-Republican Thomas Jefferson becoming vice president. Adams's presidency was marked by intense partisan disputes over foreign policy. Britain and France were at war. Adams and the Federalists favored Britain, whereas Jefferson and the Democratic-Republicans favored France.

Problems arose again in the election of 1800. Democratic-Republicans Thomas Jefferson and Aaron Burr each received the same number of electoral votes. This threw the election into the House of Representatives, which then elected Thomas Jefferson president, and Aaron Burr vice president. However, the acrimony and accusations of partisan corruption surrounding these events resulted in further movement toward a partisan electoral system.

The intentions of the founding fathers for a nonpartisan system were finally contravened with the ratification of the Twelfth Amendment in 1804. This amendment required each elector to cast two distinct votes: one for president and another for vice president. Given the low probability of partisan electors splitting their votes between candidates of different parties, this effectively created a partisan electoral system. From this point forward the political party receiving the most electoral votes elected both the president and the vice president. This has meant that the federal government has been continuously controlled by political parties since 1804, rather than by representatives from the broader community.

A Partisan Interpretation of the Jay Treaty Controversy

The Jay Treaty crisis marked the beginning of the end of the founders' vision of a nonpartisan presidency representing the larger interests of the community. Washington was selected as the first president because of his perceived consistency with this vision. He had participated in the constitutional convention and understood the founders' intentions for the presidency. More generally, he viewed himself not as a partisan, but as a caretaker of the new nation. Nevertheless, it was clear that the partisan views emerging from Washington's handling of the Jay Treaty controversy contained very different perspectives on what was in the national interest.

Political parties in the modern sense had not yet developed. However, the political arena was now divided into two groups, with very different visions of the nation's future. Each group held tightly to a set of principles upon which they thought the republic should be based. Each was firmly convinced that its principles were right, and that deviating from these principles would move the new nation down the wrong path. Thus, both Federalists and Democratic-Republicans were driven in their beliefs and actions during the Jay Treaty crisis by a sense of principled partisanship.

Federalists depicted themselves as the party most consistent with the original intent of the Constitution. Their vision was of a stronger national government that would actively promote the development of the nation. They viewed the nation as having tremendous potential for economic progress and expansion. During the Washington administration, Federalists used an elastic interpretation of the Constitution to pass far-reaching laws. These included establishing a national currency, funding the national debt, federal assumption of state debts, creation of a national bank, and a system of import tariffs and a tax on whiskey that would help pay for these measures. Federalist support tended to be higher in the Northeastern states, which were developing more urban economies. Hamilton and many other Federalists opposed the institution of slavery as inconsistent with the founding principles, but recognized that its dissolution was not possible at this time. They also tended to admire the success of the British system, particularly its strong financial and trade networks. Federalists also opposed what they saw as the excesses of the French Revolution, which had begun in 1789. They were deeply suspicious of popular government, and favored government through individuals with strong intellect and merit.

In opposition, Democratic-Republicans depicted the Federalists as favoring government by the aristocracy. They claimed that Federalists sought to establish a sort of elective monarchy that would put undue power in the hands of the president and central government. This seemed anomalous to Democratic-Republicans, because the nation had recently fought to overthrow a monarchy of a different sort. Democratic-Republicans promoted states' rights and wanted to limit the power of the central government, espousing the view that states should be primarily responsible for the nation's development. They insisted on a strict construction of the Constitution, and denounced many of the Federalists' proposals (especially the national bank) as unconstitutional. Democratic-Republicans also opposed such Federalist policies as high tariffs, military spending, a national debt, and assumption of state debt. They opposed the Federalists' urban, financial, and industrial goals. With support generally concentrated among southern states, the Democratic-Republican vision was of a nation characterized more by the relaxed agrarian lifestyle of the South and of a continuation of slavery. Democratic-Republicans opposed the Jay Treaty and were appalled at the idea of catering to British interests. Instead, they favored neutrality toward Europe or an alliance with France, especially after the French Revolution. They viewed the French Revolution as a natural extension of the American Revolution, where free men threw off the bonds of the aristocracy and absolutism. Democratic-Republicans were less suspicious of popular government, favoring government grounded in principles of liberty, rule by the people, and civic virtue by its citizens.

These contrasting visions of what constituted good government formed the backdrop for the partisan conflict surrounding the Jay Treaty. The Federalists saw the Jay Treaty as essential to the development of a strong national economy through favorable relations with Britain, or at least an absence of war, which would be crippling to the mercantile interests of the Northeast. The Democratic-Republicans saw the Jay Treaty as failing to achieve goals that were critical to the agrarian interests of the South, promoting autocracy, catering to the British monarchy, and exhibiting hostility toward the French, who had recently completed a just revolution of their own.

Neither party viewed itself as pursuing a course that was inconsistent with the national interest. Both parties espoused deeply held views about the principles upon which the republic should be based. As expressed by Thomas Jefferson in a letter to Abigail Adams on September 11, 1804,

> Both of our political parties, at least the honest portion of them, agree conscientiously in the same object: the public good; but they differ essentially in what they deem the means of promoting that good. One side believes it best done by one composition of the governing powers, the other by a different one. One fears most the ignorance of the people; the other the selfishness of rulers independent of them. Which is right, time and experience will prove. (Lipscomb and Bergh 1904a, 52)

Washington signed the Jay Treaty because he believed he was safeguarding the new nation, and in spite of strong countervailing public sentiment. However, if he had been a Democratic-Republican, he could just as easily have made the argument that the treaty with Britain was not in the national interest. Viewed in this light, Washington, the Federalist, was as much a partisan as a centrist in his manner of presidential representation.

MODERN PERSPECTIVES ON THE NATURE OF PRESIDENTIAL REPRESENTATION

Questions concerning who presidents represent and how are as timely today as they obviously were in Washington's time. The founding fathers originally intended the presidency to be a centrist representative of the community at large and an advocate of the overarching national interest. However, political parties developed soon after the new republic was launched, so that there emerged different visions of who presidents should represent and what was in the national interest. With the ratification of the Twelfth Amendment, presidents were increasingly partisan in their manner of political representation.

What about modern presidents? Do they generally feel a responsibility to represent the nation at large, as might be suggested by the founders' vision? Or do they primarily represent the interests of the partisan majority that elected them, as might be suggested by the behavior of early political parties? Do modern presidents generally follow the will of a majority in their behavior and decisions? Or do they sometimes deviate to attain what they perceive as some overarching public interest? If presidents do generally follow the will of a majority, then which majority do they represent? Are they representative of a centrist majority drawn from the middle of the political spectrum? Do they represent a partisan majority drawn from the left or right of the political spectrum? Or is presidential behavior determined by some mixture of centrist and partisan representation?

Presidential Views on the Nature of Presidential Representation

A starting point for studying the nature of presidential representation is simply to evaluate what presidents themselves have said about their representative role. Through time, many have expressed a belief that they represent the nation at large, rather than just the narrow partisan interests of those who elected them. This perspective has been advanced through their public rhetoric, as well as the writings of various presidents. Indeed, most American presidents have endorsed, at least symbolically, a centrist view of presidential representation.

We have already observed this perspective through Washington's public statements and writings, in which he claimed to be consulting "the wishes of every part of the community," administering with "the affections of the people," pursuing "the will of the nation," and performing actions driven by "the happiness of... fellow citizens." However, later presidents also suggested that they represented the nation at large, rather than just their political party.

For example, Thomas Jefferson, in his first inaugural address in 1801, said, "We are all Republicans. We are all Federalists" (Oberg 2006). Following Federalist President John Adams, this remark signified Jefferson's willingness to compromise partisan principles in the national interest. During his first years as president, he lived up to this promise. He kept Hamilton's National Bank and debt repayment plans, even though he deeply opposed these measures. Later, the monumental event reflecting Jefferson's willingness to compromise in the national interest was the Louisiana Purchase, which went strongly against his ideals of decentralized government and limited federal powers.

Abraham Lincoln stated in the Lincoln–Douglas debates in 1858, "In this and like communities, public sentiment is everything. With public sentiment, nothing can fail; without it nothing can succeed" (Angle 1991). Here Lincoln was clearly expressing the view that elected representatives depend on mass public support for the success of their policies, and should therefore either cater to it, or attempt to achieve it.

Theodore Roosevelt, writing in his autobiography about how he had viewed his role as president, said the following:

> My belief was that it was not only his right but his duty to do anything that the needs of the nation demanded unless such action was forbidden by the Constitution or by the laws.... In other words, I acted for the public welfare, I acted for the common well-being of *all our people*, whenever and in whatever manner was necessary, unless prevented by direct constitutional or legislative prohibition.... (Roosevelt 1913, 197)

In a similar vein, Woodrow Wilson wrote the following about the presidency in his book *Constitutional Government in the United States*:

> No one else represents the people as a whole, exercising national choice; and inasmuch as his strictly executive duties are in fact

subordinated.... Let him once win the admiration and confidence of the country, and no other single force can withstand him, no combination of forces will easily overpower him....

Government is competent when all who compose it work as trustees for the whole people.... It can obtain justified support and legitimate criticism when the people receive true information of all that government does.... If I know aught of the will of our people, they will demand that these conditions of effective government shall be created and maintained.... In taking again the oath of office as President of the United States, I assume the solemn obligation of leading the American people forward along the road over which they have chosen to advance.... While this duty rests upon me I shall do my utmost to speak their purpose and to do their will....

More recent presidents have also expressed their belief in the centrist nature of presidential representation. For example, President Carter, recognizing the extreme partisanship and special interest politics that had emerged during the 1980 presidential election campaign, said the following:

Because of the fragmented pressures of these special interests, it's very important that the office of the President be a strong one and that its constitutional authority be preserved. The President is the only elected official charged with the primary responsibility of representing all the people. (*Public Papers of the Presidents* 1981)

Ronald Reagan, well known for his strong partisan stands, also publicly endorsed the centrist model of presidential representation. For example, at the swearing-in ceremony for members of the White House Staff on January 21, 1981, he said, "Our loyalty must be only to this Nation and to the people that we represent. I've often said the only people in Washington who represent *all the people* are those, basically, that are found here, because we're beholden to no district, beholden to no particular section or State" (*Public Papers of the Presidents* 1981).

President Clinton, upon winning reelection in 1996, expressed similar views about who the American president represents. He said, "When I ran for President 4 years ago, I said I wanted to give our Government back to the people. I wanted a Government to represent the national interests, not narrow interests, a Government that would stand up for ordinary Americans. And I have worked hard to do that" (*Public Papers of the Presidents* 1996).

During the 2000 presidential election campaign, candidate George W. Bush adopted a theme of ending the partisan politics that so dominated the later years of the Clinton administration. He stated, "Responsible leadership sets a tone of civility and bipartisanship that gets things done. I am a uniter, not a divider and.... It is how I will lead in the White House"(Bush 2000). He made similar remarks about governing from the center following his reelection in 2004. "With that trust comes a duty to serve all Americans.... So today I want to speak to every person who voted for my opponent: To make this nation stronger and better I will need your support, and I will work to earn it.... A new term is a new opportunity to reach out to the whole nation" (*Public Papers of the Presidents* 2004).

During the 2008 presidential election campaign, candidate Barack Obama frequently repeated his famous remarks from the 2004 Democratic national convention. "... there is not a liberal America or a conservative America – there is the United States of America.... We are one people, all of us pledging allegiance to the stars and stripes, all of us defending the United States of America" (Obama 2004). Of course, these remarks were again intended to decry the increasingly partisan nature of recent presidential politics. Once again, as the framers intended, Obama was promising to represent all Americans, rather than just the partisans who elected him.

As the preceding evidence shows, most American presidents have publicly endorsed the view that they represent the community at large. There has been an expectation, at least symbolically, extending from Washington's time to the present that presidents will put partisan considerations aside after elections and that their behavior and actions while in office will reflect the larger interests of the nation.

Citizen Views on the Nature of Presidential Representation

The expectation of nonpartisan centrist presidential representation has also long been an important part of the belief system of Americans. Most citizens abhor partisanship and prefer that the president be responsive to the broader public will, rather than simply those responsible for their election.

For example, an ABC News/Washington Post poll administered on March 15, 1999 asked respondents, "How important will a candidate's position on reducing political partisanship in Washington be to you in deciding how to vote in the next presidential election in the year 2000 – very important, somewhat important, not too important, or not important at all?" Fully 76 percent of respondents answered that reducing political partisanship was either very important or somewhat important to their electoral choices in the 2000 election.

A survey reported by the Pew Research Center on November 11, 1999 asked, "If 5 represents an absolutely essential quality in a president, and 1 a quality that is not too important, where on this scale would you rate willingness to compromise?" Fully 62 percent of survey respondents answered that presidents should be willing to compromise. The identical question was asked again on September 25, 2003, with 67 percent preferring presidents who are willing to compromise.

More recently, a Democracy Corps poll conducted on May 2, 2007 approached the centrist versus partisan representation question differently by asking citizens about two opposing conceptions of presidential behavior. The questions were as follows. "Tell me whether the first statement or the second statement comes closer to your view, even if neither is exactly right. First statement: The next president of the United States should be someone who will stick to core principles and fight for what they believe is right. Second statement: The next president of the United States should be someone who can compromise and work with both parties to get things done." Fully 68 percent of respondents agreed that the second statement better reflects their view of how presidents should behave once in office.

Citizens generally believe in a centrist model of presidential representation. One possible reason is that civics textbooks consistently teach that presidents represent the nation as a whole, rather than narrow partisan interests. For example, Bond and Smith (2008, 447) write, "Several features of American politics limit the president's ability to act as party leader. First is the traditional mistrust of parties, dating back to the founding of the nation. This suspicion promotes the inclination to be 'president of all the people' and a fear of being too partisan is politically risky." In another passage they write, "Elected by a nationwide constituency, the president tends to see issues from a national perspective" (2008, 461).

Edwards et al. (2008, 391) observe that a "fundamental question regarding democratic leaders is the nature of their relationship with the public and its consequences for public policy. The president and vice president are the only officials elected by the entire nation. . . . "

Along similar lines, O' Connor and Sabato (1993, 232) note that "Much of the president's authority stems from his position as the symbolic leader of the nation and his ability to wield power. When the president speaks . . . he speaks for the nation in one voice."

Patterson (1990, 468) observes that "The president . . . is a nationally elected official and the sole chief executive. More than anything else, these features of the office – national election and singular authority – have enabled presidents to claim the position of national leader."

Consistently, Burns et al. (1990, 376) write, "The framers in 1787 perceived the presidency in the image of George Washington, the man they expected would first occupy the office. The American chief executive, like Washington, was to be a wise, moderate, dignified, nonpartisan, president of all the people."

As suggested by these civics texts, highly idealistic views of presidential representation are strongly embedded in what citizens are commonly taught about the nature of the American presidency. They are also prominent features of more scholarly textbooks on the American presidency.

For example, Cronin and Genovese (2004, 198) write "Once in office, presidents often bend over backward in an attempt to minimize the partisan appearance of their actions. This is so in part because the public yearns for a 'statesman' in the White House, for a president who is above politics. Presidents are not supposed to act with their eyes on the next election; they are not supposed to favor any particular group or party."

Similarly, Cohen and Nice (2003, 203) state that "One of the defining characteristics of the modern presidency is the relationship between the president and the mass public . . . no other politician can claim such a close and intense relationship with the mass public. That is, no other political leader can claim legitimately to be the public's leader as the president can . . . he is the sole national spokesperson and representative of the nation."

Likewise, Pika et al. (2006, 186) argue that "presidents can point to the entire nation as their constituency and thus claim to speak authoritatively on behalf of the national interest or to act for various inarticulate and unorganized interests. . . . "

Along similar lines, Edwards and Wayne (2006, 333) claim, "Only presidents (and their vice presidential running mates) are chosen in a national election. Each member of Congress is elected by only a fraction of the populace. Inevitably, presidents must form a broader coalition in order to win their office. . . . Thus, the whole that the president represents is different from the sum of the parts. . . . "

Koenig (1996, 94) notes that "The president's most profound and continuous relationship is with the American people, who not merely award the prize of election but are at once the source and affirmation of his policies. When the people are behind him, he can better withstand the lesser publics – the interest groups with their lobbyists, congressional spokesmen, and bureaucratic defenders. . . . "

Similarly, Pious (1996, 184) observes that "In the final analysis the president is of the party – but also above it and sometimes in opposition to it. He or she does not find it of any great use to attempt to be a strong party leader. . . . After two centuries of party politics, American practices remain remarkably in tune with original constitutional principles. . . . "

As the preceding references illustrate, most Americans prefer the presidency to represent the nation as a whole. They dislike partisan presidential behavior. They have a common understanding that the president is the only U.S. elected official with a single constituency, the entire nation. Citizens are taught the efficacy of a centrist model of presidential representation through their civics training. Scholars of the American presidency also promote centrist views as they describe the operation of the office. Therefore, the belief that presidents should and do represent the broader public, rather than just those partisans who elected them, is strongly embedded in American political culture.

Scholarly Views on the Nature of Presidential Representation

Scholarly research has also fostered a belief in the centrist model of presidential representation, though working through a different rationale. In theorizing about the nature of presidential representation, scholars have often relied on assessments of presidential self-interest, rather than norms and expectations. This work posits that presidents and politicians seek political advantage for themselves and their supporters. They also want to enact their most desired policies (e.g., see Fenno 1973; Mayhew 1974; Kingdon 1989). As self-interested actors, presidents need the public's approval of their performance and policies to be successful. From this standpoint, a centrist theory of presidential representation would argue that they should not stray too far from the political center, or what many scholars call the median voter.

Downs (1957) first proposed a theory whereby self-interested politicians always move toward the median voter to maximize their political support. Davis and Hinich (1966) subsequently initiated the seminal literature from this perspective, and median voter theory has manifested itself through numerous formal and empirical analyses grounded in this tradition.[1] Indeed, the notion that politicians always move toward the median voter to maximize their political support is so embedded in scholarly thinking that it could be called an established paradigm of elite political behavior.

Consistent with median voter theory, a significant body of scholarly research has stressed the importance of mass political preferences to policy outputs from American political institutions (Page and Shapiro 1985, 1992; Stimson, MacKuen, and Erikson 1995; Wlezien 1996; Canes-Wrone, Herron, and Schotts 2001; Erikson, MacKuen, and Stimson 2002; Canes-Wrone and Shotts 2004; Canes-Wrone 2006). For example, Erikson, MacKuen, and Stimson (2002) and Stimson, MacKuen, an Erikson (1995) claim that mass preferences affect policy stances by all three major U.S. political institutions, including the presidency. They report that presidents respond *dramatically* to the public's mood (a dynamic measure of overall mass

---

[1] This literature following from Downs (1957) is too voluminous to be reviewed fully here. For expository treatments see Davis, Hinich, and Ordeshook (1970), Riker and Ordeshook (1973), Enelow and Hinich (1981, 1982), Aldrich (1983), Wittman (1983), Enelow and Hinich (1984), or Austin-Smith and Banks (1988).

preferences), with a high percentage of any disequilibrium between presidential liberalism and mass preferences corrected after one year. In other words, their analyses suggest that the president's policy stances are very responsive to the political center.

However, others argue that modern presidents cater to the median voter only when they need to. According to this perspective, presidents are strategic actors who use their knowledge of public opinion to evade responsiveness to mass political preferences. For example, Jacobs and Shapiro (2000, Chapter 2) use case study evidence to argue that a sophisticated understanding of public opinion combined with a variety of factors have enabled presidents to engage in "crafted talk" *to manipulate, rather than respond to* the public. Presidents often face a tradeoff between pursuing partisan policy goals and pleasing the public. Thus, Jacobs and Shapiro (2000, 42–44) assert that it is only intermittently prior to elections and when they require broad public support that modern presidents pursue a centrist strategy. At other times, their cost–benefit calculations are weighted toward pursuit of policy goals and appeasing fellow partisans.

Consistent with this theme of conditional centrist presidential representation, Canes-Wrone and Schotts (2004) suggest that congruence between the president's policy stances and the mass public has declined through time, perhaps as a result of increasing partisan polarization. They also report statistical evidence that this congruence is conditional on the electoral cycle and the president's public approval ratings. They find that as elections approach, presidential policy proposals become more consistent with mass preferences (see also Zaller 2003).

Various other scholars suggest that presidents only respond to the public when they need to increase their approval ratings (Hicks 1984; Hibbs 1987; Manza and Cook 2002). Consistently, Canes-Wrone and Schotts (2004) find that congruence between the mass public and the president occurs only when the president's approval ratings are in their midrange. This is allegedly because both low- and high-approval presidents have little to lose by pursuing their favorite policies at the expense of the public's approval.

Yet other scholars claim there is little or no relationship at any time between presidential policy stances and mass preferences. For example, Cohen's (1999) statistical analysis finds no relationship between presidential liberalism expressed through State of the Union messages and mass political preferences. Furthermore, inconsistent with Jacobs and Shapiro's (2000) and Canes-Wrone and Schotts's (2004) arguments, Cohen also reports that presidents do not become more responsive to the public during election years or with changing presidential approval ratings. Similarly, Edwards (2007; see also Jacobson 2007) argues that President George W. Bush consistently followed a strategy of pursuing policies that lacked broad public support.

Thus, the scholarly literature on presidential representation has produced no clear image of its nature, whether centrist, partisan, or some blend of the two. The prevalent view is that presidents cater to the median voter in some measure. However, some scholars report that presidential responsiveness to the political center is conditional. Presidents are strategic actors who are driven primarily by self-interest and the interests of their political parties. They only respond to the political center when there are electoral incentives or a need to build public support. A few scholars also suggest a total lack of presidential responsiveness to mass preferences.

If these latter results are correct, then presidents can be seen as driven primarily by ideology and partisanship. Under a partisan theory of presidential representation, presidents do not cater to the larger public. Instead, they attempt to persuade the public toward their own preferences and their political party, much as was done by Washington and the Federalists in 1795–96 in the effort to secure funding for the Jay Treaty.

CONCLUSIONS

The president is the most visible and important political and economic actor in the United States. As such, it is important that we understand the president's role as a representative in American democracy. As symbolic representatives of the nation at large, presidents are expected to be problem identifiers, policy purveyors, managers of the public good, international leaders, and unifying representatives of all the people. People look to the president both to represent their views and to provide leadership on important policy issues.

The notion that presidents represent the community at large is strongly embedded in American political culture. From Washington's time to the present, virtually every president has claimed to represent all of the people. However, do presidents represent the community at large by pursuing a centrist course that responds mainly to mass citizen preferences? Or do they, as Washington did during the Jay Treaty controversy, represent the community at large by pursuing a partisan course that they view as consistent with their own vision of the national interest?

Citizens and many scholars consistently express a belief in the centrist model of presidential representation. People strongly prefer that the president put aside partisanship and be willing to compromise. Civics textbooks commonly teach that the American presidency has but one constituency, the entire nation. Textbooks on the presidency commonly depict the American president as closely connected to the American people in a nonpartisan manner.

The notion that presidents are centrist representatives is also strongly embedded in scholarly research. That self-interested presidents and politicians always move toward the political center (i.e., the median voter) to maximize their political support has achieved paradigmatic status in the social sciences. Much scholarly research advocates this perspective. However, some research also suggests a more tempered view of presidential centrism, suggesting that it is conditional on a variety of other factors.

Although a centrist theory of presidential representation is widely endorsed by presidents, the public, and social scientists, it has not been subjected to rigorous scrutiny either theoretically or through empirical analysis. This book seeks to provide a better understanding of the president's role as a democratic representative.

In this introductory chapter, I have laid out the primary research questions that guide this work. Do presidents generally adhere to a centrist model of representation? Or do they represent primarily those who elected them, as might be suggested by a partisan model? Do presidents change their mode of representation while in office, sometimes following a centrist model and at other times a partisan model? If so, under what conditions are presidents centrists versus partisans? Do presidents attempt to lead the public toward their own partisan positions, as Washington did during the Jay Treaty funding effort? If so, then how successful are they at leading the public toward their own partisan positions? What factors enhance or diminish presidential efforts at partisan persuasion? What are the consequences for presidential support of following a centrist versus partisan model of representation?

In the next chapter I lay out in more detail the theoretical implications of the centrist and partisan models of presidential representation. In subsequent chapters I evaluate expectations that flow from these competing and perhaps complementary models with empirical data.

CHAPTER 2

The Centrist and Partisan Theories of Presidential Representation

If the centrist and partisan theories of presidential representation are to be subject to rigorous empirical scrutiny, then it is first important to define each theory in detail, as well as make precise statements about their empirical implications for presidential behavior. This chapter lays out the fundamentals of the centrist and partisan theories of representation. It also formalizes each theory graphically and through simple spatial analysis. The chapter concludes with a summary of predictions about presidential responsiveness and leadership under each model, which are evaluated empirically in later chapters.

DEFINING PRESIDENTIAL REPRESENTATION

The concept of political representation has been studied extensively both by political theorists and by legislative politics scholars. As a result, there is a large literature that offers many different definitions of the concept. Classic treatments by political theorists can be found in the works of Pitkin (1967), Pennock and Chapman (1968), Schwartz (1988), and Mansbridge (2003). Pitkin (1967, 8) provides one of the simplest definitions: to represent is to "make present again." In other words, political representation is making citizens' voices, opinions, and perspectives "present again" in the policy-making process.

Pitkin identifies four different dimensions of political representation: formalistic, symbolic, descriptive, and substantive. Formalistic representation concerns the means through which a representative gains power and whether the representative can be held accountable.

Symbolic representation addresses the question of what the representative "stands for" among constituents. Descriptive representation concerns whether the representative "looks like" those who are represented. Substantive representation refers to whether the representative advances the policy preferences of those who are represented.

This study is concerned with substantive representation. Substantive representation occurs when political representatives speak, advocate, or act on behalf of others in the policy process. If a representative's constituents prefer a given policy A over another policy B, then the representative should also prefer the given policy A over B, and may also actively pursue policy A. The issue of responsiveness is the key to the definition of political representation used here. Officials who respond to citizen preferences and/or advocate citizen interests are considered better substantive representatives.

Substantive representation has been studied extensively by scholars of legislative politics. The seminal treatment of legislative representation is that of Miller and Stokes (1963), who used correlational analysis to evaluate whether legislator voting is consistent with the policy preferences of constituents. Numerous subsequent analyses evaluated this and related questions. Concise reviews of the literature on legislative representation can be found in Wood and Andersson (1998), Hill and Hurley (1999), and Box-Steffensmeier et al. (2003). Although political representation by legislators has been a frequent subject of analysis, political representation by presidents has seldom been explicitly considered.

This is puzzling, because presidents are also elected officials who speak, advocate, and act on behalf of their constituents. A major question addressed by this book is "Who is the president's constituency?" Do presidents behave as if their constituency is the nation at large, and therefore respond more to the mass public or median voter? If so, then they are behaving in a manner consistent with a centrist model of representation. Do presidents behave as if their constituency is the partisans who elected them, and therefore pursue partisan policies while remaining relatively unresponsive to the mass public and median voter? If so, then they are behaving in a manner consistent with a partisan model of representation. Of course, there may also be a middle ground where presidents sometimes behave as centrists and at other times as partisans.

It is also important to note that both the centrist and partisan models have implications for presidential leadership. Under a centrist model of representation, presidents attempt to lead from the center. That is, they express views that reflect those of the nation at large as they pursue matters of public policy. Because they mirror the political center, the public policies they pursue will generally be popular, in order to ensure success in the policy-making process. Therefore, presidents shouldn't have to do much leading to get their policies approved.

In contrast, under a partisan model of representation, presidents attempt to lead from the left or right. That is, they consistently express views reflecting their partisanship and attempt to persuade the mass public toward their positions. The public policies they propose will tend to be more partisan, with the resulting need to persuade those near the political center if they are to achieve success in the policy-making process.

A DESCRIPTION OF CENTRIST THEORY

As noted above, the centrist theory of representation posits that presidents consider their main constituency to be the entire nation, rather than just the partisans who elected them. Given this belief, presidents should behave accordingly by responding whenever possible to aggregate community preferences. They should also lead from the political center, attempting to maximize political support by appealing to the median voter. Of course, presidents are obviously elected as partisans, because they have been chosen through a partisan system since 1804. However, centrist theory posits a postelection willingness to compromise and reflect the middle of the political spectrum through words and behavior.

Why Should Presidents Be Centrists?

Why should presidents be centrists, rather than partisans? One reason to expect presidents to be centrists is the pattern of norms and expectations that surround the presidency. As noted in the introductory chapter, the norm of centrist representation was initiated by

Washington, who most observers believe conducted his administration above the political fray with a focus on the larger interests of the nation. Many presidents since Washington have also expressed similar views about presidential representation through their writings and public remarks. Thus, there is a norm extending back to the beginning of the republic that should encourage centrist behavior by presidents.

This internal norm of presidential centrism should be reinforced externally by citizen expectations and textbook orientations about the nature of presidential representation. As suggested by the survey evidence in Chapter 1, Americans strongly prefer presidents who are not partisans, but are willing to compromise in the interests of the nation at large. This citizen expectation is reinforced through textbook descriptions of the presidency. American civics training almost uniformly promotes the expectation that presidents have a close connection to the mass public. According to this view, presidential power derives from the people. Without popular consent presidents can do little; with popular consent they are almost unstoppable in the pursuit of their policies. Some textbooks even argue that presidents distance themselves from partisanship because it is inconsistent with founding principles and people's expectations about the presidency.

Another major reason to expect that presidents should be centrists is rooted in the concept of presidential self-interest. Presidents may believe that centrist representation is the most effective means of maximizing their political support. It is important to note here again the dominant social science paradigm of what motivates presidents and politicians generally. Presidents are both elected representatives and politicians. Like all politicians, they have two goals: securing political advantage for themselves and their supporters, and enacting their most desired policies (e.g., see Fenno 1973; Mayhew 1974; Kingdon 1989). Of course, these two goals are inextricably linked. Policies catering to the political center should elicit greater political support, and in order to achieve particular policies presidents must have sufficient support.

As noted in the introductory chapter, Downs (1957) first proposed a centrist theory whereby self-interested politicians and political parties move toward the median voter to maximize their political support. The Downsian version of centrist theory argues that presidents

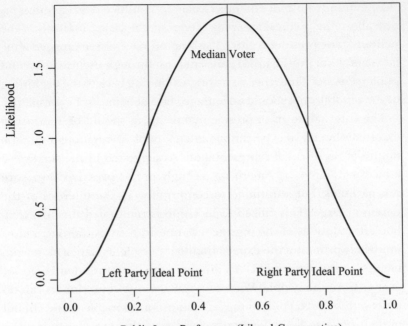

Figure 2.1. The centrist model and citizen preferences.

act strategically to tailor their public issue stances for appeal to the median voter. Presidents are basically forced to behave in this manner because of the possibility that the opposing party might also do so, thereby attracting weakly committed citizens. Presidential responsiveness to the median voter should, therefore, result in covariation between presidential issue stances and mass preferences. Presidential issue stances that are close to the median voter should result in stronger public support for presidential policies and assessments of their job performance. As a result, they should not stray too far from mass political preferences.

We can formalize these ideas graphically as shown in Figure 2.1. Suppose we assume that the probability of each distinct citizen preference is a draw from a Beta distribution.[1] The centrist model assumes

---

[1] The Beta distribution is a probability density function with index variable, x, ranging from zero to one. It is given as $P(x) = x^{p-1}(1-x)^{q-1}\frac{\Gamma(p+q)}{\Gamma(p)\Gamma(q)}$, where $\Gamma(.)$ is the Gamma function, given by $\Gamma(x) = \int_0^\infty t^{x-1}e^{-t}dt$. The variates p and q are shape parameters that jointly determine the mean, mode, median, variance, and skew of the distribution.

a unimodal and symmetric distribution of citizen preferences.[2] The distribution shown in Figure 2.1 is drawn from a Beta distribution with both shape parameters fixed at three. This parameterization produces a symmetrical distribution similar in appearance to a normal distribution.

The bottom axis of Figure 2.1 arrays people's preferences in a unidimensional policy space ranging from zero (most liberal) to one (most conservative). The vertical axis depicts the relative density of citizens having a particular preference under Downsian assumptions. Note that under this model the greatest mass of citizens is always near the center. This distribution posits that most citizens are moderate in their ideology, rather than strongly liberal or conservative. Because the distribution is symmetrical, the median voter's preference is 0.5, also coinciding with the average citizen.

Presidents are partisans of either the left or right who generally have preferences that differ from those of the median voter. The hypothetical ideal preferences for leftist and rightist parties are shown in Figure 2.1 by the vertical lines to the left and right of the median voter line. Because presidents are selected by their political parties to run for office, we can assume that presidents' true preferences are near those of their political parties.

In the aggregate, citizens always support the party with issue stances that are closer to their own. If both parties adhere to their ideal preferences, then they will each capture exactly half of total citizen support. This might be a rational scenario if there were no strategic behavior by the other party. However, if the other party wants to gain support, then it will move toward the political center. This is because its positions become closer to those of a larger mass of voters under the distribution in Figure 2.1. Thus, if presidents remain fixed at the partisan line, while the opposing party moves strategically toward the median voter, then presidents lose political support.

The Beta distribution can be used to mimic many other probability distributions and is used here because of its flexibility.

[2] Note that many formal applications have modeled preference distributions as quadratic functions, which are by definition unimodal and symmetric. The reason many analysts use quadratic functions is their mathematical simplicity for optimization problems. However, the Beta distribution with its tails actually seems more consistent with the theory discussed here.

This formalization suggests that presidents have a strategic incentive to move toward the political center. They must avoid the opposition party capturing support from their side of the preference distribution. If they do not move to the political center, then according to centrist theory their support will fall, reelection opportunities will drop for themselves and their fellow partisans, and their prospects for achieving policy success will be diminished. Thus, according to centrist theory, rational presidents should always move toward the political center to achieve the greatest support.

Once presidents have captured majority support, they should also lead from the political center in order to maintain their political advantage. Their policy stances should appeal to the broad public, rather than just their fellow partisans. Otherwise, the opposing party can undermine their leadership with more popular prescriptions by moving closer to the political center.

Thus, according to a centrist interpretation, presidents are basically forced into centrist behavior to prevent the opposing party from capturing their support relative to the median voter. Competition between the two parties for citizens near the political center is the root force driving centrist behavior. Much like supply and demand in markets, competition between the political parties provides an equilibrating force, grounded in the politics of self-interest, which attracts presidential issue positions to the political center. Any disturbance to the centrist equilibrium that pushes the president away from the political center results in losses. These losses, in turn, force presidential behavior back toward the median voter.

A Critique of Centrist Theory

Although this formalization of the centrist model is intuitively pleasing, it may not be a fully accurate description of presidential relations with the mass public. One major limitation is that it assumes a unimodal distribution of citizen preferences. Yet a unimodal distribution has not accurately depicted the American system since the time of Washington and before the Twelfth Amendment, if it did even then.

The underlying assumption of the nation's founders was obviously a unimodal distribution with no partisanship. The original institutional framework simply assumed that able representatives would emerge to represent the nation at large without concern for ideology or partisan interests. However, partisanship emerged very early in our system, evidenced by the discussion of the Jay Treaty controversy in the introductory chapter. The lesson of early American political history is that people naturally align themselves into political parties, so that the true distribution of citizen preferences facing presidents is actually bimodal.

Another major limitation is that the centrist model assumes that presidents are in continuous coequal competition with the opposing political party for citizens near the political center. Yet, after presidential elections, there is no cohesive out-party representative stating issue positions which compete with the president. The out party tends to be leaderless and without a strong focus after losing a presidential election. If an opposing actor does not exist, then presidents should be less driven to centrist behavior after elections. Accordingly, the equilibrating force becomes weaker after a president assumes office.

The unimodal distribution of citizen preferences in Figure 2.1 also does not allow for the empirical fact that many people near the political center don't care much about policy or politics. Many citizens have weak political attachments. Some are weak Democrats; some are weak Republicans; some call themselves Independents. Moreover, there is and always has been a part of the citizenry that is distinctly apolitical. They don't care whether the president's preferences match their own. Indeed, they may not even know what their preferences are on many issues, or what the president's preferences are, due to their low interest in policy and politics (Campbell et al. 1960). They may become more interested in politics near the time of elections. However, most of the time, presidents are relatively free to choose their issue stances, because citizens near the political center are often unaware of or don't care much about most presidential issue stances or policies (e.g., see Zaller 1992, 100–115; Delli Carpini and Keeter 1997). In other words, the equilibrating force associated with the pure centrist model in Figure 2.1 is significantly diminished by poorly informed, uninterested, and apathetic citizens near the political center.

Furthermore, given the characteristics of many citizens near the political center, presidents may find advantage in pursuing an alternate strategy of attempting to persuade citizens near the center toward their own positions. People near the political center are only loosely attached to either political party. As a result, they may be persuadable or at least not alienated by a partisan strategy (Zaller 1992, 100–115). Of course, it is widely recognized by presidency scholars that persuasion and leadership are important elements of presidential politics (e.g., see Neustadt 1960). Presidents are rarely passive responders to public opinion. Rather, they often attempt to lead the mass public toward their own positions.

Of course, if presidents behaved as predicted under the pure centrist model depicted in Figure 2.1, such leadership would always be from the political center and observationally indistinguishable from following the mass public. This seems unrealistic. There are greater payoffs for presidents who lead the public toward their own positions, rather than passively following public opinion. They receive greater benefits for themselves and their constituents from partisan policies. Presidents who are recognized as leaders are generally more popular, garner more political support, and acquire a more lasting historical legacy.[3] More relevant to the centrist model of representation, presidents who successfully lead can avoid having to move toward the political center to acquire political support. Instead, they can attract support to their own positions through persuasion. As Washington did in 1795–96, they can convince citizens that their vision of the public interest is more correct than that of the opposing party.

The formalization of the centrist model in Figure 2.1 also fails to take account of dynamic variations through time in factors that might condition presidential self-interest. For example, continuing public support and the composition of Congress after elections are very important to presidential success. When presidents already hold a dominant party position, they have little need to compromise by moving toward the political center. Under this scenario, presidents can achieve their preferred policies while deviating very little from their preferred issue position. Presidents may have votes to "burn," which results in little incentive to move toward the political center.

---

3 For example, see the summary of the literature on presidential ratings in Cohen (2003, 114–23).

At the other extreme, when the other political party holds a dominant position, presidents may also have little incentive to move toward the political center. Such movement will not produce victory, because the president needs to find many converts from individuals driven by different partisan ideals. Under this scenario, there may be little that presidents can do to achieve victory, so it again makes no sense to compromise partisan principles in such a hopeless situation.

It is only when presidents perceive an ability to win through centrist behavior that they have an incentive to compromise. This may occur for minority party presidents when the electorate is not too polarized. With respect to Congress, this occurs only when the partisan division of Congress is reasonably close and there is the possibility that movement toward the median voter can mobilize sufficient new support to achieve victory. The implication is that presidential responsiveness to the political center may be conditional on the partisan composition of the electorate and institutional arrangements facing the president.

A related factor that might condition the president's propensity to move toward the political center is the president's relative need for public approval and support. High public approval is a resource that presidents can use to affect policy. For example, numerous studies suggest that high public approval ratings translate into greater success in Congress (Bond, Fleisher, and Wood 2003; Brace and Hinckley 1992; Edwards 1980, 1989, 1997; Neustadt 1960; Ostrom and Simon 1985; Rivers and Rose 1985). High public approval also consistently results in a higher probability of reelection for the president and/or the president's party (Brody and Sigelman 1983; Erikson and Wlezien 2004; Holbrook 2004; Lewis-Beck and Rice 1992; Lewis-Beck and Tien 2004; Sigelman 1979). Over the long term, public approval also promotes the perception of a successful presidency, which may enhance a president's historical standing.

However, presidents' relative need for approval and support is a variable that should follow a rule of diminishing marginal returns. According to centrist theory, presidents develop high public approval ratings because they cater to the median voter. However, presidents with high public approval ratings also have less need to cater to the median voter because their approval ratings are already high. Thus, the degree of centrist presidential behavior may be conditional on preexisting public approval and support. Presidents with low approval ratings should be more responsive to the median voter than those with high approval ratings.

Consistent with these arguments, various scholars have suggested that presidents have less incentive to respond to the mass public when their approval ratings are high (Hibbs 1987; Hicks 1984; Jacobs and Shapiro 2000; Manza and Cook 2002). Interestingly, at least one study (Canes-Wrone and Shotts 2004) has also suggested that presidents have less incentive to respond to the mass public when their approval ratings are low. The assertion is that presidents have little to lose by not catering when their approval is low, because movement is unlikely to achieve sufficient support. Either way, the degree of presidential responsiveness to the political center should be conditional on the president's relative need for public approval and support.

Another related factor that might condition the president's propensity to move toward the political center is the proximity of elections. Presidents should have greater incentive to seek public support as elections approach. Consistent with these ideas, Jacobs and Shapiro (2000, Chapter 2) use case study evidence to argue that most of the time a sophisticated understanding of public opinion, combined with other factors, has enabled presidents *to manipulate, rather than respond to* the mass public. As shown in Figure 2.1, presidents face a tradeoff between pursuing partisan policy goals and pleasing the mass public. This tradeoff has become sharper with increased party polarization through time and the competing need to cater to fellow partisans in Congress and the electorate. Failing to deliver on policy promises can result in alienation of a president's core constituencies, which may impose high costs. Thus, Jacobs and Shapiro (2000, 42–44) assert that it is only intermittently during election periods that modern presidents pursue a centrist strategy.

Consistent with this theme, Canes-Wrone and Schotts (2004) use data on presidential and public spending preferences to suggest that congruence between the president's policy stances and preferences of the mass public has declined through time, perhaps as a result of increasing partisan polarization. However, they also report statistical evidence that this lack of congruence is conditional on the electoral cycle. They find that as elections approach, presidential policy proposals become more congruent with mass preferences. During other periods there is a striking lack of congruence. This study suggests that presidential responsiveness to the political center should be conditional on the president's need for political support.

The formalization of the centrist model in Figure 2.1 also fails to consider that presidential movements toward the center may be constrained by various exogenous factors impinging on presidential behavior. For example, policy movements in either a liberal or conservative direction may be inhibited by fiscal or economic constraints. Some liberal policies, such as expanding health care coverage or social benefits, might at times be politically popular. Yet they might also be difficult to achieve for either party due to fiscal constraints or a weak economy. Similarly, some conservative policies, such as increased defense spending, might also at times be politically popular. However, these can also be inhibited by fiscal constraints or a weak economy, even if there is strong public support. Thus, presidential movements toward the median voter are not always without friction.

Another major limitation of the model in Figure 2.1 is that it does not include the possibility that presidents can follow a course that is inconsistent with mass preferences, but that the president views as in the best interests of the nation. Just as Washington signed the Jay Treaty in 1795 in the face of overwhelming public opposition, presidents up through modern times have often followed courses that deviate from mass preferences. As expressed by Hamilton in Federalist 71, "The republican principle ... does not require an unqualified complaisance to every sudden breeze of passion, or to every transient impulse which the people may receive from the arts of men, who flatter their prejudices to betray their interests." Under the centrist model, presidents would automatically lose support if they followed an independent course. Yet there have been many times historically when presidents have chosen courses that were contrary to public opinion (e.g., see Beschloss 2007).

Finally, the centrist model depicted in Figure 2.1 is also limited in that it only allows the president a single strategy for bolstering political support. Citizens mechanistically give their support to the party whose preferences are closer to their own. Therefore, presidents become passive responders to what they think the public wants. The only strategy that presidents can employ to attract greater support is to mirror mass preferences. Yet this is not a realistic depiction of presidential options. As suggested in the introductory chapter, presidents may also use persuasion to attract political support, much as Washington did in 1795–96 during the Jay Treaty crisis. Indeed, presidents actually have at least two strategies for maximizing political support. They can move toward the median voter or they can choose the partisan leadership strategy of attempting to move people near the center toward their own positions.

A DESCRIPTION OF THE PARTISAN THEORY

The partisan theory of presidential representation developed in this section addresses all of these potential limitations. It posits simply that presidents are driven more by partisanship than by a thrust to reflect the larger preferences of the community. Presidents are elected by partisan majorities from either the left or the right. Although they may sometimes need those in the political center to achieve reelection or policy goals, their success is generally not based on moving toward the policy stances of the median voter. Rather, it can also be based on political persuasion, symbolism, obfuscation, and/or the stability induced by partisan loyalty.

Further, presidential self-interest is generally better served by following a partisan strategy. Having achieved electoral success, presidents are anxious to pursue their most favored policies and reward core supporters with benefits that accrue from election outcomes. Future electoral and policy success are also dependent on the continuing loyalty of fellow partisans. Given these partisan incentives, after elections presidents respond whenever possible to ideological imperatives and pursue partisan principles that reflect their own vision of the larger interests of the community.

Partisan theory also suggests that presidents try to lead from the political left or right, not from the political center. As with the centrist model, they are strategic actors. As such, they always have the option of moving toward the median voter. However, they generally view the strategy of attempting to persuade those in the political center toward their own positions as more beneficial.

As partisans, presidents strongly prefer not moving toward the median voter. Their success, past and future, comes from a partisan majority, not from a centrist majority. The median that partisan presidents care most about is the party median, not the centrist median. Thus, the fundamental difference between the partisan and centrist theories of representation is that presidents tend to respond to a partisan majority, but do not generally respond to the centrist majority.

Why Should Presidents Be Partisans?

Why should presidents be partisans, rather than centrists? One rationale stems from the natural tendency of a polity toward partisan division. People in a free society naturally divide themselves along partisan lines. In a plurality electoral system such as the United States, these partisan divisions generally involve two political parties (Duverger 1951). Accordingly, presidents naturally align themselves with one or the other side in order to attract sufficient support for election and governing.

As observed by Thomas Jefferson writing in 1813, this partisan division of civil society is as old as government itself.

> Men have differed in opinion and been divided into parties by these opinions from the first origin of societies, and in all governments where they have been permitted freely to think and to speak. The same political parties which now agitate the U.S. have existed through all time. Whether the power of the people or that of the [aristocracy] should prevail were questions which kept the states of Greece and Rome in eternal convulsions, as they now schismatize every people whose minds and mouths are not shut up by the gag of a despot. And in fact the terms of Whig and Tory belong to natural as well as to civil history. They denote the temper and constitution of mind of different individuals. (Lipscomb and Bergh 1904b, 279)

The same partisan divisions that Jefferson saw in the early republic remain with us today. Each political party is driven by different principles of governing. Republicans see government as a danger to individual liberty, and sometimes the problem itself. They view support for business and the upper classes as a means to ensure a sound economy and promote national interests. In contrast, Democrats see government as a means for promoting the common good. They tend toward support for the lower and middle classes as a means to ensure a sound economy and promote national interests. Each political party views itself as better representing the community. However, their approaches to pursuing "the public good" differ along well-defined principles that define their partisanship.

Just as people naturally align themselves with political parties, presidents naturally align themselves with one or the other vision of how best to represent the community. They are socialized toward partisanship, and this socialization guides their political behavior. They are elected while holding deeply felt partisan principles, and it becomes natural for them to pursue those principles once in office. Accordingly, presidents are natural partisans in their manner of political representation.

Extending this argument, if people and presidents naturally align themselves with political parties, then the Downsian assignment of citizen preferences to a unimodal distribution as shown in Figure 2.1 is incorrect. In a two-party system, such as has existed since the early republic, citizen preferences should be modeled as a bimodal distribution. As will be shown formally below, under a bimodal distribution of citizen preferences, most configurations suggest that little or no movement is required for presidents seeking to maintain majoritarian status.

If the president's party already holds a committed majority, then there is little incentive for such movement. Presidents only need to maintain their majorities. Moreover, even if there is a roughly even split between the parties in representing citizen preferences, they may not need to move much from their preferred positions to capture a majority. In both cases, presidents may believe that political persuasion can pull sufficient numbers of loosely affiliated citizens toward their own position.

It is only when presidents are in a minority that there might be an incentive to move toward the median voter. However, even under this configuration of citizen preferences, presidents may still be averse to centrism due to ideological imperatives. They may strongly believe that their issue stances are inherently moral or in the national interest. Additionally, movement toward the political center runs the risk of demobilizing partisans, who are also key to presidential success. Thus presidents may perceive that their interests are best served by being

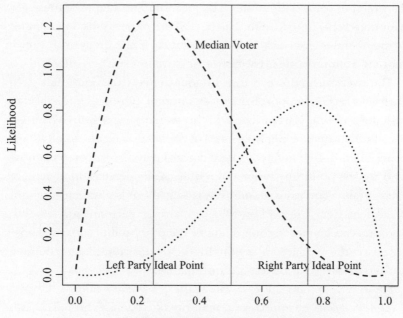

Figure 2.2. Partisan model of citizen preferences, majority president.

true to those who elected them, rather than responding to a centrist imperative.

We can formalize these arguments about presidential self-interest and partisanship graphically as shown in Figure 2.2. Again, the bottom axis arrays people's preferences in a unidimensional policy space ranging from zero (most liberal) to one (most conservative). The vertical axis depicts the relative density of citizens having a particular preference. The median voter line in Figure 2.2 is the median defined by the centrist model in Figure 2.1. However, note that the greatest density of citizens is now nearer the ends of the left–right continuum, corresponding to the idea that citizens naturally align themselves with one or the other political party.

The partisan model assumes bimodal and asymmetrical distributions of citizen preferences. The distributions in Figure 2.2 are draws from two Beta distributions with shape parameters for the left party (LP) at two and four, and shape parameters for the right party (RP) at four and two. Note that these parameterizations produce skew in both distributions toward the center. The locations and shapes of these distributions reflect the idea that there is a core of partisans on each end of the liberal–conservative scale, but that each party may also receive support from those near the center who are less strongly attached.

The overlap in the two distributions reflects the idea that each party may receive support from those whose preferences might also fit with the opposing party. Citizens in the overlapping regions of the two distributions include weak partisans of the left and right, as well as self-proclaimed Independents.[4] These citizens may also encompass those who are less politically aware and require some persuasion to achieve their loyalty. The assumption here is that there is always a reservoir of citizens near the middle who lack strong partisan attachments, and who can be moved toward one or the other political party. Those citizens in the overlapping regions for the two distributions are defined as "persuadable" for the discussions that follow.

Figure 2.2 depicts the case where the president's natural support (*NaturalSupport*) encompasses a majority of citizens. The president's *NaturalSupport* consists of a core of partisan supporters plus those aligned with the president's party in the overlapping part of the distributions. For purposes of this discussion, the president's party is always the distribution on the left (LP, dashed line), and is scaled for this example to contain 60 percent of all citizens. The right party distribution (RP, dotted line) contains 40 percent of all citizens.[5] If we separately integrate the two distributions across the range of citizen preferences ($x = 0 \ldots 1$) and then sum the two results, we have unity. That is,

$$\int_0^1 \mathrm{LP}\,dx + \int_0^1 \mathrm{RP}\,dx = 1. \tag{2.1}$$

---

[4] Note that this modeling approach assumes that the proportion of weak partisans and independents is equal for the two parties. Empirically, this is not a bad assumption, because American National Election Survey data show that the average proportion of weak partisans for Democrats since 1952 has been about eleven percent, whereas that for Republicans has been around ten percent.

[5] The scaling is accomplished by assigning a weight, p, to each of the two distributions, where the weight represents the proportion of citizens in each part. Specifically, the left party distribution is given in this example by $P(\mathrm{LP}) = p \times \mathrm{Beta}(2, 4)$, whereas the right party distribution is $P(\mathrm{RP}) = (1 - p) \times \mathrm{Beta}(4, 2)$.

Thus, the two distributions jointly capture the entire density of citizen preferences.

The cadre of strong partisans who can be counted on most of the time are in the nonoverlapping part of the left party distribution. Define this part of the left distribution in Figure 2.2 as *CoreLeft*. The president also has support from some citizens in the left party distribution whose preferences overlap with the right party distribution. These citizens are less tightly bound to the president, but are nevertheless prone to support the left party. Define this group in Figure 2.2 as *PersuadableLeft*. Then the president's *NaturalSupport* is defined by

$$NaturalSupport = CoreLeft + PersuadableLeft. \qquad (2.2)$$

The president's potential support (*PotentialSupport*) consists of *NaturalSupport* plus those who might be persuadable from the right party distribution. Citizens in the overlapping part of the right party distribution are less attached than those in the core of the right party distribution. The president may be able to pull loosely attached citizens away from the other party. Thus, a third part of the president's *PotentialSupport* is in the overlapping part of the right party distribution. Define this group in Figure 2.2 as *PersuadableRight*. Total *PotentialSupport* for the president is the sum of these three regions of the two distributions in Figure 2.2:

$$PotentialSupport = NaturalSupport + PersuadableRight. \qquad (2.3)$$

For the simulated scenario presented in Figure 2.2, we can calculate the components of *PotentialSupport* by taking the appropriate integrals for the three parts of the two distributions. The president's *CoreLeft* support is obtained as follows:

$$CoreLeft = \int_0^S LP\,dx - \int_0^S RP\,dx \qquad (2.4)$$
$$\text{where } S = x_{LP\,=\,RP}.$$

S above is the preference value on the liberal–conservative scale where the two distributions intersect. In words, *CoreLeft* is the entire distribution for the left party less those in the overlapping part of the left distribution. Performing these calculations, we find that in the majority president scenario depicted in Figure 2.2 the president's core support as a proportion of the citizenry is 0.42.

The president's *PersuadableLeft* support is obtained as follows:

$$PersuadableLeft = \int\limits_{S}^{1} LP\,dx + \int\limits_{0}^{S} RP\,dx. \qquad (2.5)$$

In words, *PersuadableLeft* is the part of the left party distribution that overlaps with the right party distribution. Performing the calculation implied by Equation (2.5), the president's persuadable partisans as a proportion of the citizenry are 0.18. Given Equation (2.2), we can also sum *CoreLeft* and *PersuadableLeft* to verify that the president's *NaturalSupport* is 0.60, corresponding with the 60 percent majority established for this example.

However, presidents also have another potential source of support through the possibility of being able to persuade loosely attached citizens from the right party distribution toward their position. Potential presidential support from *PersuadableRight* can be calculated as follows:

$$PersuadableRight = \int\limits_{S}^{1} LP\,dx + \int\limits_{0}^{S} RP\,dx. \qquad (2.6)$$

Note that by definition this is the same calculation as that used above for *PersuadableLeft*, because it is the overlapping area for the two distributions. *PersuadableRight* can also be calculated:

$$PersuadableRight = q - \left(\int\limits_{S}^{1} RP\,dx - \int\limits_{S}^{1} LP\,dx \right) \qquad (2.7)$$

where $q = 1 - NaturalSupport$.

This is just the natural support for the opposing party less those in the nonoverlapping part of the right distribution. Performing these calculations shows that the president has the potential to capture another 0.18 as a proportion of the total citizenry. Thus, total *PotentialSupport* (i.e., *CoreLeft* + *PersuadableLeft* + *PersuadableRight*) for the president is 78 percent of the citizenry. Obviously, in the majority party scenario depicted in Figure 2.2, the president needs only to play good defense

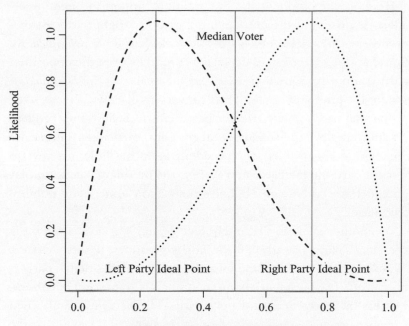

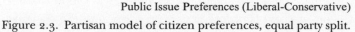

Figure 2.3. Partisan model of citizen preferences, equal party split.

to maintain majority status, and there is little incentive to move toward the median voter.

What about a scenario in which support is evenly divided between the two parties? Figure 2.3 depicts this case. The setup is the same as in Figure 2.2, except that each party now contains 50 percent of citizens holding particular preferences. The president is still from the left party. Calculating *CoreLeft* using Equation (2.4) above, we find that the president's core support is 0.31. When Equation (2.5) above is used to calculate *PersudadableLeft*, the persuadable citizens under the distribution for the left party are 0.19 as a proportion of the citizenry.

These results sum to *NaturalSupport* for the president of 0.50, which again corresponds to the 50 percent support allocated to each party for this example. From this number it is obvious that if the president can successfully maintain support from those naturally tending toward the left party, then little or no movement toward the right is required for the president to maintain an advantage. Still, presidents must engage in persuasion to maintain their advantage.

However, the president also has potential support through loosely attached citizens in the overlapping part of the right party distribution. Using Equation (2.6) or (2.7) to calculate *PersuadableRight*, we find that the proportion of persuadable citizens from the opposition party is also 0.19. Summing these results reveals that the *PotentialSupport* for the president is 0.69. This again seems like a sufficiently large proportion of *PotentialSupport* for presidents to believe they can successfully employ a persuasion strategy. Thus, even when the parties are about evenly divided, the president again has little incentive to move toward the median voter. Rather, the president can again play good defense and attempt political persuasion to maintain political advantage.

Yet another scenario that might face a president occurs when the president's party is clearly in the minority. Figure 2.4 depicts this case. Again, the setup is the same as above, and the president's party is on the left. The president's party encompasses 40 percent of citizens, whereas the opposition party encompasses 60 percent. Again, when *CoreLeft* is calculated using Equation (2.4) above, it is found that the president's core support is now 0.22 as a proportion of the citizenry. This number suggests that minority presidents might need either to move toward the center, or to be very persuasive, to attract a majority.

Is it even possible under this scenario for presidents to achieve a majority? When Equation (2.5) above is used to calculate *PersuadableLeft*, the persuadable citizens from the president's party are 0.18 as a proportion of the citizenry. Again, these results sum to reflect the 40 percent of citizens who naturally fit within the preference distribution for the president's party. Now, using Equation (2.6) or (2.7) to calculate *PersuadableRight*, we find that there are another 0.18 from the right who are loosely attached and might be movable toward the president's position. Summing the three components of *PotentialSupport*, we find that the president can achieve as much as 58 percent support by attracting loosely attached citizens from the other party.

Which strategy should presidents use in the minority party scenario depicted in Figure 2.4? They can move toward the political center, as suggested by the centrist/median voter model in Figure 2.1. However, in contrast to the centrist model, they may not have to move fully to the center to achieve a majority. Small movements away from the left party

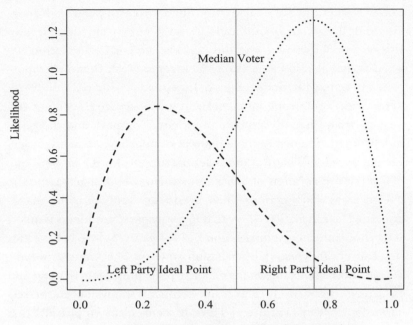

Figure 2.4. Partisan model of citizen preferences, minority president.

line may be all that is required to capture the desired proportion of persuadable citizens. There are also incentives for not moving too far. Centrist behavior runs a risk of demobilizing core partisan supporters on the left.

Presidents can also employ a strategy of political persuasion by attempting to move loosely attached citizens toward their own position. This strategy seems promising, given that *PotentialSupport* is almost 60 percent of the electorate. Indeed, it seems plausible under this scenario that presidents who have confidence in their persuasive abilities might believe they don't need to move toward the median voter at all to achieve political success. Of course, which strategy presidents actually choose when their party is in the minority is an empirical question to be addressed in a later chapter.

Is the Partisan Model Grounded in Empirical Reality?

How realistic are the scenarios depicted in Figures 2.2 through 2.4? We can explore this question using data on party identification drawn from the American National Election Survey from 1952 through 2004. This study has asked a question about respondent's party identification at least every other year over this period. The party ID question has seven potential responses: Strong Democrat, Weak Democrat, Independent Democrat, Independent, Independent Republican, Weak Republican, and Strong Republican. If we categorize the strong and weak partisan categories as core presidential support, and the three Independent categories as potentially persuadable, then we can calculate the president's natural and potential support for the modern era.

The last two columns of Table 2.1 contain these calculations. The shaded areas mark periods when presidents were from the majority party. The calculations show that majority party presidents virtually always had sufficient *NaturalSupport* and *PotentialSupport* to believe they could successfully use the persuasion strategy. The average *Natural-Support* and *PotentialSupport* for majority party presidents were 59 and 73 percent, respectively. This result is roughly equivalent to the scenario depicted in Figure 2.2. Thus, it seems clear empirically that majority party presidents may have felt little need to move to the political center.

Minority party presidents also compare well with the results from the partisan model. The lowest period of partisan support for a minority party president was for President Eisenhower. Over this period the president faced a citizenry that was overwhelmingly Democratic. The president's average *NaturalSupport* and *PotentialSupport* over this period were 41 and 54 percent, respectively. This result is roughly equivalent to the minority president scenario depicted in Figure 2.3. As a result, President Eisenhower may have been more prone to centrist behavior than later presidents. Again, this remains an empirical question.

Later minority party presidents were in a more favorable situation to use the partisan persuasion strategy. The average *NaturalSupport* and *PotentialSupport* for minority party presidents from 1970 through 2004 were 43 and 62 percent, respectively. These numbers suggest that even minority party presidents over this period could reasonably believe that a partisan persuasion strategy would be successful. They needed only to maintain their core and persuade less than a majority of loosely committed citizens toward their positions. Such persuasion may have required little or no movement toward the political center.

TABLE 2.1. *Partisanship and potential support for the president, 1952–2006*

Year	Party of president	Democrat	Independent Democrat	Independent	Independent Republican	Republican	Natural support	Potential support
'52	Democrat	47	10	8	7	28	61.0	72
'54	Republican	47	9	11	6	27	38.5	53
'56	Republican	44	6	13	8	29	43.5	56
'58	Republican	49	7	12	5	27	38.0	51
'60	Republican	45	6	12	7	30	43.0	55
'62	Democrat	46	7	13	6	28	59.5	72
'64	Democrat	52	9	8	6	25	65.0	75
'66	Democrat	46	9	13	7	25	61.5	75
'68	Democrat	45	10	11	9	25	60.5	75
'70	Republican	44	10	14	8	24	39.0	56
'72	Republican	41	11	15	10	23	40.5	59
'74	Republican	38	13	18	9	22	40.0	62
'76	Republican	40	12	15	10	23	40.5	60
'78	Democrat	39	14	16	10	21	61.0	79
'80	Democrat	41	11	15	10	23	59.5	77
'82	Republican	44	11	13	8	24	38.5	56
'84	Republican	37	11	13	12	27	45.5	63
'86	Republican	40	10	14	11	25	43.0	60
'88	Republican	35	12	12	13	28	47.0	65
'90	Republican	39	12	12	12	25	43.0	61
'92	Republican	36	14	13	12	25	43.5	64
'94	Democrat	34	13	11	12	30	52.5	70
'96	Democrat	37	14	10	12	27	56.0	73
'98	Democrat	37	14	12	11	26	57.0	74
'00	Democrat	34	15	14	13	24	56.0	76
'02	Republican	34	15	8	13	30	47.0	66
'04	Republican	33	17	10	12	28	45.0	67

Note: The shaded rows indicate periods when the president was a member of the majority party.

Source: Consecutive studies from the American National Election Survey. Question text: "Generally speaking, do you usually think of yourself as a Republican, a Democrat, an Independent, or what?" (IF REPUBLICAN OR DEMOCRAT) "Would you call yourself a strong (REPUBLICAN/DEMOCRAT) or a not very strong (REPUBLICAN/DEMOCRAT)?" (IF INDEPENDENT, OTHER [1966 and later: OR NO PREFERENCE]) "Do you think of yourself as closer to the Republican or Democratic party?"

47

This is because presidents on average needed to persuade only about 7 percent of the average 19 percent persuadable citizens in the center. Thus, minority party presidents could easily have seen an advantage in following a strategy of partisan persuasion.

When Is Partisan Persuasion Not a Feasible Strategy?

Under what configurations of citizen preferences is it not plausible for presidents to follow a strategy of partisan persuasion? One such configuration requires that the president is in the minority party and that there are insufficient persuadable citizens to achieve a majority. This scenario occurs when *PotentialSupport* < 0.50. Under the preceding setup this threshold occurs when the president's *NaturalSupport* drops below 33 percent – for example, when the president's *NaturalSupport* is 32 percent, *CoreLeft* = 0.15, *PersuadableLeft* = 0.17, and *PersuadableRight* = 0.17. Under these conditions, presidents will have great difficulty in successfully pursuing a political persuasion strategy, because the most they can expect to achieve is 49 percent. However, it should be noted that presidents also cannot be successful with a centrist strategy under this scenario, because there are too few citizens in the middle. Observing the data in Table 2.1, this scenario has never occurred for the post–World War II party system.

How do presidents behave when their *PotentialSupport* drops this low? Do they cling to their fundamental beliefs and those of their political party? Do they move toward the political center, as might be implied by the median voter model? Do they exhibit patterns of principled partisanship in attempting to pull the political center toward their own positions? More generally, do they follow a strategy of political persuasion in attempting to regain political support? If so, then what is the nature of their persuasion strategy? These are empirical questions that must be left to future research, because this scenario has not occurred in the modern era.

Another configuration under which presidents cannot reasonably follow a strategy of political persuasion occurs when the system is highly polarized. The extreme for this scenario is depicted in Figure 2.5. Two Beta distributions are again used to reflect the densities of citizen preferences for the two political parties. However, the two shape parameters for the left party are now set at two and ten,

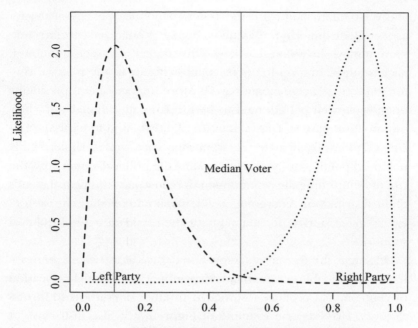

Figure 2.5. Partisan model of citizen preferences, polarized citizenry.

respectively, whereas those for the right party are at ten and two. The president's party remains the party of the left. The split between the two parties is almost even, with the president's party allocated 48 percent, and the party of the right allocated 52 percent. However, the shape and location of the two distributions now reflect a high degree of polarization.

Note that the region of overlap between the two parties is quite small. This captures the notion that under extremely polarized politics most of the president's supporters are core supporters and there are few persuadable citizens. When the calculations for *CoreLeft* and *PersuadableLeft* are performed using Equations (2.4) and (2.5), the president's *NaturalSupport* for this scenario is 48 percent. When the calculations for *PersuadableRight* are performed using Equation (2.6) or (2.7), only 1.0 percent of the right party's support is persuadable. This means that the president's proportion of *PotentialSupport* is only 0.49. Under this scenario there is no amount of political persuasion that the president can use to gain a majority.

Given their inability to use the strategy of political persuasion to gain a majority, do minority presidents facing a very polarized citizenry then move toward the political center? This strategy also seems doubtful, because there are too few persuadable citizens in the political center to produce an adequate payoff. Moreover, successful presidents under polarized politics tend to be ideologically aligned with their own political parties. That is, they are tightly bound to partisan principles and less likely to deviate from their core beliefs. Under highly polarized politics any movement toward the political center runs the risk of diminishing the commitment of fellow partisans near the ends of the distribution. As a result, presidents should see the centrist strategy as inappropriate for maintaining their natural base of political support.

Of course, this extreme example also depicts a case where there are so few persuadable citizens that no amount of presidential persuasion or centrism can produce a sufficient number of converts to form a majority. However, the example of Figure 2.5 is also instructive as to when we might expect presidents to be strong partisans who are unwilling to move from their positions.

As the overlapping region in Figures 2.2 through 2.5 gets smaller, there is progressively less potential payoff for the president in moving away from partisan positions. There are progressively fewer persuadable citizens near the center who can become supporters, so presidents have less incentive to move to the center. This is not to say that presidents will be centrists when the proportion of persuadable citizens is large. As illustrated above in Figures 2.2 through 2.4, they can either move toward the median voter or attempt political persuasion to gain political support. However, presidents should increasingly exhibit patterns of partisanship as the proportion of the citizenry that is persuadable declines.

Finally, presidents may see the strategy of political persuasion as infeasible when their persuasive abilities are too weak to persuade those who are persuadable. This scenario might occur when presidents are simply inept at political persuasion. Such ineptness may be due to rhetorical limitations specific to particular presidencies. However, given the rhetorical requirements for being elected president in the media age, this is less likely to occur in the modern era.

A more likely explanation for weak presidential persuasion is an absence of political resources for persuasion. One political resource is public approval. For example, President Truman's popular support (gauged by Gallup approval ratings) was below 33 percent from early 1951 through December 1952 due to public dissatisfaction with the Korean War. In the aftermath, Eisenhower was elected president in 1952. This scenario may also have occurred prior to the 1976 and 1980 elections. President Nixon's approval was very low during the Watergate era, falling to 25 percent. President Nixon achieved little during the Watergate period, and Jimmy Carter was elected president in 1976. Public approval was also quite low near the end of the Carter administration as a result of the president's handling of the Iran hostage crisis and the economy. From mid-1979 through December 1980 the president's popular support often registered below 33 percent. President Carter was generally regarded as an ineffective president, and Ronald Reagan was elected in 1980.

Finally, George W. Bush's public approval fell as low as 22 percent by October 2008 and averaged just 34 percent between November 2005 and January 2009. The aftermath of this drop in support for President Bush was a lack of persuasive ability and a strongly negative reaction to his issue stances on the Iraq war and the economy. Again, the public's lack of support produced a new president, Barack Obama, and a large turnover in the House and Senate. Thus, like earlier presidents with low public approval ratings, President Bush lacked the resources and persuasive ability to move citizens toward his own issue positions.

CONCLUSIONS

Political representation occurs when presidents respond to the policy preferences of their constituencies. A key question to be addressed in later chapters is "Who is the president's constituency: the nation at large or the president's partisan majority?" If we are to answer this question, we need a good theoretical base from which to work. Accordingly, this chapter has developed a precise statement of the centrist and partisan theories of presidential representation.

As observed in Chapter 1, the centrist model is the currently popular paradigm and has achieved widespread acceptance by social scientists.

However, this chapter has laid out some potential limitations of the centrist model. Presidential incentives to move toward the political center should differ with the changing need of presidents for political support. If the president holds a strong majority, then there may be less need to compromise in the direction of the median voter. If the president is already popular, then there should be less incentive to move toward the political center. If there are no impending elections, then presidents may hold more to their partisan positions because there is less need to build a majority.

Presidential responsiveness toward the center may also be constrained by various exogenous conditions. For example, fiscal or economic constraints may inhibit movements in the liberal direction for such popular policies as expanding health care coverage or social benefits. They can also diminish movements in the conservative direction for such popular policies as increased defense spending or tax relief. Thus, presidential movements toward the political center from either direction are not always without friction.

Furthermore, the centrist model is limited in that the only permissible strategy for presidents needing to build political support is movement toward the political center. Yet it is well understood by presidency scholars that leadership and persuasion are important dimensions of presidential politics. Indeed, the classic statement of the nature of presidential power asserts that "Presidential power is the power to persuade" (Neustadt 1960, 10). According to this view, presidential success depends more on leadership and persuasion than on democratic responsiveness. Therefore, an empirically accurate model should also take into account the strategy of presidential persuasion.

The preceding limitations suggest the need for an alternative model of presidential representation. The partisan model depicted in Figures 2.2 through 2.5 provides an alternative theory that is more reflective of the nature of the American system. Under the partisan model, three interdependent factors should determine presidential strategies. First and foremost, the president's level of PotentialSupport should determine whether presidents feel compelled to move toward the political center. If the president's PotentialSupport is large, then there is no incentive for such behavior. Presidents can simply play good defense and use political persuasion to attract persuadable citizens. If the president's party is in the minority, then there may be incentives to move toward the political center. However, presidents may also employ a strategy of partisan persuasion if there are sufficient numbers of persuadable citizens.

Second, and highly related to the first, the size of the persuadable part of the citizenry should be important to presidential strategies. When there are fewer persuadable citizens near the center, there is less incentive for presidents to move toward the center. Under this scenario, presidents should remain partisans. When the proportion of persuadable citizens is large, the president can potentially move toward the political center to increase political support. However, an alternative strategy is to attempt moving those near the political center toward the president's position through leadership and persuasion. Again, which strategy presidents choose is an empirical question to be addressed in later chapters.

A third factor affecting presidential strategies for building political support is the perceived risk of demobilizing core partisans. If the president believes that moving toward the political center is likely to demobilize core partisans, then it is probably more reasonable to employ partisan persuasion. In contrast to the centrist model, the highest density of supporters under the partisan model shown in Figures 2.2 through 2.5 is near the ends. So it makes little sense to risk losing supporters from the core in exchange for supporters near the political center. This is because support from the core is more numerous and dependable.

Of course, the risk of demobilizing core partisans becomes greater as the electorate becomes more polarized. Under polarized conditions, citizens care zealously about the issues, and are unwilling to compromise. If the president appears willing to compromise, then partisans may become disenchanted and unwilling to provide their support. Thus, as the electorate becomes more polarized, presidents should increasingly behave as partisan representatives.

The models developed here clearly differentiate the contrasting expectations for presidential behavior implied by the centrist and partisan models. If presidents are driven by incentives associated with the centrist model shown in Figure 2.1, then they will consistently be pulled toward the political center in their issue stances and policy behavior. Their main constituency is the mass public, reflected through the median voter. If they fail to move toward the mass public, then they will lose support and fail to achieve their political objectives.

On the other hand, if presidents are driven more by incentives associated with the partisan model shown in Figures 2.2 through 2.5, then there should be little or no presidential movement toward the political center. Given the bimodal nature of the distribution of citizen preferences, presidents generally have little incentive for movement toward the median voter. Moreover, the president's main constituency is the partisans who elected them, so they generally prefer to remain close to their partisan allies.

Neither the centrist nor the partisan model of presidential representation has been subjected to rigorous empirical scrutiny. To do so, we must develop measures to reflect presidential issue stances through time relative to citizen preferences. The next chapter lays out the methods used to construct such measures, and also provides some initial descriptive analyses.

CHAPTER 3

Measuring Mass Preferences and Presidential Issue Stances

To understand the nature of presidential representation in the American system, I must first develop empirical measures of the key concepts associated with the theories in Chapter 2. The two key concepts flowing from those theories are mass preferences and presidential issue stances, both on a left–right continuum. In later chapters I shall address the question of who presidents represent by exploring the relative responsiveness of presidential issue stances to mass preferences. In the other direction, I shall also address questions of presidential leadership by exploring how mass preferences respond to presidential issue stances.

The centrist model implies a one-way relationship between these variables. Presidential issue stances should respond to mass preferences, but should not affect them. This is because presidents mirror citizen preferences, and as a result have no need to change them. Additionally, the centrist model strongly implies that mass preferences and presidential issue stances are in one-way long-term equilibrium. Shocks may occur that push presidential issue stances away from mass preferences for a time. However, the long-term force of presidential self-interest always pulls presidential issue stances back into the centrist equilibrium with mass preferences. Additionally, if the equilibrium implied by the centrist model exists, then any disequilibrium between the two measures should result in adjustment solely by the president.

In contrast, the partisan model suggests a more complex set of relationships. Presidents can choose between two alternative strategies for achieving political support. As with the centrist model, they can respond to mass preferences. They can also attempt to persuade those near the political center toward their own positions. If presidential efforts at persuasion are successful, then mass preferences should respond to presidential issue stances. In this case, we should see supportive movements in mass preferences through time with new presidential administrations, and within presidential administrations as they pursue the permanent campaign. However, with the partisan model, there is not a competitive force of self-interest pulling the president toward the political center. Rather, the force of self-interest pulls the president toward the median partisan. Thus, presidential issue stances and mass preferences may tend toward independence through time.

Here it is important to note that the partisan model does not require responsiveness by the mass public to presidential efforts at persuasion. Rather, it requires only that presidents *reasonably believe that they can be successful.* Nevertheless, it will be interesting empirically to know whether presidents succeed at partisan persuasion.

All of these potential relationships are best explored using time series methods. Time series methods make it possible to determine whether there is a causal relationship running from mass preferences to presidential issue stances. They also make it possible to determine whether a causal relationship runs from presidential issue stances to changing mass preferences. Causal relationships could also run in both directions, or in neither direction. Time series methods also make it possible to evaluate the presence or absence of long-term equilibrium relationships between presidential issue stances and mass preferences. If we find little or no relationship between presidential issue stances and mass preferences, then there are also time series methods for evaluating the statistical independence of the two measures.

Thus, time series measures are needed for mass preferences and presidential issue stances. I now describe the core time series measures used in this study.

MEASURING MASS PREFERENCES THROUGH TIME

The theories developed in the previous chapter imply an array of citizen issue preferences running along a liberal–conservative continuum. Of course, not all issues in American politics can be arrayed along a liberal–conservative continuum. For example, public spending for national parks, disaster relief, and scientific research do not fall neatly on this scale. There is no obviously liberal or conservative position on these issues. Nevertheless, this study assumes that the most important issues in American politics can be arrayed along such a continuum.[1]

One approach to measuring citizen preferences for the various issue domains would be to use people's self-identified liberalism–conservatism. Various survey organizations have been asking people regularly about their relative liberalism–conservatism since the 1950s. A time series could be constructed using the marginals from these surveys (e.g., see Box-Steffensmeier, De Boef, and Lin 2004; Ellis and Stimson 2007). One could then simply assume the nature of mass preferences on specific issues based on self-identified liberalism–conservatism.

However, this approach to measuring people's preferences may lack validity because there is also a symbolic dimension to self-identification (Free and Cantril 1967). During recent times, many survey respondents have self-identified as conservative, but when asked about specific issues they have actually supported liberal positions (Stimson 1999, 76–77). The opposite relationship may have occurred in other eras. Thus, self-identified liberalism–conservatism can miss the true underlying issue-based preferences of the mass public.

Given this limitation, a better approach to measuring mass preferences is to use people's responses to survey questions relating to particular issue domains that can be classified along a liberal and conservative continuum. Defining liberal versus conservative positions for many issues in American politics is generally easy. Liberal issue stances reflect positions advocating larger and more intrusive government. Conservative issue stances reflect positions advocating smaller

---

[1] A single left–right array of issues is not an outlandish assumption. For example, Poole and Rosenthal (1991; see also Poole 1998) analyzed the entire set of congressional roll call votes from 1789 to the present and found that most votes align on a single left–right continuum. Their spatial modeling approach did allow extracting additional dimensions. However, the first left–right dimension was dominant over all other dimensions for the entire period of their analysis.

and less intrusive government. For example, liberals tend to advocate more government involvement in such domains as race relations, the environment, worker safety, labor relations, health care, and urban problems. Conservatives tend to advocate the opposite.

However, for some issues the distinction is less obvious and requires intuition. For example, conservatives tend to advocate greater government presence for issues such as abortion and crime. They also advocate larger government for providing national security and military spending. In contrast, liberals tend to prefer less government presence in each of these areas.

These complexities require coding survey responses intuitively, using the most common definitions of liberal and conservative for each issue. Stimson (1999) developed such a measure. He used the survey marginals (i.e., the percentage choosing a particular survey response) from 259 different issue-based questions across 4,327 surveys administered over a 53-year period. He classified responses on these questions along liberal–conservative lines. Then he constructed a time series of public liberalism/conservatism from the survey marginals using a recursive smoothing algorithm. This resulted in a continuous time series of citizen preferences for each year from 1952 through 2004.[2] Stimson labeled the measure "public mood."

The set of issues entering Stimson's measure of public mood is large. Some issues become important for a time, only to fade so that they are no longer asked about by survey organizations. Other issues tend to be present for extended periods. However, Stimson identified nine domestic issue domains that are sufficiently continuous over the measurement period to be classified as major components of public mood. The major components of public mood comprise five welfare state issues and four more recent policy concerns (Stimson 1999, 77–85). The welfare state issues are peoples' attitudes on welfare, race relations, urban problems, health care, and education. The more recent issues entering the public mood measure are "size of government," "crime, guns, and civil liberties," military spending, and the environment.

[2]   See http://www.unc.edu/~jstimson/Mood5204.xls to obtain the data and their documentation file. A more detailed description of the methods for producing the public mood measure is contained in Stimson (1999, Chapter 3).

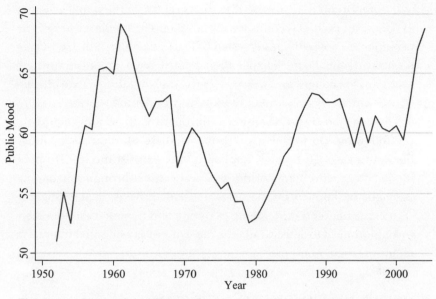

Figure 3.1. Stimson's public mood.

The definitions of liberalism and conservatism for these issues implied by Stimson (1999, Chapter 3) are straightforward and comport well with common sense and intuition. The nine major components of public mood are also consistent statistically. Stimson (1999, 85–88) showed that each of the issue domains loads consistently in a principal components analysis, with the first principal component identified as a liberal–conservative dimension. This liberal–conservative component is highly correlated with public mood.

Given the care with which Stimson constructed the measure of public mood, it has become the standard in American macro studies of public issue liberalism. Therefore, Stimson's measure of public mood is also used as the measure of mass preferences in the various statistical analyses reported in this book.

Figure 3.1 graphs Stimson's measure of public mood. Each time point on the graph reflects the average citizen issue liberalism for each year. Each time point is also a snapshot for each year of the relative issue liberalism–conservatism of the median voter. In other words, each unique measurement of public mood through time represents the corresponding center point of public liberalism–conservatism shown in Figures 2.1 through 2.5.

It is important to recognize from this graph that the political center in American politics is continuously moving. The median voter's issue positions are not static, as suggested by Figures 2.1 through 2.5, but are highly dynamic. People change their relative issue liberalism through time. These changes give us leverage for studying the relative efficacy of the centrist versus partisan models of presidential representation.

The questions I seek to answer with regard to these movements are the following. Do presidents respond to these movements in public liberalism through time, as implied by the centrist model? Do presidents affect movements of the political center through persuasion, as might be implied by the partisan model? What, if any, relationship exists between movements in public and presidential liberalism through time? Obviously, I need a measure of presidential liberalism to answer these questions.

MEASURING PRESIDENTIAL ISSUE STANCES THROUGH TIME

Prior Research

Past research has used a variety of approaches in attempting to measure the relative liberalism of presidential issue stances through time. For example, some studies have used presidential position-taking on legislation before Congress. One such strategy has been to use interest group legislation support scores. Each year, the Americans for Democratic Action (ADA) publish a list of what they consider "litmus test" legislation for support of liberal causes. The ADA scores for each legislator are calculated by taking the percentage of each member's votes supporting the ADA's position on the identified legislation.

This approach has been extended to measure presidential issue liberalism. Zupan (1992) calculated presidential ADA scores using presidential position-taking on the ADA-identified legislation as reported in the *Congressional Quarterly Almanac*. The Appendix of the *Almanac* lists whether the president supported, opposed, or took no position on legislation pending before Congress. Presidential ADA scores are then calculated by taking the percentage of ADA-identified votes during each year in which the president supported the ADA's position.

This approach has been criticized because the set of votes contained in the measure is determined by interest groups and changes each year by construction (Groseclose, Levitt, and Snyder 1999). As a result, the scales underlying the interest group support ratings can "shift" and "stretch" across institutions and time. Further, when legislative preferences change, whether due to congressional turnover or actual changes in political views, interest groups may respond by changing the scales to keep the same average score. Some scholars have attempted to adjust for this effect by calculating "shift" and "stretch" parameters and rescaling the scores (Groseclose, Levitt, and Snyder 1999; Krause 2000). This adjustment potentially improves the measure.

However, there are other limitations to using presidential ADA scores. Another limitation is that the presidential ADA approach aggregates what may be a very dynamic process within years into a single time point for each year. In other words, this approach assumes that presidential issue positions do not change within years. This may not be a reasonable assumption, given the persistent pulling and tugging that characterize American politics.

Another limitation of presidential ADA scores is that the measure is based on a sample of presidential positions taken throughout an entire year. Sampling presidential positions on a relatively small set of legislation produces sampling error. Because of the uncertainty induced by sampling error, the presidential ADA measure may not be a precise way to measure presidential issue liberalism.

Other scholars have also used presidential position-taking on congressional votes. However, they used the entire set of roll call votes for which presidents have taken a position. Poole and Rosenthal (1991; Poole, 1998) pioneered this approach for members of Congress by developing what they label Nominate scores in their various versions.[3] McCarty and Poole (1995) extended this technology to estimating issue preferences for presidents. They based their presidential liberalism measure on all *Congressional Quarterly Almanac*

[3] There are various versions of their ideal point estimation procedures that can be used for different purposes. These include D-Nominate, W-Nominate, DW-Nominate, and Common Space scores. A description of each measure is contained on their Web site at http://voteview.com/dwnl.htm.

reports of presidential support on roll call votes from 1953 through present.[4]

Their approach could be an improvement over ADA scores if their measure were aggregated to shorter time intervals. However, their methodology for estimating presidential liberalism resulted in a measure aggregated over entire presidencies. In other words, the liberalism score only changes when the president changes (see Figure 3.3, below). There is no dynamic variation to suggest whether or when presidential issue stances might have changed within presidencies. The McCarty and Poole (1995) measure is problematic in that the president's issue stances are constant for all years of a particular presidency. This is not a realistic depiction. Furthermore, it is impossible to evaluate how presidential issue stances respond to changing mass preferences with such a measure, since there is no variation within presidencies.[5]

Another approach that has been used in measuring changing presidential issue stances through time is to consider implied presidential liberalism by observing behavior toward external institutions. For example, Erikson, MacKuen, and Stimson (2002; see also Stimson, MacKuen, and Erikson 1995) employed multiple indicators that included presidential position taking on congressional roll call votes, the relative ADA average of the president's supporters in Congress, and a measure of presidential position-taking before the Supreme Court through amicus briefs filed by the Solicitor General.

Similarly, Bailey (2007) developed a measure of presidential issue liberalism based on all presidential position-taking on congressional roll call votes and on Supreme Court cases. Bailey's data on presidential position-taking for House and Senate votes were the *Congressional Quarterly Almanac* presidential position data as provided by McCarty and Poole (1995), discussed above. Presidential position-taking on

4 They have continuously updated their measure of presidential liberalism through time. The updated data are available at the Web site listed in footnote 3.

5 To be fair, McCarty and Poole (1995; see also Bailey 2007) worked within a rational choice framework. An assumption of this framework is that actors' preferences are fixed and unchanging. This is why some scholars may not find it problematic that presidential preferences remain unchanged over a four- or eight-year period. Regardless, presidents do change their public issue stances through time. What we seek to determine is whether those changes are in response to changing mass preferences. Thus, a more dynamic measure of presidential liberalism is required.

Supreme Court cases was drawn from two sources. First, like Erikson, MacKuen, and Stimson (2002), Bailey coded the relative liberalism of Solicitor General amicus briefs. The assumption here is that Solicitor General briefs truly reflect presidential positions. Given the influence of the president in the selection of the Solicitor General and the power of the president to overrule or remove him or her, Bailey argued that these could be treated as administration positions. Second, Bailey coded all public statements by presidents on Supreme Court cases, as reported in *Public Papers of the Presidents.* This is a more direct approach to reflecting presidential issue positions.

As with the McCarty and Poole (1995) measure discussed above, the Bailey measure contains little or no variation in presidential liberalism within most presidencies (see Figure 3.3, below). The measure is constant for each presidency prior to 1981. It is also a constant for both Bush presidencies. There is annual variation for the Reagan and Clinton presidencies. Interestingly, Presidents Reagan and Clinton become more and more conservative for every year of their presidencies, and in a smooth, exponential manner. These patterns for Reagan and Clinton suggest some mathematical effect that does not reflect the underlying reality of changing presidential liberalism. The description of Bailey's methodology offers no clue as to why most presidents do not vary in their relative liberalism through time, or why the Reagan and Clinton presidencies do vary in such an interesting manner. For whatever reason, such a measure is again inappropriate for evaluating presidential responsiveness to mass citizen preferences, which are continuously changing through time.

Past studies have also attempted to study presidential issue liberalism using annual budget proposals through the Office of Management and Budget (OMB). These studies have not actually placed presidential issue stances on a liberal–conservative scale. Rather, they have attempted to position the president relative to either the mass public or Congress. For example, Canes-Wrone and Schotts (2004) studied congruence between proposed changes in presidential budgetary authority and public preferences on spending for ten specific budgetary domains. They defined congruence coarsely as occurring any time a proposed change in presidential budget authority (irrespective of magnitude) was in the same direction as public preferences for change (irrespective of magnitude). Similarly, Kiewiet and McCubbins

(1988) and Canes-Wrone (2006) studied the president's budget proposals for particular policies relative to what they actually received in the congressional appropriations process.

These approaches to evaluating presidential issue liberalism finesse the question of presidential responsiveness to public or congressional liberalism by factoring out citizen or congressional liberalism at each point in time. This is a clever solution.

However, using budgetary data to measure presidential preferences also has serious limitations. Executive budget proposals are part of a strategic bargaining game between the president, the bureaucracy, Congress, and other political actors (Kiewiet and McCubbins 1988; Wildavsky 1984). Changes in proposed presidential budget authority may be due as much to bargaining by the bureaucracy or interest groups acting through the presidency as to true presidential preferences. Strategic presidents may also request more from Congress than they actually want in order to achieve some lower preferred level of spending. They may also request less than they actually want in order to temper what might be authorized by Congress. Thus, OMB budget proposals may not always reflect true presidential issue stances.

Finally, one study constructed an annual measure of presidential liberalism based on presidential rhetoric. Cohen (1999) coded each sentence in presidents' annual State of the Union messages from 1953 through 1987 using the liberal–conservative criteria defined by the ADA. In these addresses presidents propose and give their positions on legislation. They also provide more general statements about their positions on various issues. Cohen's measure was the percentage of liberal sentences in each State of the Union address for each year through time.

Unlike the other studies considered in this section, Cohen attended seriously to the reliability and validity of this measure (1999, 126–132). The limitation of Cohen's (1999) measure is that it is aggregated annually, enabling only 35 observations. Annual data miss dynamic variations that occur within years. Cohen's measure also produces too few observations to evaluate with statistical confidence the causal dynamics of presidential responsiveness to the mass public.

I turn now toward describing a new measure, which overcomes these limitations.

A New Measure of Presidential Issue Liberalism

Erikson, MacKuen, and Stimson (2002, 297) state, "The beginning point of dealing with the presidency is noting the near impossibility of direct measures of presidential liberalism from what presidents say and do." Their assessment is correct in recognizing the difficulty of constructing a direct measure of presidential liberalism. However, it is incorrect that the task is nearly impossible.

Accordingly, this project set about the task of developing a measure of presidential liberalism based on all presidential activities reported in *Public Papers of the Presidents.* The project involved coding every presidential remark about nine domestic policy issues from April 1945, when President Truman assumed office, through January 2005, when President George W. Bush began his second term.

The nine domestic policy issues chosen for the study are the same issues that are the main components of Stimson's (1999) measure of public mood: race, welfare, the environment, crime, education, urban problems, health care, military spending, and size of government. This is not the universe of issues that could be considered. For example, Cohen (1999) also included foreign policy issues. There are also various social values issues that could be considered, such as abortion, school prayer, flag-burning, and more recently same-sex marriage. However, selecting these nine issues does provide strong relevance to the best available measure of mass citizen preferences through time.

The presidential issue liberalism measure developed in this study is grounded in presidential rhetoric in each of the nine issue domains. Why use presidential rhetoric, rather than reports of legislative position-taking from the Appendix to *Congressional Quarterly Almanac,* Solicitor General amicus briefs, or budget proposals? Presidential rhetoric provides a direct reflection of presidential issue stances. Rhetoric is also the primary tool that presidents use in attempting to persuade the mass public. Presidents are engaged in a permanent campaign of public rhetoric that attempts to persuade the mass public. Therefore, it seems reasonable to employ presidents' rhetorical liberalism, rather than just their reported stances on legislation, court decisions, or budget proposals, which may be obscure to the average American.

It is also important to note that presidential rhetoric has both symbolic and substantive dimensions. Symbolically, using rhetoric to measure presidential liberalism should make it easier to observe presidential centrism. It is relatively quick and easy for presidents to generate issue stances through public remarks. Also, presidential remarks can occur independent of presidential position-taking on legislation, judicial decisions, or budget proposals, perhaps reflecting presidential manipulation of symbols instead of substance.

However, there is also a substantive dimension to the measure. Consistent with past measures, presidential remarks are very often associated with presidential position-taking on legislation, Supreme Court cases, and other external policy decisions, as well as within the administration. The source of the data, *Public Papers of the Presidents*, contains all public remarks by presidents relating to their positions on legislation, court decisions, and budget proposals (the main measures used in prior research). In addition, the *Public Papers* contain every presidential State of the Union message and budget transmittal message, and public appeals for passage of legislation, executive orders, directives, signing and veto statements, speeches to interest groups, news conferences, news briefings, and other policy-relevant remarks. Thus, utilizing the *Public Papers* to measure presidential issue liberalism is far more encompassing than earlier approaches.

Utilizing the *Public Papers* also makes possible a more dynamic and finely divided time series measure than legislative position-taking or budget proposals. A budget proposal or legislative key vote position occurs at one point in time. However, presidents don't simply propose budgets or register their positions on legislation at single points in time. They advocate their budgets and favored legislation over extended periods of time. Such advocacy occurs dynamically through time as presidents make speeches, hold press conferences, issue news briefs, etc. In some cases presidents campaign hard for public support of their issue stances; in other cases they may campaign little. As a result, the measure used here captures both the intensity of presidential advocacy and the changing dynamics of presidential advocacy through time.

Presidential rhetoric occurs hour by hour, daily, weekly, monthly, quarterly, annually, by administration, and by presidency. Presidential remarks can be aggregated over any time interval for statistical analysis. Past research has uniformly employed annual data due to measurement limitations. Much past research has also employed measures that do not vary within presidential administrations. However, using data from the *Public Papers*, one can choose the desired time interval to match the requirements of the analysis.

This more dynamic and finely divided time series should also be preferred because rhetoric reflects the face of the presidency most familiar to the public. Presidents are on a permanent campaign of public rhetoric, which makes them highly visible through the mass media. Citizens may be unaware of the president's legislative, judicial, or budgetary positions, but the media continuously report the stream of presidential remarks and speeches on these and other issues that flow through time. More generally, the president's rhetorical liberalism is an integral part of attempting to persuade the public.

Measurement Methodology

The specific methodology for measuring the president's issue liberalism involved an interaction between electronic and human coding. To begin, an electronic file was developed containing the entire *Public Papers of the Presidents* from Truman through the first term of the George W. Bush presidency.[6] Then PERL (Practical Extraction and Report Language) was used to extract from the *Public Papers* every sentence spoken publicly by the president that contained keywords relevant to each of the nine issue domains.[7] The resulting nine sentence

---

[6] The electronic file was constructed by extracting the ASCII text from a CD-rom marketed commercially by Western Standard Publishing Company (2000). This medium contained the entire *Public Papers* through 1999, including appendices that contain supplemental materials from the *Weekly Compilation*. In order to complete the electronic file through January 2005, the remaining years' materials were downloaded from the Web through OriginalSources.com. The resulting electronic file consisted of around 360 megabytes of ASCII text.

[7] PERL is a public domain open access code software package for logical manipulation of text. The overall structure of Perl derives broadly from C, but it also borrows from other programming languages such as sed, awk, the Unix shell, and at least a dozen other tools and languages (Schwartz, Olson, and Christiansen 1997). A full description of PERL, as well as various user support functions, is available at http://www:perl.com. PERL can be downloaded free from a link on this Web site. The language was originally developed for text manipulation, but is now also used for a wide variety of other tasks, including system administration, network programming,

files represent distinct issue dimensions of presidential rhetoric on U.S. domestic policy.

Next, PERL was used to list every *unique* word in the sentence files for the purpose of creating dictionaries of liberal and conservative words and phrases when the president spoke about each issue dimension. The words for each file were first sorted by frequency of use. Then human coders were used to identify liberal and conservative words and phrases. Specifically, the human coders assessed each entry intuitively, and then evaluated the proportion of correct "hits" from the previous sentence files when using the identified words and phrases. *Every unique word was evaluated* in constructing the dictionaries, and *every unique word was validated* using both machine and human analysis.

The coding unit was the sentence. After a dictionary of liberal and conservative words and phrases had been developed, PERL was used again to extract every liberal and every conservative sentence spoken by the president for each issue. Human coders were again used to read each sentence to verify that presidential liberalism and conservatism were accurately coded. Coding rules are in Appendix 3.1 at the end of this chapter. Based on a repetitive combination of machine and human coding, near-perfect validity was obtained in defining the liberal–conservative tone of presidential remarks for each issue domain. This iterative coding process required more than 2 years.[8]

Table 3.1 contains illustrative examples of the extracted sentences drawn from the sentence files and their coding for each of the nine issue domains. Note that each sentence is identified using numbers indexing the sentences by year, month, day, paragraph number, and sentence number. This detailed sentence identification system enabled human coders to return to the entire text when there was doubt about coding that arose from the context of the president's remarks.

software development, and Web site development. In fact, if you use the Internet, then it is virtually impossible not to have encountered PERL, because many Web sites are based on this language.

[8] Over the entire coding period there were a total of 173,316 sentences across the nine issues. More often than not, presidential rhetoric was neither liberal nor conservative. A total of 9,158 sentences were coded as definitively liberal, whereas 7,720 were coded as definitively conservative. Thus, presidents were somewhat more liberal than conservative over the entire time span.

TABLE 3.1. *Liberal and conservative sentences from* Public Papers of the Presidents

19620922.012.02   Liberal Race
Much remains to be done to eradicate the vestiges of discrimination and segregation, to make equal rights a reality for all of our people, to fulfill finally the promises of the Declaration of Independence.

19810129.076.05   Conservative Race
I think there are some things, however, that may not be as useful as they once were or that may even be distorted in the practice, such as some affirmative action programs becoming quota systems.

19640108.038.01   Liberal Welfare
Unfortunately, many Americans live on the outskirts of hope, some because of their poverty, and some because of their color, and all too many because of both.

19760706.002.03   Conservative Welfare
I applaud the efforts of the Congress in enacting this legislation to make food stamp vendors accountable for food stamps that they hold as well as for the funds collected.

19700202.032.01   Liberal Environment
• Launch a major effort to improve environmental quality by attacking air and water pollution, by providing more recreation opportunities, and by developing a better understanding of our environment and man's impact upon it.

19810910.020.01   Conservative Environment
Now, I'm going to stop making a speech because, unfortunately, the clean air board wouldn't give us permission to light the barbecue – [laughter] – so you're all invited inside for refreshments.

19620405.121.01   Liberal Urban Affairs
Specifically, I recommend that the Congress authorize the first installment of a long-range program of Federal aid to our urban regions for the revitalization and needed expansion of public mass transportation, to be administered by the Housing and Home finance Agency.

19980130.014.02   Conservative Urban Affairs
Whether we can empower all of our urban areas and our urban citizens to make the most of their own lives will be critical to determining whether we can, in fact, take all this success that our country has had and reach every neighborhood, every block, every family, every child.

19630308.003.01   Liberal Crime
To diminish the role which poverty plays in our federal system of criminal justice, I am transmitting for consideration by the Congress proposed legislation to assure effective legal representation for every man whose limited means would otherwise deprive him of an adequate defense against criminal charges.

(continued)

TABLE 3.1 *(continued)*

19730310.017.01   Conservative Crime
I am further proposing that the death penalty be restored for certain Federal crimes.

19630129.137.03   Liberal Education
In many areas school dropouts, or the education of the economically disadvantaged, the culturally deprived, the physically or mentally handicapped, and the gifted require specially designed programs which simply are not available.

19701020.008.01   Conservative Education
We do not believe the constitutional mandate that schools be desegregated requires compulsory busing for the sole purpose of achieving an arbitrary racial balance.

19610224.007.01   Liberal Health Care
The other bill which I am transmitting will help expand and improve community facilities and services for the health care of the aged and other persons.

20041029.052.11   Conservative Health Care
Government-run health care is the wrong prescription for health care for America's families.

19521006.060.01   Liberal Size of Government
Sometimes the Republicans aid their clientele by special favors, like the rich man's tax cut bill which was passed by the 80th Congress over my veto, or like their attempts to give away the Nation's oil resources to all the big oil interests.

20020430.018.02   Conservative Size of Government
America doesn't need more big Government, and we've learned that more money is not always the answer.

19930702.004.02   Liberal Military Spending
Now that the cold war is over, we see the opportunity around the world and in this country to reduce defense spending rather dramatically and to devote our attention to rebuilding our country here at home.

19850306.021.02   Conservative Military Spending
And now that I've vetoed this bill, I hope the Congress will get the message and work with me to reduce spending in a responsible way that does not threaten our national security.

Assessing Reliability and Validity

Reliability refers to whether or not coders (machine and human) coded each sentence the same way a high percentage of the time. Of course, machines are very reliable, and are made even more reliable when humans check their work. Also, using a *single* human coder to validate each issue domain means that reliability *within* each issue domain is not a concern. Within issue domains one can be sure that reliability is quite high, because the sentences were first coded by machine and then validated by a *single* human coder. Questionable sentences were flagged and resolved through joint decision-making.

There are, however, cross-issue coding reliability concerns with this methodology. Across the nine issue domains, three human coders were used to validate the machine coding. Occasional cross–human coder checks revealed very high agreement across coders in validating the machine coding. Nevertheless, because there were nine distinct issue domains and three different human coders, one cannot be sure that the same degree of coding precision was obtained across issue domains. In other words, the coding precision may have differed across issues, perhaps due to the differential efficiency of the keywords supplied for the machine coding, or to the differential efficiency of the human coders in validating the machine coding.

Although this may be a concern at the sentence level, it becomes less of a concern after the sentences are aggregated into time series. The liberal and conservative sentences spoken by the president were counted and aggregated by appropriate time intervals to produce liberal and conservative time series for each issue. Aggregating the coded sentences into time series means that any lack of precision at the sentence level is swamped by the total count of sentences in each time interval. Coding inaccuracies, to the extent that any remain, become part of the time series noise.

The final measure of the president's issue liberalism is the difference between the number of liberal and conservative sentences spoken by the president during each time interval, converted into standard deviation units for each issue and then summed.[9] Expressing each issue

---

[9] In plain English, the standard deviation is a measure of the average deviation of a set of numbers from their mean, in this case a time series. The standard deviation of a variable X is usually denoted by the symbol S_X. To convert a measure into standard deviation units is commonly referred to as standardizing. Specifically, the standardization transformation is $X_{std} = \frac{X - \overline{X}}{S_X}$, where X_{std} is the standardized variable, X is the original variable, $\overline{X}$ is the mean of the X variable, and S_X is the standard deviation of the X variable. This transformation is most useful when one wants to compare or combine variables that have no natural metric or are in different measurement units, such as we have here.

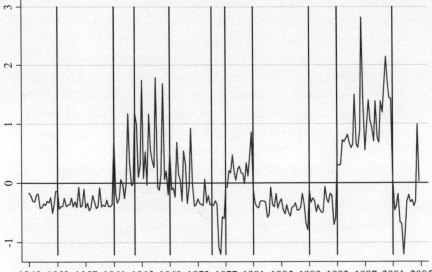

1949 1953 1957 1961 1965 1969 1973 1977 1981 1985 1989 1993 1997 2001 2005

Figure 3.2. Presidential issue liberalism.

in standard deviation units rather than the count metric provides yet another control for differential coding across issue domains. The standardized issue domains are summed into the final measure of presidential issue liberalism because there is no obvious rationale for artificially weighting the separate issue domains. Each issue has differed in relative importance to presidents through time, so summing the time series expressed in standard deviation units provides a natural weighting scheme reflecting their differential importance, but not overemphasizing the respective counts of presidential remarks.

Figure 3.2 contains a graph of the quarterly version of the presidential issue liberalism time series, with a marker for the start of each new presidential administration. By construction, the graph shows that the measure captures movements in presidential liberalism through time occurring within years. This is different from earlier proposed measures discussed above that vary only annually (Bailey 2007; Cohen 1999; Erikson, MacKuen, and Stimson 2002; Stimson, MacKuen, and Erikson 1995; Zupan 1992) or remain constant for entire presidencies (Bailey 2007; McCarty and Poole 1995).

At the sentence level, one can be sure that the measures underlying the aggregated time series in Figure 3.2 are reasonably valid because of using iterative electronic and human coding. However, one might also ask whether the time series itself is a valid measure of changing presidential issue liberalism.

Consider first whether the time series in Figure 3.2 has face validity. Face validity refers to whether a measure comports with conventional understandings of what the data should look like. Observing the dynamics of the presidential liberalism series in Figure 3.2 suggests the obvious importance of partisanship to presidential issue stances. President Truman was more conservative than might be expected from his partisanship. However, Democratic Presidents Kennedy, Johnson, Carter, and Clinton generally track to the liberal side. President Nixon straddled the zero line until his second term, when he turned more conservative. Republican presidents Eisenhower, Ford, Reagan, George H.W. Bush, and George W. Bush generally track to the conservative side. Thus, the new measure of presidential liberalism is reasonably consistent with what might be expected from Democratic and Republican presidencies.

One might also ask whether the new measure has construct validity. Construct validity refers to whether the measure compares favorably with other indicators which theory says it should relate to. For example, the new measure can be compared to some of the measures discussed earlier which have been used in past research. For validation purposes, Zupan's (1992) measure discussed above was updated through 2004 using his same methodology.[10] The new measure can also be compared to that proposed by Bailey (2007), and to an updated version of the measure developed by McCarty and Poole (1995). Given that earlier measures were uniformly at annual time intervals, the new measure of presidential issue liberalism must also be aggregated to annual time intervals for comparison.

Figure 3.3 contains graphs of the different time series measures of presidential issue liberalism.[11] One cannot expect the new measure to correlate perfectly with the other measures. This is because, by

[10] Zupan's presidential ADA score for a particular year is the percentage of ADA key votes in which the president took a position that was the same as that of the ADA, not counting abstentions. Presidential positions were identified using the *Congressional Quarterly Almanac*'s report on key votes for consecutive years.

[11] We cannot directly compare the new measure with that used by Erikson, MacKuen, and Stimson (2002). This is because they did not have a single measure, but used

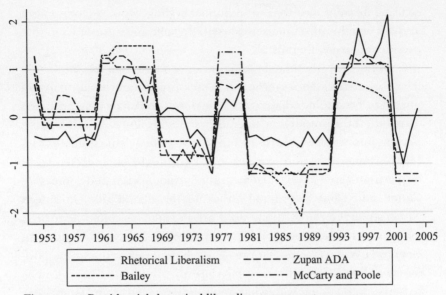

Figure 3.3. Presidential rhetorical liberalism versus past measures.

construction, the other measures have less variation through time. Nevertheless, the simple correlations between the president's rhetorical liberalism and the Zupan (1992), McCarty and Poole (1995), and Bailey (2007) measures are respectively 0.77, 0.78, and 0.65.

Visual comparison of the four plots shows that all of the time series track well with respect to changing presidential administration. However, the president's annual rhetorical liberalism shows more dynamic variation through time than the other three. This enables us to see that what presidents say in public may not perfectly coincide with their fixed averages on legislative and/or judicial support contained in the other measures.

Some variations in the new measure also reveal interesting within-presidency dynamics. During the Truman–Eisenhower years, the rhetorical liberalism measure suggests that these presidents were more conservative than suggested by the other measures. The rhetorical liberalism of Kennedy during his first two years is also more conservative

multiple indicators in a measurement model. However, Bailey (2007) used some of the same indicators and his measure should be comparable to the measure used by Erikson, MacKuen, and Stimson.

than reported by the other measures. This may reflect Kennedy's well-known early reluctance on issues of race and social justice (e.g., see Beschloss 2007, 235–79). However, as shown by the new measure, in the year before his assassination he became decidedly more liberal. This is consistent with case study evidence suggesting that Kennedy became more active on race and social justice issues in 1963 (e.g., see Wood and Huss 2008).

President Johnson declined in rhetorical liberalism through time and was quite moderate by 1968. This may reflect moderation due to Republican gains in the 1966 midterm elections. As will be discussed, such moderation due to changing institutional alignments is supported by the evidence reported in the next chapter. Johnson's moderation may also reflect public disenchantment with civil rights and the Great Society, or general weariness with his presidency (Bullion 2008, 165–204).

Nixon is more moderate during the early part of his presidency than suggested by the other measures. This is consistent with the large amount of social legislation Nixon proposed and signed into law during his first term. He proposed environmental regulation for clean air and signed legislation on clean air, clean water, safe drinking water, endangered species, protection of marine mammals, noise pollution, worker safety, and equal employment opportunity. By executive order, President Nixon created the Environmental Protection Agency and the National Oceanic and Atmospheric Administration. President Nixon also used administrative tools to revitalize the Federal Trade Commission, particularly in regard to consumer protection. He also proposed expanding the Food Stamp program and signed legislation increasing Social Security, Medicare, and Medicaid benefits.

Ford is more conservative than even Reagan during the 1976 election year. Carter begins as a moderate, but grows increasingly liberal through his term. Reagan is consistently conservative throughout both terms with little variation, as is George H.W. Bush. Clinton stands out as the most liberal democratic president, perhaps reflecting his strong emphasis on issue-based rhetoric. During 2002 George W. Bush is more conservative than even Reagan as he increasingly pushes for higher military spending in response to 9/11 and more tax cuts.

However, he becomes markedly less conservative during the 2004 election year.

Given the ocular and statistical similarity of the four time series across administrations, and the consistency of the new measure with well-known within-presidency behaviors, the measure of the president's rhetorical liberalism used in this study also has construct validity. Therefore, the new measure is appropriate for the statistical analyses reported in later chapters.

CONCLUSIONS

In this chapter, I have described the core measures used in later chapters for evaluating the centrist versus partisan models of presidential representation. Evaluating these competing theoretical models requires measuring two concepts: mass citizen preferences and presidential issue liberalism.

Mass citizen preferences are measured using an updated version of Stimson's (1999) measure of public mood. This is the most common time series measure of mass citizen preferences in modern public opinion research. Public mood measures citizen issue preferences through time using over 4,000 public opinion surveys conducted between 1952 and 2004. The resulting time series is based on public attitudes across a range of issues, the most continuous and important of which are the nine issues used to construct the new measure of presidential issue liberalism. Each time point on the public mood measure can be viewed as a one-period snapshot of the median voter depicted in Figures 2.1 through 2.5. The time interval for each snapshot in subsequent analyses will vary depending on whether we use Stimson's annual or quarterly measure of public mood.

Presidential issue liberalism is measured by constructing a time series of all presidential remarks on the nine issues recorded in *Public Papers of the Presidents*. Using an approach involving iterative machine and human coding, the time series reflects every public presidential remark about welfare, race, education, urban problems, health care, crime, the environment, military spending, and size of government. These issues are reported by Stimson (1999, 77–85) as the most important and continuous components of public mood.

The presidential issue liberalism measure used here is grounded in presidential rhetoric. Presidential rhetoric is an important indicator of how presidents stand on the issues. It is also the president's primary tool of political persuasion. Modern presidents are on permanent campaigns of public rhetoric that attempt to persuade the mass public toward their own issue positions.

It is also important to recognize that the measure used here encompasses earlier measures of presidential issue liberalism. The data source, *Public Papers of the Presidents*, contains all public remarks by presidents relating to their positions on legislation, court decisions, and budget proposals. It also contains every presidential State of the Union message and budget transmittal message, and continuing public appeals for passage of legislation, executive orders, directives, signing and veto statements, speeches to interest groups, news conferences, news briefings, and other general policy-relevant remarks.

Utilizing the *Public Papers* also allows analysis of more finely divided and dynamic measures of presidential issue liberalism than those used in past research. Presidential rhetoric occurs hour by hour, daily, weekly, monthly, quarterly, annually, and by administration. We can aggregate presidential remarks to any time interval for statistical analysis.

The graphs of presidential issue liberalism reported in this chapter provide an important first look at the relative efficacy of the theoretical models discussed in Chapter 2. The centrist model discussed in the previous chapter strongly implies that presidents of both political parties should converge on the median voter when they express public issue stances. Competition for political support between the two political parties should presumably force presidents toward the median voter if the centrist model is correct.

However, the graphs reported in Figures 3.2 and 3.3 suggest that presidents do not converge. Rather, they suggest the overarching importance of partisanship to presidents' public issue stances. There are sharp changes in presidential liberalism associated with each new presidential administration. Both Democratic and Republican presidents appear to be partisans after elections, with little or no evidence of convergence through time.

Although this result suggests that the centrist model is incorrect, this evidence is not definitive. Presidents may be partisans who show tendencies toward centrism through time as a function of elections, the need for additional support, economic or institutional constraints, or the partisan division of the electorate. The next chapter turns toward a more systematic analysis of the relationship between presidential issue stances and mass preferences.

APPENDIX 3.1

Following are the lists of keywords and coding rules for the nine issue dimensions of presidential liberalism reported in this study. Note that Boolean searches were used to eliminate irrelevant sentences brought up by many of the keywords.

Issue domain	Keywords	Liberal/conservative coding rules
Education	educat, school, teacher, voucher, integration, segregation, busing, affirmative action	Liberal statements favor increased federal spending on education, increased federally sponsored or spurred education services, federal intervention to promote school integration, and generally a larger federal role in education. Conservative statements favor a decreased role for the federal government in all of these areas.
Health	health, medic, hospital, doctor, physician, disease, illness	Liberal statements support a greater role for the federal government in providing or supporting health care, opposition to health privatization, greater information on birth control, efforts to reduce the costs of health care, and greater government versus private responsibility. Conservative statements favor a decreased role for the federal government in all of these areas.

Crime	crime, gun, death penalty, victim's right, sentencing, sentenced, criminal, prison, penitentiar, capital punishment, death row, Brady bill, trigger lock	Liberal statements oppose capital punishment and promote defendants' rights, gun control, and a rehabilitation approach to addressing problems of crime. Conservative statements support capital punishment, oppose gun control, and favor greater spending to address problems of crime and get-tough approaches in dealing with criminals.
Urban Problems	urban, ghetto, inner city, inner-city, innercity, riot, big city, large city, big cities, large cities, central city, central cities, barrio, skid row, slum	Liberal statements favor correcting problems of poverty, unemployment, ghettos, and race in big cities. Conservative statements favor a restricted federal role in these areas. Conservative statements also favor using force to maintain law and order in cities.
Welfare	welfare pay, welfare recip, welfare prog, welfare mo, welfare pol, social welfare, relief pay, single mo, supplemental income, food stamp, AFDC, WIC, TANF, Aid to Families with Dependent Children, poverty, low income, low-income, poor, indigent, destitute, impoverish, deprived, deprivation, needy, underprivilege, under-privilege.	Liberal statements favor a greater federal role in helping the poor, increased welfare spending, improving the lives of those in poverty, and promoting greater economic equality in America. Conservative statements favor federal restraint, and suggest greater individual responsibility for economic circumstances.
Race	race, racial, negro, African American, Hispanic, Latino, Native American, segregation, affirmative action, minorit, slavery, colored, Jim Crow, voting rights act, discrimination, busing, riot, Black Panther, Martin Luther King, Malcolm X	Liberal statements imply that the administration should be pushing racial integration, fair housing, voting rights, equal jobs, education, nondiscrimination, and greater opportunity for minorities. Conservative statements favor a decreased role for the federal government in all of these areas.

(*continued*)

Issue domain	Keywords	Liberal/conservative coding rules
Environment	Environment, global warming, climate change, pollut, Kyoto, forestation, acid rain, emission, smog, ozone, greenhouse, pesticide, hazardous waste, superfund, clean air, clean water, EPA, toxic, noxious, contamin, atmosphere.	More liberal statements advocate greater spending on the environment or increased efforts to protect the environment. Conservative statements advocate reduced environmental regulation and spending and approaches grounded in markets.
Military Spending	national defense, national security, military spending, military budget, military expenditure/outlay, defense spending/budget/expenditure/outlay, arms spending/budget/expenditure/outlay, security spending/budget/expenditure/outlay.	Liberal statements favor reducing expenditures for national defense, security, and the military. Conservative statements advocate increasing these expenditures.
Size of Government	big government, small government, reduce tax, tax cut, cut tax, lower tax, high tax, over-regulat, over regulat, government waste, bureaucratic waste, red tape, reduce spend, cut spend, lower spend, excessive regulat, excessive government, limited government, reduce government, reduced government, wasteful government.	Liberal statements advocate measures that would increase the size of government, regulation, spending, or taxation. Conservative statements advocate reduced government, regulation, spending, taxation, or waste.

CHAPTER 4

Evaluating the Centrist versus Partisan Models of Presidential Representation

In this chapter the measures of presidential issue liberalism and public mood described in Chapter 3 are used to evaluate the theoretical models of presidential representation described in Chapter 2 empirically. In particular, I shall be concerned with whether and how mass preferences affect presidential issue stances through time.

From either a centrist or a partisan standpoint, changing presidential issue stances can be viewed as an aspect of democratic representation. Under centrist theory the president is the single nationally elected representative in the American system and should express issue stances that appeal to the larger public. To do otherwise invites loyalty to the opposing party and a reduction in popular support. Thus, centrist theory would predict that presidential issue stances should remain reasonably consistent with mass preferences.

Under partisan theory presidents represent narrower interests that they may feel are consistent with their own conception of the national interest. Presidents are elected to lead. Leadership often implies moving the mass public away from their current issue stances. Under partisan theory presidents are not passive responders to the mass public, but should often attempt to persuade the public toward their own positions and those of their political parties. Thus, the question of how presidents fulfill their role as democratic representatives, either as responders or leaders, is the overarching concern.[1]

---

[1] Here I am referring to substantive leadership. However, leadership can take either a substantive or a symbolic form. Presidents can lead the public substantively as discussed here. They can also respond to mass preferences, but do so in a way that reinforces pre-existing public preferences through symbolic messages. Substantive

Given that the measure of presidential liberalism used in this chapter is grounded in presidential rhetoric, an ancillary concern is to understand why modern presidents engage in a permanent campaign. Is it simply because we are now in an age of mass media, and presidents are expected to communicate with the public? Or is the permanent campaign something presidents use to accomplish political ends? It seems reasonable to believe that presidents do not pursue the permanent campaign simply to hear themselves talk. Therefore, they must pursue the permanent campaign for political reasons.

Given this assertion, do presidents use the permanent campaign to bolster their public support? Do they somehow sense mass preferences and cater to them by reflecting what they perceive as the median voter's position? Or do presidents attempt to build their public support by convincing persuadable citizens of the worth of their own issue positions?

At the core, if presidential liberalism responds to the mass public, then there should be statistical covariation through time between Stimson's measure of public mood and the measure of presidential liberalism. Public mood gauges average citizen liberalism at each point in time. It also measures the changing issue stances of the median voter depicted in Figures 2.1 through 2.5 in Chapter 2. If the centrist model is correct, then presidential issue stances should change with movements of the political center. Thus, public mood and presidential liberalism should track consistently through time.

However, the discussion of the centrist model in Chapter 2 also suggested a number of potential factors that might condition covariation between presidential liberalism and mass preferences. Presidential liberalism may only respond to mass preferences when presidents have incentives to build their public support. This need may occur when public approval of the president's job performance or issue stances is low. It may also occur during presidential election years, when voters must be convinced that incumbent presidents or their political parties best reflect citizen preferences. Thus, a conditional centrist model would predict that covariation between public mood and presidential liberalism may exist only during certain periods.

leadership implies moving the public toward the leader's preferences, whereas symbolic leadership may not.

Further, the spatial analysis of the partisan model in Chapter 2 suggested that presidents may feel a stronger need to bolster their political support during minority party presidencies. Under these conditions presidents seek support from those near the political center, because their governing majorities are more fragile. Presidents may bolster their support either through partisan persuasion or through movement toward the political center.

The partisan model also suggested that presidents have a greater incentive to attempt to bolster their political support when the percentage of persuadable citizens is larger. Consistent with this argument, as the electorate becomes more polarized, there should be less incentive for presidents to move toward the median voter. This chapter evaluates all of these predictions.

This chapter also addresses the more general question of what determines changes in presidential liberalism through time. Presidents are pragmatists, as well as democratic representatives. Therefore, presidential liberalism may be conditional on various contextual factors. Presidents facing a weak economy should be reluctant to pursue a liberal agenda. Presidents facing a hostile Congress should also have more difficulty pursuing a liberal agenda. Thus, as pragmatists, presidents should temper their relative liberalism and conservatism in response to the changing economic and institutional context.

EVALUATING CORE EXPECTATIONS ABOUT THE CENTRIST AND PARTISAN MODELS

Simple Graphical Analyses

A simple starting point for evaluating the centrist versus partisan models is to graph the time series of presidential liberalism and public mood on the same plot. Figure 4.1 contains such a graph. As discussed in Chapter 3, the presidential liberalism time series is expressed in standard deviation units. To provide comparability, the public mood time series is also standardized.[2] For ease of exposition, Figure 4.1 also contains a marker for the start of each new presidency.

Readers should closely examine movements in the two time series as an initial test of the centrist versus partisan models. Examining

[2]   See footnote 9 in Chapter 3 for a discussion of what it means to standardize a variable.

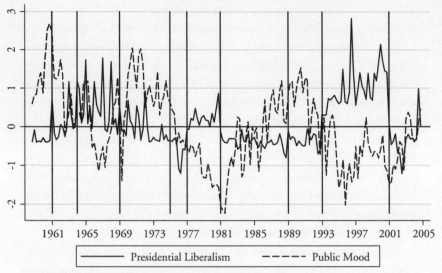

Figure 4.1. Presidential liberalism and public mood.
Note: Pearson's $r = -0.23$; Granger Independence Test ChiSqr$(4) = 2.56$, p-value $= 0.63$.

the within-presidency intervals suggests that there must be little or no long-term relationship between public mood and presidential liberalism. During the Eisenhower administration (1958–1960), public mood (dashed line) moved in a sharply liberal direction while President Eisenhower (solid line) remained consistently conservative. During the Kennedy and Johnson administrations (1961–1968), public mood moved in a conservative direction, while presidential liberalism moved in a liberal direction. During the Nixon administration (1969–1974), public mood moved toward liberalism and remained quite liberal, while the president was moderate to conservative. The Carter presidency (1977–1980) was characterized by a sharp conservative shift in public mood, while the president remained moderately liberal. During the Reagan and George H. W. Bush administrations (1981–1992), public mood moved sharply from very conservative early in the Reagan administration to quite liberal during the middle Bush presidency, followed by a reversal. At the same time, presidents remained steadily conservative with little movement. During the Clinton administration (1993–2000), public mood exhibited dynamic variation, but was mostly conservative. At the same time, presidential liberalism grew increasingly liberal. It was only during the Ford administration

(1975–1976) and the last two years of the George W. Bush administration (2003–2004) that public mood and presidential liberalism moved in the same direction. Thus, an ocular test of whether presidents systematically cater to mass preferences suggests that they do not.

More often, presidential issue liberalism and public mood actually move in *opposite* directions. Confirming these opposite tendencies, Pearson's correlation coefficient, reported at the bottom of Figure 4.1, is negative at −0.23. Additionally, the test of Granger independence reported at the bottom of Figure 4.1 shows that the null hypothesis of statistical independence of presidential liberalism from public mood cannot be rejected.[3] Thus, the statistical evidence from Figure 4.1 strongly supports the partisan over the centrist model. Presidents generally buck the trends of changing mass preferences. They do not cater to the mass public, but remain partisans in their public issue stances.

However, it may be that there is a relationship between public mood and presidential liberalism once we have removed the obvious fluctuations through time due to partisanship. In other words, presidents may be partisans, but still respond to centrist forces at the margins.

To check this possibility, a new variable was created that removed effects from presidential liberalism due to changing presidential partisanship. Specifically, the presidential liberalism time series was regressed on indicator variables for each new presidential administration.[4] The residuals from this regression were then saved for further analysis. The residual series contains the original presidential liberalism time series, but purged of effects due to partisanship or ideology that are unique to each presidency. Therefore, it represents movements in presidential liberalism independent of presidential partisanship.

Figure 4.2 contains the purged presidential liberalism time series graphed against public mood. Considering the within-presidency

---

[3] Granger independence is defined here as a lack of Granger (1969) causality. The notion of Granger causality states that if after controlling for the history of a set of variables, one variable statistically affects another, then the variable is said to Granger cause the other. In the analysis reported at the bottom of Figure 4.1, presidential liberalism was regressed on four quarterly lags of both presidential liberalism and public mood. The four lags of public mood are not jointly significant in the regression. Therefore, presidential liberalism is statistically independent of public mood.

[4] Indicator variables are also called dummy variables and are coded zero or one, depending on the presence or absence of a condition of interest.

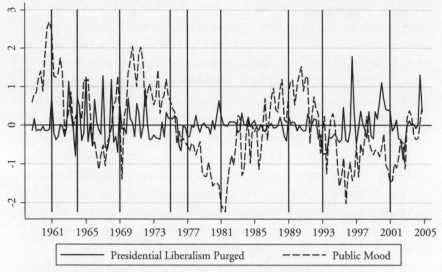

Figure 4.2. Presidential liberalism purged and public mood.
Note: Pearson's $r = -0.01$; Granger Independence Test ChiSqr(4) = 4.63, p-value = 0.33.

intervals, it is again clear that presidents do not follow the long-term fluctuations in public mood. Presidential liberalism purged of individual presidency effects is fairly stable around a mean. In contrast, public mood continuously drifts dynamically from liberal to conservative over the entire time frame. There is a period during the Kennedy and early Johnson administrations when the two time series appear to track together. This could relate to the civil rights era or the Great Society programs. We shall evaluate this assertion below. Again, the two time series also move together for certain periods of the Ford and George W. Bush administrations. However, the overall pattern of covariation is not systematic. Thus, the ocular test again suggests that presidential liberalism is oblivious to changing mass preferences.

Further, as reported at the bottom of Figure 4.2, the Pearson's correlation between purged presidential liberalism and public mood is near zero. The test of Granger independence between public mood and purged presidential liberalism is also nonsignificant, again confirming that there is no systematic relationship from public mood to presidential liberalism through time. Thus, the graphical and statistical evidence is clearly supportive of the partisan over the centrist model.

Multivariate Statistical Methods

Although suggestive, these graphical and statistical results are not a rigorous standard for assessing the relationship between public mood and presidential liberalism. These are bivariate tests. However, it may be that there are suppressor effects,[5] requiring multivariate regression methods for exposition. Therefore, further analyses must be done to confirm these nonrelationships.

Of course, the measures of interest in this study are time series, and it is well known that regressions involving such measures are often characterized by autocorrelation, and perhaps heteroskedasticity. Accordingly, throughout this chapter and the next, most of the statistical analyses rely on regressions with measures of coefficient precision calculated using Newey–West (1987) autocorrelation and heteroskedasticity-consistent standard errors.[6]

The estimated coefficients from this procedure are identical to those produced by ordinary least squares (OLS) regression. This is appropriate because it is well known that OLS coefficient estimates are unbiased in the presence of either autocorrelation or heteroskedasticity. However, in the presence of either anomaly, measures of the precision of OLS coefficients (i.e., standard errors) can be biased upward or downward.

The Newey–West (1987) procedure is quite general in producing the correct measures of coefficient precision. In the absence of

[5] Suppressor effects occur in a bivariate analysis when an omitted variable is correlated with included variables in directions that cancel the actual effect. Such effects can also be called spurious nonassociation effects (e.g., see Healey 2008, Chapter 17). Note that this differs from suppressor effects in multivariate analysis, which commonly refers to the inclusion of variables that, although uncorrelated with a dependent variable, can actually magnify the effects of independent variables due to correlation with those variables (e.g., see Cohen and Cohen 1983).

[6] To apply time series regression methods to these data, it is first necessary to determine whether the time series are stationary. To be deemed weakly stationary, a time series must meet three criteria. It must be mean-reverting, have non-time-varying variance, and have a non-time-varying autocovariance function. When a time series is not stationary, this causes problems with statistical inference, the so called "spurious regressions" problem (Granger and Newbold 1974). Thus, time series stationarity tests were performed, including computation of correlograms, augmented Dickey–Fuller (1979), and KPSS (Kwiatkowski et al. 1992) tests. All stationarity tests showed definitively that the presidential liberalism and public mood time series are stationary. Given this stationarity, it is appropriate to apply regression methods to evaluate the multivariate relationships.

autocorrelation and heteroskedasticity, Newey–West standard errors reduce to OLS standard errors. In the absence of autocorrelation, Newey-West standard errors reduce to the standard errors from White's (1980) heteroskedasticity-consistent estimator. In the absence of heteroskedasticity, Newey–West standard errors become autocorrelation-consistent standard errors. Thus, the Newey–West approach is sufficiently flexible to handle the most common anomalies associated with OLS regression applied to time series data.[7]

A Replication

First, consider a replication of the analyses contained in Erikson, MacKuen, and Stimson (2002; see also Stimson, MacKuen, and Erikson 1995). Using annual data and indirect measures of presidential liberalism, they report strong statistical relationships between public mood and presidential liberalism. Table 4.1 presents an analysis that replicates their analyses, but using quarterly data and a more direct measure of presidential liberalism.

The first replication, reported in the first column of Table 4.1, is similar to that in Erikson, MacKuen, and Stimson (2002, Table 8.3, second column). The dependent variable is presidential liberalism. The independent variables are presidential liberalism lagged one quarter, public mood lagged one quarter, and an indicator variable switched on for presidents who are Republican.

Consistent with Erikson, MacKuen, and Stimson (2002), the statistical results in Table 4.1 show that past presidential liberalism and presidential partisanship are strong predictors of current presidential liberalism. Lagged presidential liberalism is statistically significant (marked with asterisks as described in the table notes hereafter). Concerning partisanship, the results for Republican also show a statistically significant relationship. Republican presidents are 0.57 standard deviations less liberal than Democrats.

Erikson, MacKuen, and Stimson (2002) also find that each unit increase in public mood produces 0.52 units increase in presidential

[7] Alternative approaches to estimation would be to employ estimated generalized least squares or ARIMA techniques. The Newey–West approach was chosen over these approaches because of its simplicity and weak demands on the limited number of time series observations. However, Wood and Lee (2008) report parallel analyses for many of the analyses in this chapter using ARIMA methods.

TABLE 4.1. *Presidential liberalism as a function of mass preferences*

Model variable	Erikson, MacKuen, and Stimson (2002, Table 8.3)	Erikson, MacKuen, and Stimson (2002, Table 8.7)
Presidential liberalism$_{t-1}$	0.40* (5.03)	−0.60* (−7.50)
Republican	−0.57* (−6.33)	−0.57* (−6.41)
Public mood$_{t-1}$	−0.00 (−0.47)	−0.00 (−0.19)
Δ Public mood		0.01 (0.86)
Constant	0.56 (1.46)	(0.45) (1.18)
Diagnostics		
N	184	184
p(LM χ^2_1)	0.38	0.28
p(F)	0.00	0.00

Note: The numbers in the table are coefficients and *t*-statistics (in parentheses). The *t*-statistics are calculated using Newey–West (1987) autocorrelation and heteroskedasticity consistent standard errors.

  * Indicates statistical significance at the 0.01 level.
 ** Indicates statistical significance at the 0.05 level. N is the number of observations. p(LM χ^2_1) is the probability of rejecting the null hypothesis of no residual autocorrelation using the Breusch (1979)–Godfrey (1978) autocorrelation test. p(F) is the probability for the overall model F statistic.

liberalism. However, inconsistent with their analysis, the results in Table 4.1 show that public mood produces no statistically significant change in presidential liberalism. There is no systematic relationship between public mood and presidential liberalism.

The second analysis is an error correction specification (Davidson et al. 1978; Engle and Granger 1987; Bannerjee et al. 1993) positing an equilibrium between public mood and presidential liberalism. This analysis is similar to that reported in Erikson, MacKuen, and Stimson (2002, Table 8.7, first column). This model is just an alternative autoregressive form to that reported in the first column (e.g., see De Boef and Keele 2008). However, this specification allows one potentially to account for both short- and long-term relationships. The dependent variable is change in presidential liberalism. The independent variables are Republican, presidential liberalism lagged one quarter, change in public mood (short-term component), and public mood lagged one quarter (long-term component).

Erikson, MacKuen, and Stimson (2002) report that public mood and presidential liberalism are in long-term equilibrium with each other, and that when shocks occur to this equilibrium, about 87 percent of the disequilibrium is corrected each year after the shock. However, the results reported in the second column of Table 4.1 reveal no evidence of equilibrium between presidential liberalism and public mood. Neither the short- nor the long-term coefficient for public mood is statistically different from zero.

Of course, Figures 4.1 and 4.2 also cast serious doubt on the notion that presidential liberalism is in any sort of equilibrium with public mood. The simple correlation between the two time series is actually negative at −0.23, and they typically move in different directions. Consistently, the statistical results in Table 4.1 show no significant relationship between presidential liberalism and public mood, either short- or long-term.

The results of the graphical and statistical analyses reported above provide strong evidence that presidents' relative liberalism is grounded in partisanship. The graphs show substantively important movements in presidential liberalism with each new presidential administration where there is a shift from one political party to the other. Further, Republican partisanship is statistically significant and strongly negative in both statistical specifications, showing a major difference between Republicans and Democrats in public issue stances. On the other hand, there is virtually no covariation between presidential liberalism and public mood in either the graphical or statistical analysis.

These results are inconsistent with some past work seeking to explain presidential liberalism (Canes-Wrone 2006; Canes-Wrone and Shotts 2004; Erikson, MacKuen, and Stimson 2002; Stimson, MacKuen, and Erikson 1995; but see Cohen 1999). What accounts for the difference? One possibility is that past work relied on annual measures that may not adequately capture the within-presidency dynamics of presidential liberalism. This study uses quarterly measures based on a more complete record of presidential issue stances. Presidents and the public can shift significantly within years and across presidencies.

Adequately modeling these effects requires data that have not been available to past research.[8]

Another possible reason for the difference is that past work relied on measures that only indirectly reflect presidential liberalism. Erikson, MacKuen, and Stimson (2002; see also Stimson, MacKuen, and Erikson 1995) used a measurement model with a dependent variable that combined two annual Congress-based measures and a court-based measure that were not closely related to the underlying concept.[9] Canes-Wrone and Shotts (2004) collapsed presidential and public issue stances into a binary variable and did not actually measure presidential liberalism.

In contrast, this study measures presidential liberalism directly using presidents' public issue stances across nine issue areas. Of course, it is impossible to compare results from past studies with those reported here, because earlier work did not graph presidential liberalism against mass preferences for comparison. Also, it did not report the presidential liberalism data upon which its analyses were based. Nevertheless, the results reported here should cast serious doubt on prior work positing a consistent pattern of presidential responsiveness to changing mass preferences through time.

Issue-Specific Public and Presidential Liberalism

The results in the preceding section imply that presidents do not respond systematically to changing mass preferences as defined by Stimson's aggregate measure of public mood. However, recall that public mood is a combination of public opinion responses across multiple issue domains. Thus, it may be that by combining the multiple issue domains into aggregate measures of public and presidential liberalism, presidential responsiveness to the mass public has been obscured for single issues. The president may respond for some issues, but not others, ultimately damping the statistical results for the

---

[8] However, note that in separate unreported analyses there is also no relationship between presidential liberalism and public mood when Zupan's (1992) annual presidential ADA scores, the McCarty and Poole (1995) measure, or Bailey's (2007) measure for any of the specifications reported in Table 4.1 is used.

[9] Their Solicitor-General measure had communality of only 0.05 with the latent construct.

aggregates reported in the preceding section. Presidential responses to mass preferences may also be time-bound in the sense that presidents may respond for only part of a particular time series.

Do presidential issue stances respond to mass preferences when the single-issue domains that compose aggregate public and presidential liberalism are considered? To answer this question we must isolate and analyze separate time series for the various issue domains of public mood and presidential liberalism.

In considering the presidency, isolating the separate issues is not a problem for any time interval (i.e., weekly, monthly, quarterly, annually). Presidents have spoken about the issues comprising the measure of public liberalism with sufficient frequency through time to allow time series to be constructed for any interval.

In considering public mood, the underlying public opinion data for the separate dimensions of public mood are too sparse to construct quarterly time series for each issue. Indeed, the sparseness of public opinion data on each issue through time is arguably the very reason that an aggregate measure of public mood was constructed in the first place.

However, annual measures can be constructed for most issue domains for both public and presidential liberalism. Constructing the annual measures for presidential liberalism is just a matter of choosing a different aggregation interval for the sentences used to code presidential liberalism. Instead of the liberal and conservative sentences spoken by the president being summed during each quarter as described in Chapter 3, they are now summed annually to produce annual time series.

Constructing the annual measures for mass preferences requires more consideration. Stimson (1999) reported a separate annual time series for each of the nine issue domains in the appendix to his treatise on public mood. However, the reported time series are short, sometimes starting in the 1970s and running only through 1996. Stimson later utilized an extended version of the same data in another study (2004, Chapter 2), with many of the time series running from the 1950s through 2000. Although he reported data for only six of the nine original time series, the longer time series do enable a more robust test of how presidents respond to changing public liberalism through time.

The separate annual public issue liberalism time series utilized in this section are drawn from Stimson (2004) and measure the percent public support for greater federal involvement in urban affairs, welfare, education, health care, the environment, and race relations.[10] Greater public support for federal involvement in each issue domain constitutes a more liberal public issue stance, whereas the opposite constitutes a more conservative stance.

The statistical specifications for the separate issues differ from the replications reported above. Following Erikson, MacKuen, and Stimson (2002), the replications reported above employed a lagged dependent variable (LDV) to control for inertia in presidential liberalism, as well as autocorrelation. However, statistical specifications with an LDV provide a difficult standard against which to evaluate the effects of other variables. This is because changes in independent variables through time tend to be highly collinear with the LDV, because it contains the independent variables in the prior time period. Consequently, many analysts would argue that an LDV should only be used when there is some theoretical rationale (e.g., adaptive behavior, error correction, VAR). Other than providing a strong control for autocorrelation, there is no strong theoretical rationale for using an LDV in this analysis. Thus, to provide the most amicable statistical environment for public mood to affect presidential liberalism, the LDV is omitted from the analyses below.[11]

Results of the issue-specific statistical analyses are reported in Table 4.2. They confirm once again the overarching importance of partisanship to presidential issue stances. Republican presidents are

[10] In a separate unreported analysis, the public opinion data from Stimson (1999) were used in an analysis similar to that reported below. The results for the omitted issue domains show no relationship between mass public opinion liberalism and presidential liberalism.

[11] There are also many other compelling reasons to be cautious about using an LDV. Using an LDV significantly alters the interpretation of model coefficients (i.e., the LDV captures the dynamics for all variables jointly, whereas the independent variables capture only the instantaneous effects). All of the independent variables are constrained to have the same lag dynamic, which seems unreasonable in most cases. Further, if autocorrelation remains after their inclusion, then using an LDV can lead to inconsistent coefficient estimates. Additionally, including an LDV in a time series analysis where the dependent variable is stationary ALWAYS produces a noninvertible moving average autocorrelation process. A proof of this statement is in the explanation of the Koyck model in most standard econometrics texts. In other words, an LDV can actually generate unwanted autocorrelation.

TABLE 4.2. *Issue-specific presidential liberalism and issue-specific public liberalism*

Variable	Support greater federal involvement to solve problems involving					
	Urban affairs	Welfare	Education	Health care	Environment	Race relations
Republican	−1.27*	−1.38*	−1.30*	−1.53*	−1.94*	−1.14*
	(−3.95)	(−3.92)	(−3.44)	(−4.16)	(−3.87)	(−4.77)
Public liberalism$_{t-1}$	−0.07**	−0.01	−0.00	0.06	0.08**	0.09*
	(−2.03)	(−0.27)	(−0.01)	(1.19)	(1.91)	(3.15)
Constant	5.02*	1.21**	0.92	−3.87	−4.43	−3.47*
	(2.56)	(1.70)	(0.37)	(−1.02)	(−1.44)	(2.51)
Diagnostics						
N	36	37	45	45	30	45
$p(F)$	0.00	0.00	0.00	0.00	0.00	0.00

Note: The numbers in the table are coefficients and *t*-statistics (in parentheses). The *t*-statistics are calculated using Newey–West (1987) autocorrelation and heteroskedasticity consistent standard errors. N is the number of observations. $p(F)$ is the probability for the overall model F statistic.

* Statistical significance at the 0.01 level.
** Statistical significance at the 0.05 level.

uniformly more conservative than Democratic presidents in their public remarks for each of the six issue domains. This systematic response again suggests the efficacy of the partisan over the centrist model in explaining presidential liberalism through time.

With regard to presidential responsiveness to public issue liberalism, the second row of Table 4.2 shows that presidents are again unresponsive to the mass public for four of the six issue domains. Coefficients reflecting presidential responses to public sentiment favoring greater federal involvement in urban affairs, welfare, education, and health care are either signed in the wrong direction or not statistically different from zero. However, the estimated coefficients reflecting presidential responsiveness to public sentiment favoring greater federal involvement in the environment and race relations are statistically significant in the direction predicted by the centrist model.[12] Each 10 percent change in public liberalism on the environment and race relations produces about 0.8 and 0.9 standard deviation units of change in presidential liberalism on the environment and race relations, respectively.

What do these presidential responses to public sentiment on the environment and race relations look like in terms of time series covariation? We can show this covariation graphically using the same strategy as for Figure 4.2. First the presidential environmental and race relations time series are purged of the effects of partisanship by regressing each on the Republican indicator and saving the resulting residuals. Then the purged presidential liberalism time series are graphed jointly with the public opinion time series for comparison. Again, the measures are standardized to place them in a common metric. Figures 4.3 and 4.4 contain the resulting graphs.

Consider first the relationship for environmental liberalism shown in Figure 4.3. The Pearson's correlation between the two time series is 0.28, suggesting the same positive relationship as reported in Table 4.2. However, the Granger independence test from public environmental liberalism to presidential environmental liberalism shows

---

[12] Note that in separate analyses using Stimson's (1999) measures for the environment and race relations, the relationships between presidential and public liberalism are statistically zero.

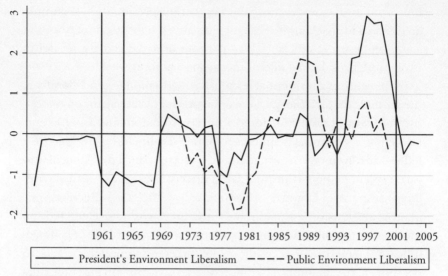

Figure 4.3. Presidential and public environmental liberalism.
Note: Pearson's $r = 0.28$; Granger Independence Test ChiSqr(1) $= 0.03$, *p*-value $= 0.86$.

that the two time series are statistically independent. In other words, once we control for inertia, the relationship reported in Table 4.2 disappears.

Nevertheless, the graph in Figure 4.3 shows that there was an isolated period when public and presidential liberalism on the environment tracked through time. In particular, the decade of the 1970s shows a common trend for the public and the president. However, this common trend disappears with the Reagan administration and after. Other segments of the two time series occasionally move together, but one would be hard pressed based on the graphical evidence to claim that presidents are systematically responsive to public opinion on the environment.

Consider now the graph containing public and presidential liberalism on race relations. Again, confirming the result in Table 4.2, the Pearson's correlation between presidential and public liberalism is positive at 0.47. The Granger independence test also confirms that the two time series are not statistically independent. However, the graphical evidence again suggests that the relationship is time bound.

Considering Figure 4.4, starting with the Kennedy administration in 1961 and continuing through the early Nixon administration, the

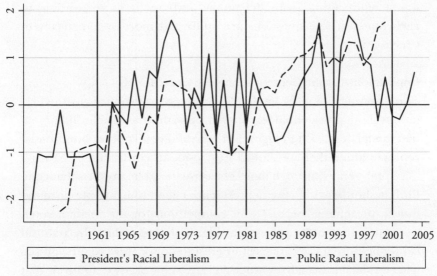

Figure 4.4. Presidential and public racial liberalism.
Note: Pearson's $r = 0.47$; Granger Independence Test ChiSqr(1) $= 5.29$, p-value $= 0.02$.

public became increasingly liberal on the issue of race relations. At the same time, presidents became increasingly liberal. Beginning in 1972, the public initiated a pattern of increasing racial conservatism that lasted until the election of Ronald Reagan in 1981. During this same period, presidents became more moderate in their public statements on race relations. Beginning in 1981, the public reversed course and became increasingly liberal, with a peak of racial liberalism occurring in 2000. During this same period, presidents were less responsive in their public issue stances. Thus, the graphical analysis of covariation between public and presidential liberalism on race relations again suggests a relationship that is restricted to certain eras. As with the environment, most of the covariation occurred prior to 1981, with the period from 1961 through 1972 (i.e., the civil rights era) being the heyday of presidential responsiveness on race relations.

What is unclear from these graphical analyses is who responded to whom through this period. Did presidents respond limply to the median voter as predicted by the centrist model? Were presidents also participants in this process, attempting to persuade the mass public on the issues of the environment and race? Was the relationship unidirectional as assumed by the model in Table 4.2, or was it bidirectional, with the public and president responding to each other? These questions are addressed more systematically in Chapter 6.

Implications for the Centrist versus Partisan Models

The theoretical models developed in Chapter 2 produce clear expectations about presidential responsiveness to the mass public. If the centrist model described in Figure 2.1 is a valid depiction of presidential representation, then we should see presidents consistently mirroring mass preferences through time. The centrist model predicts that equilibrium should exist between presidential liberalism and public mood due to the glue associated with competition for the median voter. According to centrist theory, presidents should reflect the political center because it is in their self-interest to do so. However, the graphical and statistical analyses reported here show pretty definitively that presidents do not passively and limply track the median voter in their public issue stances.

On the other hand, if the partisan model described in Figures 2.2 through 2.5 is a valid depiction of presidential representation, then presidents should find little advantage in moving to the political center. Majority party presidents do not need to do so. Presidents from the minority party may choose to do so. However, they may also attempt the strategy of partisan persuasion. The evidence reported above suggests that under most circumstances they choose the latter strategy, because there is little or no evidence of systematic presidential centrism in the graphical or statistical analyses reported above. Rather, partisanship appears as the most important factor determining presidential behavior.

EVALUATING THE CONDITIONAL PRESIDENTIAL CENTRISM MODEL

The preceding analyses show that presidents do not *generally* respond to democratic signals flowing from the mass public. However, it is still possible that they may *sometimes* respond to signals when they have especially strong needs for support or due to contextual factors. We saw evidence above of presidential responsiveness on environmental and race relations issues during one era. However, can we find more systematic evidence of conditional presidential responsiveness to the mass public?

Under the conditional presidential centrism model proposed by some past research, presidents are strategic actors who have a sophisticated understanding of public opinion. They use this understanding to evade responsiveness to mass preferences. As expressed by Jacobs and Shapiro (2000, Chapter 2), they utilize their understanding of public opinion to engage in "crafted talk" *to manipulate, rather than respond to* the mass public.

Of course, presidents often face a tradeoff between pursuing partisan policy goals and pleasing the political center. This tradeoff has become sharper with increased party polarization through time and the competing need to cater to fellow partisans in Congress and the electorate. As suggested by the discussion of the partisan model in Chapter 2, failing to deliver on policy promises can result in alienation of a president's core constituencies, which may impose high costs. Thus, it is only periodically, before elections and when they require broad public support, that modern presidents may feel they must pursue a centrist strategy. At other times, their cost–benefit calculations are weighted toward pursuit of ideological goals and appeasing fellow partisans.

Consistent with this theme of conditional presidential centrism, some scholars argue that congruence between the president's policy stances and the mass public has declined through time as a result of increasing partisan polarization (Canes-Wrone and Shotts 2004; Jacobs and Shapiro 2000; Zaller 2003). They also report statistical evidence that this congruence is conditional on the electoral cycle and the president's public approval ratings. Canes-Wrone and Schotts (2004) use budgetary data to find that as elections approach, presidential budgetary proposals become more consistent with mass preferences. Various other scholars suggest that presidents only respond to the public when they need to increase their public approval ratings (Hibbs 1987; Hicks 1984; Manza and Cook 2002). Consistently, Canes-Wrone and Schotts (2004) find that congruence between the mass public and the president occurs only when approval ratings are in their midrange. This is allegedly because both low- and high-approval presidents have little to lose by pursuing their favorite policies at the expense of the public's approval.

We can test for these strategic presidential behaviors by creating indicator variables and interactions for certain ranges of public approval with public mood.[13] Table 4.3 contains statistical analyses that explore these potential effects. The dependent variable is again presidential liberalism. The first two columns of Table 4.3 report statistical analyses intended to explore presidential responsiveness to public mood during low and midrange public approval periods. The regressions contain public mood lagged one quarter, an indicator for Republican presidencies, indicators for when public approval is low (first column) or in the midrange (second column), and the interactions of the public approval range indicators with public mood.

Public approval of the president's job performance is measured as the percentage of survey respondents approving of presidential job performance in consecutive Gallup surveys from 1958 through 2004. This is the standard Gallup measure that has been used in past research. The Gallup survey organization regularly asks the question, "Do you approve or disapprove of the way [president's name] is handling his job as president?" This question has been asked at least quarterly (on an irregular basis) since 1949, and at least monthly (sometimes more than once in the same month) since 1978. These survey data were used to extract quarterly public approval time series using the procedure and software WCALC developed by Stimson (1991).[14]

Using the quarterly time series of public approval, two indicators were created for the different ranges of approval. Low public approval was coded as one for any time the president's approval rating was below

---

[13] Interaction variables are commonly used to uncover conditional effects between variables. To interact variables means to multiply them together. When the interaction variable is zero, due to either variable in the interaction being zero, then the interaction variable drops out of the regression equation. When the interaction variable is nonzero, then the interaction coefficient represents the added effect due to conditioning.

[14] WCALC recursively produces a smoothed and averaged time series. The irregular surveys prior to 1978 were smoothed and the near-monthly surveys after 1978 were averaged to produce the quarterly data.

TABLE 4.3. *Presidential liberalism, public approval, and elections*

Model variable	Conditional centrism (low approval)	Conditional centrism (midapproval)	Conditional centrism (elections)	Conditional centrism (elections II)
Republican	−0.90*	−0.94*	−0.90*	−0.79*
	(−9.46)	(−10.62)	(−9.74)	(−8.64)
Public mood$_{t-1}$	−0.04	−0.07	−0.01	−0.02
	(−0.93)	(−1.40)	(−0.30)	(−0.48)
Approval$_{t-1}$ low/mid	−0.20**	0.17**		
	(−2.16)	(2.36)		
Approval$_{t-1}$ low/mid × mood$_{t-1}$	−0.02	0.10		
	(−0.18)	(1.55)		
Election year			0.15	0.42**
			(1.35)	(1.91)
Election year × public mood$_{t-1}$			−0.07	
			(−0.76)	
Republican × election				−0.46*
				(−1.88)
Constant	0.61*	0.53*	0.56*	0.50*
	(7.14)	(5.97)	(7.00)	(6.10)
Diagnostics				
N	184	184	184	184
$p(F)$	0.00	0.00	0.00	0.00

Note: The numbers in the table are coefficients and *t*-statistics (in parentheses). The *t*-statistics are calculated using Newey–West (1987) autocorrelation and heteroskedasticity consistent standard errors. *N* is the number of observations. $p(F)$ is the probability for the overall model *F* statistic. The presidential liberalism and public mood variables are standardized to facilitate interpretation.

* Statistical significance at the 0.01 level.
** Statistical significance at the 0.05 level.

40 percent, and zero otherwise. This number is arbitrarily selected but consistent with the earlier theoretical discussion in Chapter 2.[15] Midrange public approval was coded as one for periods during which public approval was between 40 and 60 percent, and zero otherwise.

The analysis for presidential responsiveness to public mood when public approval is low is contained in the first column of Table 4.3. The coefficient for public mood in the second row now represents presidential responsiveness to public mood for periods when public approval was above 40 percent.[16] The coefficient for public mood for low-approval periods is contained in the interaction variable in fourth row. The statistical results show no change in presidential liberalism through time as a function of public mood for either low- or high-approval periods. In other words, presidents do not strategically adjust their public issue stances to bolster their public support during low-approval periods.

However, Canes-Wrone and Schotts (2004) assert that this relationship should be nonmonotonic. Presidents have little incentive to cater to the median voter when their approval ratings are high. This is because they have support to burn. According to their argument, presidents also have little incentive to cater to the median voter when their public approval ratings are low. This is allegedly because there is little they can do to alter those low ratings. Under this logic, presidents only have a strategic incentive to cater to the median voter when their public approval ratings are in the midrange.

Given this assertion, the second column of Table 4.3 contains an analysis to isolate periods when public approval is in its midrange. The coefficient on public mood in the second row now reflects periods when public approval is in its low or high range (<40 or >60).[17] The coefficient on the interaction variable in the fourth row represents periods when approval is in its midrange (>40 and <60). Neither coefficient is statistically significant at conventional levels. The interaction coefficient is positive and in the predicted direction at 0.10.

---

[15] Results reported below are unchanged whether one selects 20, 30, or 50 percent for low approval.

[16] The coefficients for Approval$_{t-1}$ Low/Mid in the third row are descriptive only, showing the relative liberalism of low and nonmidrange approval presidents after controlling for other factors.

[17] The results reported here are the same for limits between 35 and 65.

However, this substantive effect (if it exists) is very small. It would take a ten–standard deviation movement in public approval coupled with a one–standard deviation shift in public mood to produce a one–standard deviation shift in presidential liberalism. Again, this is a very small effect, suggesting little or no movement by the president toward the median voter during midrange approval periods.

Another assertion flowing from past work on conditional centrism is that presidents cater more to the median voter during election years. The third column of Table 4.3 tests for the differential responsiveness of presidential liberalism to public mood during election years. The election year variable is measured as an indicator switched on during the first three quarters of presidential election years, and zero otherwise.[18] The coefficient for public mood in the second row now represents presidential responsiveness to public mood in nonelection years. The interaction coefficient in the fourth row represents election year responsiveness. Neither coefficient is statistically different from zero. Since neither coefficient is statistically significant, we can conclude that presidents are no more responsive to public mood during election years than during nonelection years.

Consistent with this result, if we look back at the graphs in Figure 4.1, it is easy to see that the gap between presidential liberalism and public mood actually widens during election years for some presidents, and narrows for others. Thus, presidential responsiveness to mass preferences does not change systematically as a function of election year incentives.

Another approach to evaluating presidential responsiveness during election years is to consider movements by Republicans and Democrats either toward or away from their respective party medians. The conditional centrist model predicts that both Republicans and Democrats should move away from their respective party medians during election years. However, such movements also run the risk of demobilizing fellow partisans. Therefore, presidents may also have a strategic incentive NOT to move away from their party medians during election years. Contrary to the centrist model, where both Democrats and

---

[18] An alternative election year coding was also tried, in which the election variable is coded as on during the quarter prior to the presidential election and off for all other quarters. The results do not differ either substantively or statistically from those reported here.

Republicans are expected to move toward the median voter during election year, a prediction from the partisan model would be that they each either stick to or move closer to their respective party medians. In other words, we should expect Republicans either not to move or to become more conservative during election years. Democrats should either not move or become more liberal.

To test for these potential effects, the election year indicator was interacted with the party of the president. This interaction variable makes it possible to observe the direction of changing presidential liberalism for both Republicans and Democrats as a function of election year incentives.

The estimated coefficients in the fourth column of Table 4.3 suggest the partisan over the centrist interpretation. The constant at 0.50 represents the relative liberalism of Democratic presidents during non-election years in standard deviation units from zero.[19] The coefficient for Republican represents the difference for Republicans during non-election years. It shows that Republicans during nonelection years are on average about −0.79 standard deviations more conservative than Democrats. This means that the average nonelection year liberalism for Republicans is about −0.29 standard deviation units from zero. The coefficient for election year at 0.42 represents the change in liberalism for Democrats during election years. In other words, Democrats become more liberal during election years to about 0.92 standard deviations above zero. The coefficient for the interaction at −0.46 shows the change for Republicans during election years. In other words, Republicans also shift toward their respective party medians to about −0.75 standard deviations below zero. These are large differences, again suggesting the importance of partisanship to presidential behavior.

More generally, this analysis suggests that the conditional centrist model of presidential behavior that has been advocated by some past presidency research (Canes-Wrone, Herron, and Shotts 2001; Canes-Wrone and Shotts 2004; Hibbs 1987; Hicks 1984; Jacobs and Shapiro 2000; Manza and Cook 2002; Zaller 2003) does not work. Instead,

---

[19] Zero is by definition the average presidential liberalism, because the variable is standardized.

presidents of both parties become even more partisan during election years, rather than moving toward the median voter.

EVALUATING PARTISAN MODEL EXPECTATIONS ABOUT PRESIDENTIAL CENTRISM

The preceding analyses suggest that partisanship is the dominant explanation for changing presidential liberalism through time, whether core expectations of the centrist model or a conditional centrist model is being considered. However, there are also expectations about presidential centrism that flow directly from the partisan model developed in Chapter 2. The partisan model suggests that presidents may (or may not) move toward the political center when they need additional support. Again, presidents have two possible strategies: they can move toward the political center; or they can attempt to persuade those near the political center toward their own positions.

In either case, the partisan model described in Figures 2.2 through 2.5 suggests certain situations in which presidents should be more likely to seek additional support. First, under the partisan model, we should expect minority party presidents to be more needful of additional support than majority party presidents. This is because minority party presidents govern with a smaller committed base than majority party presidents (e.g., see Figure 2.4). Therefore, they have greater incentive to attempt bolstering their political support by moving toward the political center, through political persuasion, or by some combination of the two strategies. The particular strategy they use is what we seek to determine empirically.

Second, presidents have stronger incentives to seek additional support when the percentage of persuadable citizens is higher. By definition, when a higher proportion of the electorate are persuadable, the president's governing coalition is smaller and potentially more fragile (e.g., see Figure 2.3 relative to Figure 2.2). Again, under this scenario, presidents have an incentive to attempt to bolster their support either by moving toward the political center or through political persuasion.

Third, presidents have fewer incentives for centrist behavior when the electorate is more polarized. In part, this is because there are fewer persuadable citizens (e.g., see Figure 2.5). When there are few persuadable citizens, it makes little sense to move to the center, because the potential payoff is small. Additionally, any movement toward the political center runs the risk of alienating core constituents. This means that under polarized conditions presidents should be reluctant to engage in centrist strategies. Rather, they should rely on partisan persuasion. This strategy energizes the president's core support and may also persuade some of the few persuadable citizens.

This section now turns toward testing these predictions with empirical data. Consider first whether minority party presidents exhibit more centrist behavior than majority party presidents. The analysis in Chapter 2 shows that the average *NaturalSupport* and *PotentialSupport* for majority party presidents since 1952 have been 59 and 73 percent, respectively. This suggests that majority party presidents have almost no need to move toward the political center to maintain their majority status. They have support to "burn." However, minority party presidents have averaged less, with *NaturalSupport* and *PotentialSupport* at 42 and 60 percent, respectively. This means that there may be incentives for minority party presidents to cater to the median voter, instead of relying exclusively on a partisan persuasion strategy. Which of the two strategies do minority party presidents generally use?

Again, we can evaluate this question by interacting an indicator for minority party presidencies with public mood. The only minority party presidents of the modern era have been Republicans, and they have never been in the majority with respect to party identification (see Table 2.1). Therefore, we must interact the partisanship variable (Republican) with public mood to achieve the desired variable. The first column of Table 4.4 reports the statistical results.

The coefficient for the public mood variable now represents responsiveness for majority party presidents. The coefficient for the interaction variable represents the responsiveness for minority party presidents. Consistent with predictions from the partisan model, majority party presidents (i.e., Democrats) are completely unresponsive to public mood. Indeed, the significant negative coefficient in the first row of Table 4.4 shows that they even move away from the mass public. The obvious reason for this divergence is that they have no need to move from the party median toward the electoral median. Majority party presidents have adequate support to maintain their majority status

TABLE 4.4. *Presidential liberalism and the partisan model*

Model variable	Minority party presidents	Electoral percent persuadable	Electoral polarization
Public mood$_{t-1}$	−0.21*	−0.03	−0.03
	(−2.80)	(−0.72)	(−0.86)
Minority party president	−0.86*	−0.91*	−0.97*
	(−10.33)	(−9.85)	(−10.75)
Minority party president × mood$_{t-1}$	0.28*		
	(3.47)		
%Persuadable		−0.03	
		(−0.70)	
%Persuadable × mood$_{t-1}$		0.08*	
		(2.61)	
Polarization			0.09*
			(2.58)
Polarization × mood$_{t-1}$			−0.17*
			(−4.07)
Constant	0.54*	0.64*	0.48
	(7.15)	(7.79)	(1.18)
Diagnostics			
N	184	184	184
$p(F)$	0.00	0.00	0.00

Note: The numbers in the table are coefficients and *t*-statistics (in parentheses). The *t*-statistics are calculated using Newey–West (1987) autocorrelation and heteroskedasticity consistent standard errors. *N* is the number of observations. $p(F)$ is the probability for the overall model *F* statistic. Presidential liberalism, public mood, and electoral polarization are standardized to facilitate interpretation.

 * Statistical significance at the 0.01 level.
** Statistical significance at the 0.05 level.

without such responsiveness. Indeed, they even have leeway to pursue contrarian policies.

Also consistent with the partisan model, the interaction coefficient for minority party presidents is strongly significant and positive. We can interpret this effect in relation to the minority party indicator variable. The coefficient for this variable shows that minority party presidents (i.e., Republicans) are on average more conservative than majority party presidents (Democrats) by about −0.86 standard deviations. However, under minority party presidencies, each one-standard-deviation increase in public liberalism produces an average 0.28 standard deviations increase in presidential liberalism. Thus, minority party presidents moderate their relative conservatism through time in response to increasing public liberalism.[20]

Another prediction flowing from the partisan model developed in Chapter 2 is that presidents have a greater incentive to move toward the political center when the number of persuadable citizens is larger. A larger percentage of persuadable citizens implies a greater potential for building political support. It also implies a greater need for support, because the president's coalition is by definition less committed. However, it may also be that presidents do not generally move toward the political center under this condition, choosing instead to rely on a strategy of partisan persuasion.

We can evaluate whether presidents employ either strategy by constructing a measure of citizen persuadability. The measure of persuadability used here is based on citizens' voting behavior in recent elections. An electorate that rarely defects from its partisanship when voting can be thought of as not very persuadable. It is driven more by party identification. In contrast, an electorate characterized by a high percentage of defectors who sometimes cast votes for candidates from the other political party can be thought of as more persuadable. Using this conceptualization, data from consecutive ANES studies can be used to calculate the prevalence of straight party voting versus defection. This variable is labeled *electoral percent persuadable*. It is defined as the percentage of party defectors for each House election since 1952 relative to the vote predicted by respondents' party identification. Defectors will have voted for House members from the party opposite from their party identification.[21]

Again, this variable is interacted with public mood to evaluate the effect of electoral persuadability on presidential responsiveness. The

---

[20] I say "generally" here because the steady conservatism of Presidents Reagan and George H. W. Bush in Figure 4.1 belies this result. One can only say that these results would have been even stronger if these two presidents followed the typical pattern of Republican presidents.

[21] This measure relates to the strength of partisanship data presented in Table 2.1. However, it is based on reported actual behavior, rather than self-reported party identification. Because the measure is based on actual behavior, it is probably somewhat of an understatement of the true percentage persuadable in the electorate. This is because many who are persuadable may have decided to vote for their own party's candidate. Nevertheless, using a measure based on behavior avoids measurement error concerns about survey respondent arbitrariness in reporting the strength of their partisanship.

second column of Table 4.4 contains results for this analysis. Presidential liberalism, public mood, and electoral percent persuadable are again standardized to facilitate interpretation. Given this standardization, the public mood variable now represents presidential responsiveness to public mood when the electoral percent persuadable is at its average. This occurs when 18.05 percent of partisans defect to candidates from the other political party. When this percentage of the electorate is persuadable, the results in the second column show that presidents are completely unresponsive to public mood. The mood coefficient is not statistically different from zero.

When this result is compared with the analysis in Figure 2.2 of Chapter 2, this percentage of persuadable citizens occurs when the president's *NaturalSupport* is almost exactly 60 percent. Under this scenario presidents have no need to seek additional support. Thus, the statistical results in the second column confirm the scenario in Chapter 2.

The interaction variable in the fifth row of the second column represents the effect of public mood on presidential liberalism as we move away from the average electoral percent persuadable of 18.05 percent. When the electoral percent persuadable is one standard deviation higher at 21.6 percent, a one–standard deviation increase in public liberalism produces an increase in presidential liberalism of about 0.08 standard deviation. In other words, presidents do employ a strategy of moving more toward the political center as the electoral percent persuadable becomes larger.

However, note that this is not a very large movement, also suggesting that presidents use a mixed strategy for building political support. Using the estimated coefficients for calculation, it would take roughly a twelve–standard deviation increase in the electoral percent persuadable for a one–standard deviation increase in public mood to produce a one–standard deviation increase in presidential liberalism. Consistent with this result, the analysis of the partisan model in Chapter 2 shows that presidents of either party generally don't have to move very far to achieve majority status. Thus, this small change is highly consistent with predictions from the partisan model.

Finally, the partisan model predicts little or no presidential movement toward the political center as the electorate becomes more polarized. Indeed, presidents may move more toward their respective party medians under this condition to energize their political base. As shown in Figure 2.5, polarization means fewer persuadable citizens, as in the preceding analysis. Movement to the political center with a polarized citizenry also implies a greater risk of alienating core constituents. Therefore, as polarization increases, presidents have less incentive to move to the political center.

We can measure polarization of the electorate using the ANES survey data shown in Table 2.1. As depicted in Figure 2.5, polarization can be thought of as occurring when the distribution of Democrats and Republicans is skewed toward the respective ends. Those near the ends of the two distributions are strong identifiers, whereas those closer to the center and tails are weaker identifiers. Under polarization, the greatest masses of identifiers are concentrated at the ends of the distribution and consist of strong Republicans and strong Democrats. Therefore, using the data from Table 2.1, we can define polarization as the sum of the proportion of strong Republicans and Democrats for each consecutive survey.

The third column of Table 4.4 contains the statistical analysis using this measure of electoral polarization. Given that the variables are standardized, the coefficient for public mood now represents presidential responsiveness to public mood when electoral polarization is at its average. This occurs when the proportion of strong Democrats and Republicans is roughly 30 percent. Again, the coefficient for public mood in the first row shows that with polarization at its average, presidents are unresponsive to public mood.

The interaction coefficient between polarization and public mood gives the president's relative responsiveness to mood as we move polarization above or below the average. For example, if the degree of polarization is higher by one standard deviation, then each one–standard deviation increase in public mood makes the president 0.17 standard deviations less responsive. Conversely, if the degree of polarization is lower, then presidents become more responsive to public mood by the same amount. This result confirms once again the prediction of the partisan model. As polarization increases, presidents are less prone toward moving toward the political center. Instead, they increasingly cater to the median partisan, rather than the median of the electorate.

WHAT OTHER FACTORS AFFECT
PRESIDENTIAL LIBERALISM?

The evidence in the preceding sections speaks loudly about the importance of partisanship to presidential representation. However, there may also be variations in presidential liberalism through time due to other factors. This section considers how the different economic and institutional contexts facing each president affect presidential liberalism.

The Economic Context

Some past research suggests that presidential liberalism should depend on economic factors (e.g., see Cohen 1999, Chapter 5). Under economic constraints, presidents may be less able to pursue a liberal agenda. It becomes more difficult to finance such an agenda when the economy is weak. Conversely, it should be easier for a president to be liberal when the nation is flush with resources and the government is not ridden with fiscal problems. As expressed by Durr (1993), "... expectations of a healthy (or improving) economy contribute to the willingness within the American public to underwrite a liberal domestic policy agenda."[22] A similar argument might also pertain to the presidency. Presidents should be more liberal when they are not constrained by a weak economy, and when the nation has the economic confidence to support a liberal agenda.

It could also be argued that certain other aspects of the economic environment may produce incentives for presidents to favor government expansion or contraction. For example, in contrast to Durr's assertion, strong economic growth can be inflationary, producing incentives for smaller government. Weak economic growth favors the Keynesian solution of government expansion. Similarly, unemployment produces a need for more generous government programs along the welfare dimension. In contrast, inflation produces a bias toward reduced government spending in an attempt to cool a robust economy.

Considering these contrasting perspectives, the effect of the economic context on presidential liberalism is evaluated by entering a

---

[22] Chapter 5 explicitly tests Durr's hypothesis about economic expectations and public mood.

set of economic variables into a base model containing presidential partisanship and public mood. The economic variables are economic growth, change in unemployment, the inflation rate, and a generalized index of the current state of the economy.

Economic growth is measured as the real annualized percent change in U.S. gross domestic product (GDP in 2000 dollars), as reported quarterly by the Commerce Department. Change in unemployment is measured as the average change in the unemployment rate during each quarter, as reported by the Bureau of Labor Statistics. Inflation is measured as the annualized quarterly percent change in the consumer price index for urban consumers, as reported by the Bureau of Labor Statistics.

The general state of the economy is gauged by the Conference Board's Composite Index of Coincident Indicators. This index is constructed from four time series chosen by the Conference Board because they are consistently in step with the current state of the economy.[23] The four time series composing the Coincident Index are payroll employment, personal income, industrial production, and manufacturing and trade sales, the last three in 1996 dollars. According to the Conference Board (2001, 13), the Coincident Index is a "broad series that measures aggregate economic activity; thus they define the business cycle."

The economic context model is reported in Table 4.5. Observe that all of the economic variables are statistically significant. As economic growth gets stronger, presidents become more liberal. Further, a stronger coincident index of current economic conditions corresponds with greater presidential liberalism. Both variables suggest that Durr (1993) is correct in asserting that strong economic conditions support a more liberal government.

The variables reflecting specific economic outcomes also make sense. Table 4.5 shows that as unemployment rises, presidents become

---

[23] The Conference Board also publishes the Composite Index of Leading Indicators and the Composite Index of Lagging Indicators. I chose the Composite Index of Coincident Indicators because the concern here is how the economy is currently doing. The Leading Indicators is used mainly for forecasting how the economy will be doing in the future, while the Lagging Indicators is used for confirmation of peaks and troughs in the business cycle.

TABLE 4.5. *Presidential liberalism and the economic context*

Variable model	Economic effects
Public mood$_{t-1}$	−0.01**
	(−1.75)
Republican	−0.86*
	(−9.42)
Δ GDP	0.03**
	(1.95)
Index of coincident indicators$_{t-1}$	0.26**
	(1.88)
Δ Unemployment	0.52*
	(3.31)
Inflation	−0.03**
	(−2.06)
Constant	1.42*
	(2.65)
Diagnostics	
N	184
$p(F)$	0.00

Note: The numbers in the table are coefficients and *t*-statistics (in parentheses). The *t*-statistics are calculated using Newey–West (1987) autocorrelation- and heteroskedasticity-consistent standard errors. *N* is the number of observations. $p(F)$ is the probability for the overall model *F* statistic.
 * Statistical significance at the 0.01 level.
 ** Statistical significance at the 0.05 level.

more liberal. In other words, presidents tend to favor more liberal Keynesian welfare solutions when unemployment is increasing. Consistently, higher inflation produces less presidential liberalism and support for smaller government. These results are also consistent with standard economic prescriptions, because government should get smaller and presidents less liberal when there is an inflationary economy.

The Institutional Context
There may also be variations in presidential issue liberalism because of the different institutional contexts facing each president. Presidents may feel constrained in their relative liberalism by their practical ability to achieve a liberal agenda. Specifically, political pragmatism may be important because presidents may not push a liberal agenda as hard

when there is little possibility of achieving that agenda due to the partisan composition of Congress. In other words, presidents should be more liberal when it makes political sense to push a liberal agenda.

Social scientists have long understood that the most important determinants of congressional behavior are cues arising from partisanship, ideology, and constituency (Jackson 1974; Kingdon 1989; Matthews and Stimson 1975). Presidents can affect congressional behavior only to the extent that these cues are weak, and then only at the margins (Bond and Fleisher 1990; Bond, Fleisher, and Wood 2003; Edwards 1989). Therefore, presidents are constrained by the composition of Congress and its relative sympathy with the president's ambitions.

One way to test for this effect on presidential behavior is to create a set of indicator variables reflecting the changing partisan alignment between the president and Congress through time. Accordingly, indicators were created for each potential institutional configuration that a president might face. For example, an indicator variable Democratic President/Republican Congress is switched on when there is a Democrat in the White House and Republicans are in control of both the House and Senate. Similarly, Republican President/ Democratic Congress, Republican President/Divided Congress, and Republican President/Republican Congress represent periods consistent with their respective labels. The alignment Republican President/Republican Congress is rare within the sample, occurring only during the last two years of the George W. Bush presidency. There has been no period when there was a Democratic president facing a divided Congress. The category Democratic President/Democratic Congress is relegated to the constant term in the regression.

The statistical results using these indicator variables are reported in the first column of Table 4.6. They show clearly that presidents are more conservative when facing high institutional constraints. The constant shows that the average liberalism of Democratic presidents facing Democratic congresses has been about 0.24. Democratic presidents facing Republican congresses are significantly less liberal than those facing Democratic congresses by about 0.83 standard deviations. Republican presidents facing Democratic congresses are also lower in issue liberalism by about 0.65 standard deviations, and Republican

TABLE 4.6. *Presidential liberalism and the institutional context*

Model variable	Institutional alignment	Ideological divergence	President's party hegemony
Public mood$_{t-1}$	0.00	−0.03*	−0.02**
	(0.23)	(−3.20)	(−1.87)
Democrat president/Republican congress	−0.83*		
	(−5.94)		
Republican president/Democratic congress	−0.65*		
	(−6.31)		
Republican president/Divided congress	−0.76*		
	(−9.15)		
Republican president/Republican congress	0.46*	0.34	0.26
	(2.63)	(1.44)	(1.57)
Ideological distance president-Congress		−0.41*	
		(−2.58)	
President's party percent seats in Congress			0.02*
			(4.34)
Constant	0.24	2.18*	0.37
	(0.46)	(3.78)	(0.41)
Diagnostics			
N	184	184	184
$p(F)$	0.00	0.00	0.00

Note: The numbers in the table are coefficients and *t*-statistics (in parentheses). The *t*-statistics are calculated using Newey–West (1987) autocorrelation- and heteroskedasticity-consistent standard errors. *N* is the number of observations. $p(F)$ is the probability for the overall model *F* statistic.

 * Statistical significance at the 0.01 level.
** Statistical significance at the 0.05 level.

presidents facing divided congresses are lower in liberalism by about 0.76 standard deviations.[24]

At first glance, the result for Republican President/Republican Congress appears anomalous. Republican presidents facing Republican congresses are estimated to be more liberal by about 0.46 standard deviations. Note, however, that the number of observations associated with this institutional alignment is very low, consisting only of the last two years of the George W. Bush presidency (2003 and 2004). Note also that Figure 4.1 shows that George W. Bush turned quite liberal during the 2004 election year, a movement toward the center that

[24] A test of the null hypothesis that Democratic President/Republican Congress = Republican President/Democratic Congress = Republican President = Divided Congress cannot be rejected.

does not generally hold across presidents (see the fourth column of Table 4.3). Moreover, Bush pressed for passage of a variety of spending programs during this period that substantially increased the size of government (e.g., prescription drug coverage for seniors, "no child left behind" education spending, the Emergency Plan for Aids Relief in Africa). As a result, George W. Bush was often accused of betraying conservative fiscal principles. Therefore, this result is not as anomalous as it might initially appear.

Another approach to evaluating how institutional constraints affect presidential liberalism is to consider how presidential liberalism changes as a function of ideological divergence from Congress. Presidents who diverge ideologically from Congress should be less able to pursue a liberal agenda. We can use Poole and Rosenthal's (1991) DW-Nominate scores to construct such a measure of institutional divergence.[25] They measure presidential and congressional liberalism using the set of all roll call votes in Congress. The measure used here takes the absolute value of the president's DW-Nominate score minus the average of the House and Senate majority party DW-Nominate medians. Because the president's DW-Nominate score does not vary within presidencies, and only varies biennially for Congress, this is a fairly coarse measure. We must also control for the fact that Republican presidents facing Republican congresses (i.e., George W. Bush in 2003 and 2004) might actually be rhetorically different as a result of ideological convergence. Therefore, an indicator variable is also included to control for this potential effect.

Consistent with the results in the first column of Table 4.6, the results in the second column show that as the ideological distance between the president and Congress increases, presidents become less prone toward pursuing a liberal agenda. In other words, presidents are pragmatists who temper their relative liberalism when there is little chance of achieving their partisan goals.

Finally, Bond and Fleisher (1990; see also Peterson 1990) show that presidents are advantaged or disadvantaged in their dealings with Congress by the magnitude of their co-partisan support. As presidents observe stronger supporting coalitions in Congress, they should feel

---

[25] See footnote 3 in Chapter 3 for a reference to Poole and Rosenthal's (1991) methodology in computing the various Nominate scores.

more freedom to pursue their particular agendas. To evaluate this potential effect, a variable was created to measure the president's support in Congress. The measure is constructed simply as the average percentage of seats held by the president's party in each house of Congress, and is labeled President's Party Percent Seats in Congress. Again, we must take into account the possibility that Republican presidents facing Republican congresses may behave differently as a result of having strong co-partisan support.

Again consistent with the results in the first and second columns of Table 4.6, the results in the third column show that as the president's legislative coalition becomes stronger, presidents become more prone toward pushing a liberal agenda.

From these statistical results it becomes obvious that presidential partisanship is tempered by a dose of pragmatism when presidents face an unwilling and powerful Congress. Although presidents do not alter their public issue stances based on responsiveness to the median voter, they do alter their public issue stances based on the realities of partisan institutional politics.

CONCLUSIONS

As democratic representatives, centrist theory predicts that presidents should take issue stances during the permanent campaign that are reasonably consistent with mass preferences. However, presidents are also elected to lead and may also attempt to move the public toward their own issue stances and those of their political parties.

Past research has highlighted the centrist model in its various forms as explaining presidential issue stances. Some have claimed that presidents respond to mass preferences generally, whereas others have viewed the president as more strategic, responding to mass preferences only when required by periods of low approval or elections. These studies are part of a more general pattern in American politics of highlighting the importance of the median voter to institutional behavior and representation. Yet past research on the presidency has not subjected the centrist model to rigorous scrutiny.

In this chapter, measures of presidential liberalism derived from the president's permanent campaign have been utilized to evaluate expectations flowing from the centrist and partisan models. The statistical results reported here suggest that presidents do not cater systemat-ically to mass preferences. Rather, they consistently express partisan issue stances that are intended to persuade the public toward their own positions. The analysis of the partisan model shows that presi-dents do move slightly toward the political center when they are from the minority party, and when there are a larger proportion of per-suadable citizens. However, their primary strategy is to build support by persuading those near the political center to move toward their own positions.

Graphically, of the ten presidencies examined here, only two moved for brief periods in the same direction as dynamic movements in mass preferences. The analyses contained no statistical model in which the public mood variable was statistically significant in the direction predicted by the centrist model. These results stand in stark contrast to the conclusions of past research that has used more indirect measures and annual data.

Presidents also appear unresponsive to incentives from changing public approval and elections. Some advocates of the centrist model have concluded that presidents are more responsive to mass pref-erences during election years and for certain ranges of their pub-lic approval ratings (Canes-Wrone, Herron, and Shotts 2001; Canes-Wrone and Shotts 2004; Hibbs 1987; Hicks 1984; Jacobs and Shapiro 2000; Manza and Cook 2002; Zaller 2003). However, neither the graphical nor the statistical evidence from this study supports such conclusions. Indeed, the results reported here show that presidents actually become *more* partisan during election years, instead of moving toward the median voter.

What does drive the president's issue-based liberalism? Partisan-ship is the primary determinant, but presidential partisanship is also tempered by pragmatic concerns. The graphical and statistical results show clearly that the president's issue liberalism shifts sharply when a new president of a different political party assumes office. Within presidencies, issue liberalism flows in apparent independence from changing mass preferences. During some presidencies, the president's issue liberalism moves little, if any, perhaps due to ideological behav-ior (e.g., Reagan, George H. W. Bush). During others, the president's issue liberalism actually moves in a direction opposite from that of the public, perhaps due to efforts to lead (e.g., Kennedy, Johnson, Clinton).

Presidential liberalism also changes with the economic and institutional contexts facing each president. Previous research has suggested that presidents and the public respond to economic incentives (Cohen 1999; Durr 1993; Erikson, MacKuen, and Stimson 2002). The analysis reported here confirms this earlier research. Presidential liberalism also changes in response to the institutional alignment facing each president. As the partisan environment relative to Congress becomes more conducive to achieving a liberal agenda, presidents espouse more liberal issue stances.

What are the implications of these results for understanding presidential representation? As discussed in Chapter 1, one of the core questions of democratic theory is who our elected officials represent and how well. As discussed in Chapter 2, representation implies responsiveness and some degree of following mass preferences. The many analyses reported here suggest that modern presidents don't do much following of mass preferences. Rather, the image that emerges from this chapter is one of presidents playing to the median partisan, rather than to the median voter. However, their partisanship is moderated by political pragmatism. Of course, our constitutional design implies that presidents should both follow and lead. The next chapter examines whether presidents successfully lead.

CHAPTER 5

Presidential Persuasion and the Mass Public

Presidents are elected while making promises from either the left or right. As a result, they are initially *by definition* out of synch with the political center. They generally do not consider moving very far toward the political center, because of promises and strongly held beliefs. However, they recognize that without support from the political center their policy leadership can fail. Presidents need public support to achieve their political goals. Thus, they are forced by fear of failed partisan leadership to attempt to persuade the mass public toward their own positions.

After they assume office, new issues continually arise from the ongoing flow of events and problems. They are expected to lead in formulating and achieving solutions to these issues. Whether an issue derives from the president's incoming agenda or from the continuing flow of policy problems, partisanship virtually always colors the president's perception of how to address the many issues that must be confronted. Thus, presidents pursue permanent campaigns to convince people of the rectitude of their partisan stances and their particular approaches to serving the national interest.

Just as George Washington attempted to persuade the mass public to support funding for the Jay Treaty in 1795–96, modern presidents also seek to persuade the mass public. As detailed in the introductory chapter, Washington successfully used public persuasion to bolster support for his position on the Jay Treaty. With shifting popular support, opposing members of the House of Representatives who had previously blocked funding for the treaty switched their positions.

The measure was approved by a vote of 56–48, reflecting bipartisan support in a House dominated by the opposing party.

Of course, as the nation's first president, Washington had some unique political resources. He was a war hero, charismatic, viewed broadly as a wise leader, and a national father figure. As commander-in-chief during the American Revolution, he was almost unanimously agreed upon at the constitutional convention as suited to become the nation's first president. Most viewed him as selfless in serving the nation and above the partisan fray. Washington was held in almost religious awe by people of all political persuasions. Because of these unique political resources, Washington wielded considerable influence as he attempted to persuade the mass public toward what was initially a very unpopular stance.

Washington and the Jay Treaty controversy provide anecdotal evidence that presidents can be successful at public persuasion. However, can we find more than anecdotal evidence that presidents are successful at public persuasion? Modern presidents lack most of Washington's unique attributes. None have been national heroes of Washington's stature. Most lack personal charisma of the type that would evoke blind commitment. Virtually all modern presidents have been self-interested partisans whose view of how to pursue the national interest conflicted with the views of a sizeable segment of the population. As a result, they cannot count on the deference given to Washington during the Jay Treaty controversy. Rather, modern presidents must use cultivated images, control of their message, and tools of mass communication if they are to successfully persuade the mass public.

We do not know whether modern presidents are *systematically* successful at public persuasion. Do modern presidents generally succeed or fail when they attempt to persuade the public toward their own positions? If they do succeed, then what is the typical magnitude of the public response to presidential efforts at leadership? If modern presidents generally fail at public persuasion, then are there at least some occasions and circumstances when they are more successful? What determines the degree of success or failure of presidential efforts at public persuasion? This chapter addresses these questions, again using the measures developed in Chapter 3.

Of course, it is important to reiterate that the partisan model developed in Chapter 2 does not *require* presidents to be successful at partisan persuasion. Under the partisan configurations described in Figures 2.2 through 2.4 of Chapter 2, presidents governing from the left or right need to convince only a minority of persuadable citizens. Given their typical level of public support after elections and the typical number of persuadable citizens near the political center, presidents may be able to use the prestige, symbolic status, and resources of the presidency to convince the few who must be persuaded. However, presidential resources are finite and diminishing through time, so presidents may also fail over the long term. This should especially be true during periods when there are few persuadable citizens or the electorate is highly polarized, as depicted in Figure 2.5 of Chapter 2. We turn now toward empirically evaluating the relative success of modern presidential efforts at public persuasion.

EXISTING EMPIRICAL EVIDENCE ON PRESIDENTIAL PERSUASION

The Intuitive Evidence

From a strictly intuitive standpoint, presidents must believe that their efforts at public persuasion can be successful, or they would not engage in them so routinely. It is well established that modern presidents actively campaign for public support long after elections (Blumenthal 1982; Ornstein and Mann 2000). They maintain staffs of political consultants and pollsters in the White House who give advice on how to persuade the public (Heclo 2000; Jacobs and Shapiro 2000). They employ "outreach" offices to buttress their public support (Tenpas 2000). They speak in public literally thousands of times during a presidential administration to espouse their issue positions publicly. Further, presidential efforts at public persuasion have been increasing through time (Hart 1989; Kernell 1997). Indeed, the permanent campaign has changed the mode of governing in America, perhaps permanently (Heclo 2000; Tenpas 2000).

The rationale for the modern increase in presidential efforts at public persuasion is probably the campaign mentality through which presidents achieve the White House in the first place. In an earlier era, candidates were chosen by party insiders and owed their loyalty to the organization that would mobilize public support on their behalf. However, with the decline of political parties and the rise of candidate-centered selection processes, the need for candidates with strong communications skills became more important. As expressed by David Gergen (2000, 348), "Even through Truman and Eisenhower, it was more important to be a good broker among interests than a good speaker." However, the evolution of communications technology produced an expectation that a candidate for president would be a strong rhetorician. Mass communications and the television age have meant that an inability to speak in public makes it very difficult to be elected in the first place (Heclo 2000).

The decline of political parties as an organizing force in American politics has also meant that presidential success while in office depends on the president's ability to get a message out and appeal directly to the public (Brace and Hinckley 1992; Edwards 1983; Kernell 1997). Accordingly, the White House has through time developed a sophisticated communications apparatus (Grossman and Kumar 1981; Hinckley 1990; Kumar 2007). Modern presidents speak in a public setting more and more often than ever before (Edwards 1983, 2003; Hart 1989; Tulis 1987; Wood 2007).

Of course, it is widely believed that presidents have differed in their capacity for effective public communications. For example, Gergen (2000, 348) argues that "Kennedy and Reagan now stand out in the public mind as the most memorable speakers in the late twentieth century because they were masters of the medium. They both had a capacity to persuade a mass audience through television. . . . " Similarly, Blumenthal (1982, 284) suggests that Reagan had "stunning success in shaping public opinion" and used it to achieve policy goals. Jacobs and Shapiro (2000) support this view with evidence obtained from interviews with White House and congressional staff during the 1990s. Interviewees typically expressed great confidence in the president's ability to lead public opinion.

Greenstein (2004) categorized differences in presidential leadership style from FDR through George W. Bush. He also observed an increased reliance of presidents on public communication through time. In this regard, Greenstein noted that "Most presidents have not addressed the public with anything approximating the professionalism of countless educators, members of the clergy, and radio and television broadcasters. Roosevelt, Kennedy, and Reagan – and Clinton at his best are the shining exceptions" (2004, 217).

President Kennedy had a casual manner that made him appear comfortable and confident when speaking to an audience (Silvestri 2000). Greenstein characterized Kennedy's oratory as eloquent and his press conference performances as "intelligent and stylish" (2004, 70). As a former media personality, President Reagan was often referred to as the "Great Communicator" (Ritter and Henry 1992). According to Greenstein (2004, 155), Reagan "carried off his rhetorical responsibilities with a virtuosity exceeded only by FDR." President Clinton, at his best, was "an outstanding public communicator." At his worst "he was long-winded, unfocused, and 'off message' . . . " (Greenstein 2004, 185). However, President Clinton carried the rhetorical presidency strategy to new extremes, speaking on average 550 times per year and traveling around the country every fourth day (Edwards 2003, 3).

In contrast, other presidencies have seemed less adept at public communication, perhaps due to the absence of an effective strategy (Rozell 2003). Early modern presidents such as Truman and Eisenhower lacked a strong public relations apparatus within the White House. These presidencies occurred before the media and political transformations that made it essential for presidents to cultivate their public image. They may also have lacked the natural ability for effective public communications (Greenstein 2004, 39, 54).

Other presidents also seemingly lacked the natural ability to communicate well in public. For example, Greenstein observed that President Johnson's oratory came across as "bombastic and long-winded." During news conferences "he was stiff and defensive . . . revealing little of the vividness that made him memorable in less formal settings" (2004, 87). President Nixon "was patently ill at ease in press conferences, and his formal addresses came across as strained and stilted" (Greenstein 2004, 106). President Carter began well as a public communicator, but after the first year his rhetoric suffered because of an absence of organizing principles. He read his lines "in an uninflected voice, barely moving his lips, and pausing at inappropriate points" (Greenstein 2004, 140).George H. W. Bush "seemed to go out of his way to avoid the rhetorical emphasis that led Reagan to be dubbed the

'Great Communicator'" (Greenstein 2004, 164). And George W. Bush "seemed insensitive [early on] to the importance of public communication in presidential leadership." However, following September 11, 2001 he "became a rhetorical activist, addressing the public regularly, forcefully, and sometimes eloquently . . . " (Greenstein 2004, 206).

These variations in presidential communication skills suggest potential differences through time in presidents' ability to persuade the public. Less rhetorically gifted presidents may have been less able to persuade the public. Thus, it may be that only certain presidents have been successful at public persuasion. If this is true, then statistical analysis of a time series encompassing multiple presidencies may suffer nullification bias, with short-term success at public persuasion by some presidents being nullified by less successful presidencies.

Past Scholarly Research on Presidential Persuasion

Scholarly research on presidential success at public persuasion reaches mixed conclusions. Early experimental work showed that when the president's name is attached to specific policy proposals, some members of the public are more likely to support those proposals (Conover and Sigelman 1982; Sigelman 1980a). However, subsequent experimental research suggested that identification of the president as supporting particular policies can fail to increase support, and may even diminish public support (Sigelman and Sigelman 1981). These contradictory findings have been construed to mean that support for the president on particular policies depends on presidential popularity or credibility (Mondak 1993).

The work on aggregate public opinion lends some support to this conclusion. For example, Page and Shapiro (1985; see also Page, Shapiro, and Dempsey 1987) found that presidents can produce small short-term effects on aggregate public opinion by making repeated appeals, but only when they are popular. This effect is probably bipolar, though, because those who approve of the president are more likely to approve of the president's policies than those who disapprove (Kernell 1984; Sigelman 1980b).

Consistently, Zaller (1992, 97) found that President Nixon was able to move public opinion on wage and price controls by making a major televised address. However, the effect of the president's speech was primarily restricted to fellow partisans. Those in the opposing party were already predisposed and were therefore generally unresponsive to the president's effort.

Some research has suggested that presidents can persuade the public more effectively on issues involving foreign policy or military intervention. For example, Cohen (1999) found that presidents' ability to influence public opinion on issues of foreign policy was persistent and strong, a result that did not hold for domestic policy issues. This differential movement is consistent with the two presidencies thesis, which suggests that presidents receive more deference on matters of foreign than of domestic policy (Wildavsky 1966). As expressed by Edwards (1983, 43), "people tend to defer more to the president on [foreign policy] issues than on domestic ones that they can directly relate to their own experience."

Similarly, Meernik and Ault (2001) found that the president's foreign policy appeals routinely move current public opinion about six percentage points toward the president's position. Theoretically, on matters of foreign policy, the president's unique status as the nation's leader in international affairs lends him greater credibility. Further, the prospect of military intervention produces even greater deference to the president, because presidential popularity consistently rises during such periods due to rally effects (Brody and Page 1975; MacKuen 1983; Mueller 1973).

Several qualitative case studies suggest that the president's ability to move public opinion for all types of issues is limited by the political environment facing the president. For example, Kernell (1997) points to Woodrow Wilson's exhaustive and failed trip across the nation to drum up support for the Treaty of Versailles and League of Nations at a time when Congress was controlled by the president's political adversaries. This anecdotal evidence suggests that presidential efforts at public persuasion are less likely to succeed when there are competing voices. In contrast, they are more likely to succeed when there is a chorus of voices singing the same message.

Finbow (1998) documents President Carter's failed (and forgotten) campaign to reform the nation's health care system during a period of constrained economic and fiscal resources. Along similar lines, Jacobs and Shapiro (2000) analyze President Clinton's first few years in office and find him to have been an ineffective leader on multiple issues, with the most glaring evidence being the failed presidential effort to reform health care policy after the president had spent much political capital pursuing other issues.

The most prominent and systematic work examining presidential success at public persuasion is that of Edwards (2003, Chapters 2 and 3). He examined public opinion polls on a variety of domestic and foreign policy issues before and after major presidential speeches. He found little or no evidence that presidents had been successful in moving public opinion during either the Reagan or Clinton presidencies. Rather, the pattern of changing public support before and after major speeches was random. When changes did occur in the expected direction, they tended to be small and of brief duration. Of course, if any presidency should have been successful at moving public opinion, it should have been these two, because both Reagan and Clinton were highly acclaimed as effective communicators and for their strong standing with the public. Therefore, Edwards (2003, 241) concluded that "[P]residents typically do not succeed in their efforts to change public opinion. Even 'great communicators' usually fail to obtain the public's support for their high-priority initiatives."

If presidents have difficulty altering public opinion, can they at least affect what issues people pay attention to? Again, past research arrives at mixed conclusions. Cohen (1995) examined annual State of the Union messages to find that increased presidential attention to economic, foreign, and civil rights policy leads to increased public attention to these same issues. However, Hill (1998) observed that Cohen's work ignored potential reverse causality associated with presidential rhetoric and public attention. In other words, presidential rhetoric may be a response to pre-existing public attention, rather than a cause. In his reanalysis, Hill's results suggested that the relationship is two-way for economic and foreign policy attention. Presidents both affect and are affected by public attention in these issue domains. However, the relationship is one-way for attention to civil rights. Presidents affect public attention to civil rights issues, but they are not affected by increased public attention.

In contrast, Wood and Peake (1998) and Edwards and Wood (1999) used weekly time series data to cast doubt on the extent to which presidential rhetoric leads media (and therefore public) attention to various policy issues. They examined six issues, three in the foreign policy domain and three in the domestic policy domain. Their results for the foreign policy domain challenged earlier work suggesting that presidents strongly affect systemic attention. Rather, they found that presidential issue attention *follows* the stream of foreign policy events and media attention. In other words, presidential attention to foreign policy issues tends to be reactive, rather than leading. In domestic policy, they found that presidents are in a more interactive relationship. Presidents both follow and lead for certain domestic policy issues. The results for both domains suggest that presidents are not dominant actors in persuading the media (or public) about what issues it should attend to.

Thus, much prior research casts doubt on presidential ability to persuade the mass public. Some work suggests that presidents are leaders in the foreign policy arena, but not in the domestic policy arena. Other work casts doubt on the notion that presidents lead systematically in either arena. Consistent with this muddled picture, we can point anecdotally to cases of both success and failure of presidential leadership in both the foreign and domestic policy arenas.

For example, in foreign policy, as noted in the introductory chapter, George Washington was stunningly successful at moving public opinion to secure funding for the Jay Treaty in 1795–96. In contrast, Woodrow Wilson was an abject failure in achieving public support for passage of the Treaty of Versailles and League of Nations in 1919. In domestic policy, Presidents Kennedy and Johnson were successful in garnering sufficient public support to secure passage of the spate of civil rights legislation through the mid-1960s. However, President Clinton was glaringly unsuccessful in persuading the public to support his health care reform proposals in 1993, as was George W. Bush in attempting to privatize the Social Security system in 2005.

EVALUATING PRESIDENTIAL PERSUASION OF THE MASS PUBLIC

Modern presidents have occasionally been successful at public persuasion. However, do modern presidents *systematically* persuade the public toward their own issue positions? To answer this question we shall explore whether presidents successfully move public mood. As discussed in Chapter 3, public mood measures the average issue-based

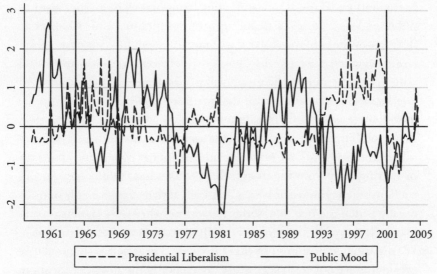

Figure 5.1. Presidential liberalism and public mood.
Note: Pearson's $r = -0.23$; Granger Independence Test ChiSq(4) $= 4.21$, p-value $= 0.38$.

liberalism of the mass public through time. Each time point on the public mood measure reflects the political center. However, the graphs of public mood in Chapter 3 show that the political center is continuously moving through time. What we seek to determine is whether presidents affect these movements, either in whole or in part. If presidents are responsible for movements in public mood, then we should see statistical covariation between changes in presidential liberalism and public mood. Such covariation would be strong evidence that modern presidential efforts at public persuasion are *systematically* successful.

Reconsidering the Earlier Graphical Analyses
Of course, the graphical results already reported in Chapter 4 cast serious doubt on the notion that presidents are overwhelmingly successful in this endeavor. For discussion purposes and reader convenience, the same graph that was reported as Figure 4.1 is now repeated as Figure 5.1, but with some small changes. The reference series (solid line) is now public mood, whereas the presidential liberalism series is overlaid (dashed line). Also, the Granger independence test reported

at the bottom of the figure now runs from presidential liberalism to public mood, instead of in the opposite direction, as in Chapter 4. Both series remain in standardized metrics to enable comparison.

The detailed narrative in Chapter 4 relating to each presidential administration and public mood will not be repeated here. However, it is important to reemphasize that presidential liberalism and public mood often seem to be moving in opposite directions. In particular, there are sharp reversing movements in public mood during most presidential administrations. Many presidents appear consistently partisan or moving away from the mass public. Observing the changes during each presidency as was done in Chapter 4 reveals that the only periods during which the two time series moved together were the Ford presidency and the last two years of the George W. Bush administration.

This absence of shared trends for the two time series suggests that presidents are not very successful at persuading the mass public at the aggregate level. Indeed, the public appears to react in the opposite direction from what would be expected if presidents were successful at public persuasion. As noted at the bottom of Figure 5.1, the Pearson's correlation between the two time series is negative at −0.23. Additionally, a test of Granger independence reported at the bottom of Figure 5.1 shows that the null hypothesis of statistical independence of public mood from presidential liberalism cannot be rejected. Thus, the statistical evidence from Figure 5.1 clearly suggests that presidents are not very successful at persuading the mass public.

A Strategy for Multivariate Analyses

The graphical results, although revealing, are not a rigorous standard for assessing the relationship between presidential liberalism and public mood. It may be that after appropriate statistical controls are included, significant covariation between the two time series will emerge. Thus, a multivariate base model through which to assess the relative effectiveness of presidential efforts at public persuasion is required.

Past research has produced at least two credible studies that can serve as base models for explaining public mood. Both focus on the economy. First, Durr (1993, 158) argued that "shifts in domestic policy sentiment along a liberal–conservative continuum may be understood in part as responses to changing economic *expectations* [emphasis added]." Specifically, when citizens expect the economy to be strong, they are more inclined to support a liberal domestic policy agenda. When citizens expect the economy to be weak, the system is biased against a liberal policy agenda. Using Durr's approach, it is the nation's economic capacity to achieve liberal programs that determines public propensity toward those programs.

In evaluating his model statistically, Durr constructed an error correction model (Bannerjee et al. 1993; Davidson et al. 1978; Engle and Granger 1987) containing various economic variables. His model also included a separate measure for a political component of public mood. No effort is made here to replicate Durr's error correction model. Instead, the notions of economic capacity and expectations are directly operationalized in a more standard time series framework.[1]

This Durr-like model to explain public mood is constructed by including a variable to capture citizens' expectations about the economic future. A measure is also included for the robustness of the current economy. Presidential liberalism is the political component of the model. Initially, in order to produce very strong statistical control, this base model includes an LDV. Later, the LDV will be dropped, again to provide the most amicable statistical environment for presidential liberalism to affect public mood, and for the other reasons discussed at length in Chapter 4.[2]

Second, in contrast with Durr's emphasis on economic capacity and expectations, Erikson, MacKuen, and Stimson (2002, 230–35) emphasize economic need as important to changing public mood. They argue that it is specific economic conditions that are most important to changing public liberalism. As the economy produces outcomes that are a hardship, the public in turn demands a governmental response that is either more liberal or more conservative. For example, rising unemployment produces stronger demand for increased governmental activity along the welfare dimension. Unemployment reflects an economy that is not spending enough to maintain full employment.

[1] As discussed in footnote 6 of Chapter 4, public mood is a stationary time series. As shown by Bannerjee et al. (1993; see also De Boef and Keele 2008), when an error correction model is constructed from stationary variables, it can be considered as just a transformation of the more standard autoregressive distributed-lag model. This fact serves as a statistical justification for using the more standard approach employed here.

[2] See Chapter 4, footnote 11 and related discussion in the text.

The remedy is often seen as more government spending. This stronger demand for government spending is, in turn, reflected through a more liberal public mood. In contrast, inflation is often caused by an economy that is too robust. Government can combat this tendency by instituting a policy of fiscal austerity. Understanding this, the mass public in turn curtail their demand for more government, which is reflected in a more conservative public mood.[3]

Given these two alternative theories, this chapter uses two base models against which to evaluate public responsiveness to presidential efforts at public persuasion.[4] The first model incorporates variables to reflect Durr's (1993) emphasis on economic capacity and economic expectations. This model contains lagged public mood, a measure to capture the current state of the economy, and another to capture the public's expectations about the economic future.

As in Chapter 4, the current state of the economy is measured using the Conference Board's Composite Index of Coincident Indicators. Again, this variable is an index constructed from four time series chosen by the Conference Board because they are consistently in step with the current state of the economy. Using the Coincident Index provides a better measure of current economic performance than often used individual series such as GDP, which is released only quarterly and often revised, or unemployment and inflation, which are lagging indicators. According to the Conference Board (2001, 13), the Coincident Index is a "broad series that measures aggregate economic activity; thus they define the business cycle."

---

3   The Erikson et al. arguments assume a mass public that is well educated in how to affect weak and strong economies. In my view, this assumption is dubious. The public is probably quite ignorant of the details of controlling an economy. Additionally, these arguments ignore the fact that the public may support reduced taxes as a remedy for a weak economy. Reducing taxes is generally associated with a more conservative public mood. Similarly, inflation can be reined in through higher taxes, as was done through the income tax surcharge in the late 1960s. Higher taxes are generally associated with a more liberal public mood. These counterarguments make the Erikson et al. approach seem ad hoc. Nevertheless, their model is used as a base model for the analyses to follow.

4   One might reasonably ask why a single base model that combines the two approaches is not used here. One reason is that high multicollinearity results in a model in which none of the economic variables is statistically significant. In terms of statistical control, this should make no difference. However, the explanatory power of the separate models does not differ significantly from that of the combined model. Therefore, the two models are applied separately.

Public expectations about the future of the economy are measured using the quarterly version of the University of Michigan's Survey of Consumers Expectations Index.[5] The expectations index is constructed by taking a weighted average of the survey marginals from three questions reflecting consumer expectations about their personal finances and future business conditions.[6]

The second statistical specification simply replicates the analysis reported in Erikson, MacKuen, and Stimson (2002, Table 6.4). Their statistical analysis used annual data. This study employs quarterly data. They included annual public mood lagged one year, change in unemployment, and the annual inflation rate. This study uses quarterly public mood lagged one quarter, quarterly change in unemployment, and the annualized quarterly inflation rate.

As in Chapter 4, unemployment is taken as the averaged monthly unemployment rate during each quarter as reported by the Bureau of Labor Statistics. Inflation is measured as the annualized quarterly percent change in the consumer price index for urban consumers as reported by the Bureau of Labor Statistics.

Both the Durr-like and the Erikson, MacKuen, and Stimson (EMS) statistical specifications exhibit moderate residual autocorrelation when using ordinary least squares regression. Therefore, as discussed in Chapter 4, standard errors and t-statistics are again calculated using Newey–West (1987) robust standard errors.

Do Presidents Successfully Persuade the Public?
Given these alternative base models as statistical controls, do presidents successfully persuade the mass public toward their own liberal or conservative issue stances? We can evaluate this question by estimating the two base models, while also including the measure of

---

[5] This measure has sometimes been labeled "prospective evaluations." For example, see Clarke and Stewart (1994), MacKuen, Erikson, and Stimson (1992), or Norpoth (1996).

[6] The questions are as follows. (1) "Now looking ahead – do you think that a year from now you (and your family living there) will be better off financially, or worse off, or just about the same as now?" (2) "Now turning to business conditions in the country as a whole – do you think that during the next twelve months we'll have good times financially, or bad times, or what?" (3) "Looking ahead, which would you say is more likely – that in the country as a whole we'll have continuous good times during the next five years or so, or that we will have periods of widespread unemployment or depression, or what?"

TABLE 5.1. *Explaining public mood as a function of economic variables and presidential liberalism*

Model variable	Durr-like capacity model	EMS needs model
Public mood$_{t-1}$	0.78*	0.77*
	(17.69)	(17.27)
Conference Board Coincident Index	−0.39**	
	(−2.38)	
Michigan Economic Expectations Index	0.01**	
	(2.21)	
Δ Unemployment		0.30**
		(2.42)
Inflation		−0.04*
		(−3.06)
Presidential liberalism$_{t-1}$	−0.11**	−0.10*
	(−2.56)	(−2.67)
Constant	−0.54**	0.17**
	(−2.05)	(2.44)
Diagnostics		
N	180	184
$p(\mathrm{LM}\chi_1^2)$	0.31	0.40
$p(F)$	0.00	0.00

Note: The numbers in the table are coefficients and t-statistics (in parentheses). The t-statistics are calculated using Newey–West (1987) autocorrelation- and heteroskedasticity-consistent standard errors. N is the number of observations. p(LM) is the probability for rejecting the null hypothesis of no residual autocorrelation using the Breusch (1979o–Godfrey (1978) autocorrelation test. $p(F)$ is the probability for the overall model F statistic. Public mood and presidential liberalism are standardized to facilitate interpretation.
 * Statistical significance at the 0.01 level.
 ** Statistical significance at the 0.05 level.

presidential liberalism lagged one quarter. Using this approach, we seek to determine whether presidential liberalism impinges on the economic models of public mood. The public mood and presidential liberalism variables are again standardized to facilitate interpretation. The estimation results are reported in Table 5.1.

Note first that both the Durr-like and EMS economic models do a credible job of explaining public mood. Predictably, the LDV explains most of the variation in public mood through time. This models the obvious inertia in public mood that is visible in Figure 5.1. On top of this dynamic, the economic variables in both models are statistically significant. A weaker economy and higher consumer expectations produce more public liberalism. This confirms Durr's (1993) analysis positing that economic expectations drive public mood, but not his finding for economic capacity. The negative coefficient for the coincident index shows that declining economic conditions result in greater public demand for government expansion, a finding consistent with Keynesian prescriptions. Also, consistent with the EMS (2002) analysis, increasing unemployment produces greater public liberalism as the public seeks relief along the welfare policy dimension. Inflation produces less public liberalism as the public approves measures for fiscal austerity as a remedy for inflation. Thus, either of the economic specifications for explaining public mood provides a good base against which to evaluate the impact of presidential liberalism.

Using these alternative economic models as controls, consider now the coefficients for presidential liberalism in the sixth row of Table 5.1. Regardless of the statistical specification, the coefficient for presidential liberalism is statistically significant in the *opposite* direction from what would be expected if presidents were successful in persuading the mass public. The coefficients for presidential liberalism are negative in both statistical specifications.

These results confirm the graphical analyses above. The evidence from both analyses shows that the public regularly and systematically moves in the opposite direction from presidential issue stances during most presidencies. In other words, not only are presidents unsuccessful at public persuasion, but also the public reacts against presidential efforts at persuasion, whether those efforts are liberal or conservative.

Why Should the Public Move Away from the President?
Why should this dynamic of negative public reaction to presidential liberalism occur? One possible explanation for the negative reaction is rooted in the expectations gap that commonly affects each presidency. Many scholars have alluded to this expectations gap as explaining the decline in public support after the president's initial honeymoon period (Edwards and Wayne 2006, 106–10; Lowi 1985, 11; Stimson 1976, 1976–77; Waterman, Jenkins-Smith, and Silva 1999; Wayne 1982).

New presidents enter office in an environment that highlights the symbolism and pageantry of American democracy. Americans play out the drama of democratic renewal every four years by selecting a new person to occupy the nation's highest office. The winner is expected to be a savior from problems past and an inspiration for the nation's future. Given the public relations effort required for election, new seekers of the presidency play a large role in building high public expectations of hope and future performance. With great pomp and circumstance, presidents are inaugurated, and they begin office with an agenda designed to deliver on their promises and symbolic sentiment.

As a result of this process, most incoming presidents enjoy an initial rally in public approval of their job performance. For example, every modern president except Reagan and George H.W. Bush has benefitted from a "positivity bias" in the first public approval poll after his initial election (e.g., see Edwards and Wayne 2006, Table 4.3). Public approval tends to go up substantially after a president's initial election. The average initial postelection public approval for new presidents since Eisenhower has been 62 percent. Compared with electoral margins, this reflects an average postelection jump of about 11 percent. These numbers suggest that many Americans of both political parties are prone to give new presidents leeway early in their administrations.

This high early public support for presidents constitutes a disturbance to the normal equilibrium of partisan support. For example, using Table 2.1 in Chapter 2, the average *NaturalSupport* for presidents since 1952 has been 49 percent, whereas the average *PotentialSupport* over the same period has been almost 66 percent. This means that early in a new administration, presidents are typically achieving almost all of the potential support that they can reasonably expect to achieve, given the partisan composition of the electorate.

Consistent with this argument, many scholars allude to the president's "honeymoon" period as the most important time for presidential success. Approval ratings may also be higher early on because of friendly treatment by the press (Brody 1991, 28–44; Cook and Ragsdale 2000; Edwards and Wayne 2006, 364; Grossman and Kumar 1979; Grossman and Kumar 1981, 259–65, 275–79; Stimson 2004, 146–47).

Thus, early in a presidential administration, presidential partisans approve of the president's performance, as do a sizeable proportion of persuadable citizens. The public holds high expectations for virtually all incoming presidents. However, most presidents fail to satisfy those expectations, resulting in subsequent movement by the public away from the president.

Said differently, a new president is not a George Washington who enjoyed public adulation over a long period. Although modern presidents receive much adulation in the beginning, they cannot expect to receive such deference and respect over the long term. The inevitable result is that presidential support declines through time after elections. As support returns toward the normal partisan division, presidential efforts at public persuasion become less successful. Modern presidents are powerful figures, but they simply do not have the ability to meet the public's high expectations resulting from election campaigns and the beginning of a new presidency.

However, the expectations gap can only be part of the explanation for the observed negative reaction by the public to presidential issue stances. The graphical and statistical evidence show that public liberalism is not fully stable around a mean (as would be required by an expectations gap theory rooted in a partisan equilibrium). Rather, the public often continues drifting away from the president through time. This means that at least some of the electorate (i.e., the persuadables) must be reacting in strong opposition to the new president's policies.

This continuing reaction suggests the efficacy of a thermostatic explanation of the public response to presidential issue stances (Erikson, MacKuen, and Stimson 2002, 326–28; Wlezien 1995, 1996). According to the thermostatic theory of public opinion, when government policy moves too far in either the left or right direction, there is a response from the electorate aimed at moving it back in the other direction. If policy becomes too liberal, relative to the thermostat, the public becomes more conservative. If policy becomes too conservative, relative to the thermostat, the public becomes more liberal. Given the public's movements, either public officials respond to public demands, or someone else is elected who the public thinks will respond. Through this thermostatic process, public policy is forced to pursue a more moderate course over the long-term.

Of course, in a two-party presidential system with periodic elections, institutional and public preferences will often be out of equilibrium.

Presidents are partisans of either the left or right who espouse issue stances that differ from those near the political center. As shown in Chapter 4, the prescriptions they pursue are those that flow primarily from their respective party medians, not from the electoral median. As a result, presidents are almost always out of synch with those near the political center.

But, of course, presidents need support from those near the political center. They attempt to achieve that support through partisan persuasion. However, as long as presidents pursue partisan prescriptions and employ partisan rhetoric, their ability to persuade the mass public will be unstable. As expressed by Stimson (1999, 123), "as the parties constantly miss the center in their policies, the electorate constantly pulls back in [the other] direction."

Thus, the dynamic of negative public reaction to presidential efforts at mass persuasion is easy to explain if we understand that presidents are partisans, rather than centrists, in their manner of political representation. They rarely cater to the median voter. Instead they consistently attempt to persuade the mass public toward their own partisan positions. This strategy can succeed early in an administration when a president has broad popular support and the aura of democratic legitimacy. However, the typical pattern for partisan presidents is that they must buck the opposing tide of centrist opinion. The dynamic of drift away from the president is, therefore, as regular and predictable as the American electoral cycle. And it will remain so as long as we elect partisan presidents in a system with centrist expectations.

PRESIDENTIAL RESOURCES AND PUBLIC PERSUASION

The preceding statistical analyses and theoretical explanations suggest that most of the time presidents will fail at persuading the mass public toward their own partisan positions. However, given the preeminence of the permanent campaign in American politics, we also know that presidents persistently continue trying to persuade the public (Blumenthal 1982; Kernell 1997; Ornstein and Mann 2000). This would be irrational behavior if presidents were never successful. However, presidents are not irrational actors. They and their advisors are well informed about the dynamics of public opinion (e.g., see Jacobs and Shapiro 2000) and generally believe that they can persuade the public at least some of the time (e.g., see Edwards 2003, 1–8). Thus, there must be certain times during a presidential administration when they can expect to be successful, or at least to slow movements of public opinion in the other direction.

What are the conditions under which presidents can expect to be successful (or less unsuccessful) at public persuasion? Obviously presidents need political resources for this endeavor, including symbolic status, public support, political allies, an untarnished image, and a friendly partisan environment (Neustadt 1960).

Honeymoons and Public Persuasion

Consider first *when* during a presidential administration a president is most likely to be successful at public persuasion. The preceding discussion suggests that the early part of a new presidential administration is a critical time for presidential success. During this period a new president wields power with an aura of democratic legitimacy, is enabled by the recent pageant of democratic renewal, generally receives favorable treatment by the mass media, and enjoys higher approval ratings on average than during any other part of their presidency. Do presidents more readily persuade the mass public during honeymoon periods relative to other stages of their administrations?

We can evaluate this question by returning to the data for a multivariate analysis of how honeymoon periods alter the relationship between presidential liberalism and public mood. If presidents are more successful at public persuasion during the early parts of their administrations, then we should expect liberal presidents to achieve liberal movements in public opinion and conservative presidents to achieve conservative movements during this period. Thus, there should be a positive statistical relationship between presidential liberalism and public mood during honeymoon periods. During other times the relationship should be negative.

To test this pair of hypotheses, an indicator variable was created that assigns a one for honeymoon periods and a zero for non-honeymoon periods of each new presidency. The honeymoon period is arbitrarily defined for most presidents as the first three temporal quarters of a new presidential administration.[7] Note that the honeymoon period pertains only to newly elected presidents, and does not apply to second-term presidents. This is consistent with the qualitative literature, which suggests that second-term presidents do not receive special treatment by the press following their reelection (e.g., see Brody 1991). They also achieve little or no increase in public approval following a second election.

Presidents who were not elected to office require special treatment in constructing this measure. President Johnson, because of the special circumstance of assuming office after the Kennedy assassination, was assigned honeymoon status for all remaining time periods of the expected Kennedy presidency through the third quarter of 1965. The Kennedy assassination produced a strong symbolic reaction among Americans that elevated the unelected president to near-unassailable status, and probably resulted in the landslide election of 1964. Therefore, this assignment is consistent with the theory outlined above. However, President Ford was not assigned honeymoon status following his assumption of the presidency after the Nixon resignation. He was not elected, and the circumstances of his elevation to the presidency did not impart extraordinary status to the office.[8]

The honeymoon variable is interacted with the presidential liberalism variable to reflect the possible differential relationship between presidential liberalism and public mood during honeymoon versus non-honeymoon periods of a new presidency. The interaction variable and its components are then included in two regressions containing only the economic variables from the Durr-like and EMS base models.[9] The public mood and presidential liberalism variables are again standardized to facilitate interpretation.

[7] Some have alluded to a legislative honeymoon as lasting around 100 days. This would argue that the first two quarters should be used. However, we actually don't know how long the honeymoon lasts with the mass public. To be sure, three temporal quarters of the first year is at the upper end of what is likely. However, if the honeymoon period is actually shorter, then this long duration should actually work against finding significant presidential persuasion, producing a more conservative test.

[8] In fact, his early pardon of President Nixon for the Watergate crimes should have produced the opposite effect.

[9] As in Chapter 4, the LDV is omitted to provide an amicable statistical environment for presidential liberalism to affect public mood. See footnote 11 in Chapter 4 for additional discussion.

TABLE 5.2. *Presidential effects on public mood during honeymoon periods*

Model variable	Durr-like capacity model	EMS needs model
Conference Board Coincident Index	−0.57	
	(−1.47)	
Michigan Economic Expectations Index	0.02*	
	(3.05)	
Δ Unemployment		0.59**
		(1.92)
Inflation		−0.12*
		(−3.72)
Presidential liberalism$_{t-1}$	−0.40*	−0.36*
	(−5.55)	(−5.34)
Honeymoon	−0.13	−0.05
	(−0.54)	(−0.21)
Honeymoon *presidential liberalism$_{t-1}$	0.71**	0.57**
	(2.21)	(2.00)
Constant	−1.82*	0.51*
	(−2.99)	(2.94)
Diagnostics		
N	180	184
$p(F)$	0.00	0.00

Note: The numbers in the table are coefficients and *t*-statistics (in parentheses). The *t*-statistics are calculated using Newey–West (1987) autocorrelation- and heteroskedasticity-consistent standard errors. N is the number of observations. $p(F)$ is the probability for the overall model F statistic. Public mood and presidential liberalism are standardized to facilitate interpretation.
* Statistical significance at the 0.01 level.
** Statistical significance at the 0.05 level.

Results of the statistical analyses are reported in Table 5.2. Note first that the coefficients for the presidential liberalism variable in each specification now reflect non-honeymoon periods of each presidency. The coefficients for the interaction variable reflect honeymoon periods. Given that the public mood and presidential liberalism variables are standardized, we can interpret the results substantively.

As in Table 5.1 above, the non–honeymoon period coefficients continue to be negatively signed, but are much larger and more strongly significant. During non-honeymoon periods, each one-standard-deviation increase in presidential liberalism through time corresponds with about a 0.40 (column one)- or 0.36 (column two)-standard-deviation decline in public mood. This is a strong effect, showing that the public reacts thermostatically during non-honeymoon periods to perceptions that presidents are either too liberal or too conservative in their issue stances.[10]

The much stronger relationships than in the models reported in Table 5.1 manifest two factors. First, the specifications no longer contain the LDVs, which are by definition collinear with the dynamics of presidential liberalism. Collinearity with other variables always reduces the size of estimated coefficients, as well as the precision of estimation. Second, the new specifications differentiate between honeymoon and non-honeymoon periods, which produce effects running in opposite directions. These opposite tendencies for the two periods necessarily damp any effects with the periods estimated together as reported in Table 5.1.

As predicted, the coefficients for the honeymoon–presidential liberalism interaction variable are positive and statistically significant in both specifications. The positive relationship shows that during honeymoon periods, presidents on average successfully persuade the mass public toward their own positions. Each one-standard-deviation increase in presidential liberalism during honeymoons corresponds to about a 0.71 (column one)- or 0.57 (column two)-standard-deviation increase in public mood. The public is obviously more sympathetic to presidents during the period immediately following campaigns and elections. This is again a very strong effect, showing that a thermostatic reaction does not occur during presidential honeymoon periods. Rather, the public systematically responds favorably to presidential efforts at persuasion. This makes theoretical sense because presidential resources are at a maximum during this period.

Public Approval and Presidential Persuasion
Of course, modern presidents campaign for public support throughout their administrations, not just during elections and honeymoon

---

[10] The honeymoon indicator coefficient is small and not statistically significant in either specification. This estimated small effect shows that the public is no more liberal or conservative during honeymoon periods than during non-honeymoon periods. This is as it should be. We should not expect honeymoons by themselves to produce a change in public liberalism, because there is a mix of Democratic and Republican presidents through time in the sample.

periods. Obviously, they must believe that they can be successful at public persuasion during non-honeymoon periods as well, or they would not bother to extend their campaigns for public support beyond the early parts of their administrations.

Thus, a more general explanation of presidential success at public persuasion should take account of continuing presidential resources. In this regard, various scholars have pointed to public approval as an important resource for presidents seeking to persuade the public (e.g., see Edwards 2003; Kernell 1984; Neustadt 1960; Page and Shapiro 1985; Page, Shapiro, and Dempsey 1987; Sigelman 1980a; Zaller 1992). Presidents with the reputation and prestige afforded by high public approval ratings are more likely to command respect from those near the political center, as well as from loosely affiliated opposing partisans who might also be persuadable. In contrast, presidents suffering from low public approval ratings tend to be ignored and become irrelevant to the political process. Therefore, we should expect that public approval would also condition the president's ability to persuade the mass public.

As discussed above, public approval is often, though not always, highest in the early part of a presidential administration. It tends to decline through time as the media and public become more familiar with and critical of the president. However, public approval is also highly dynamic within presidencies, tending to rally in response to dramatic events, decline with scandals or foreign policy failures, increase with strong economic performance, and decline with unemployment, inflation, and war deaths (Chappell and Keech 1985; Erikson, MacKuen, and Stimson 2002; Hibbs 1974; Kenski 1977; Kernell 1978; MacKuen 1983; MacKuen, Erikson, and Stimson 1992; Mueller 1970, 1973; Monroe 1978, 1979; Wood 2000).

Thus, the general pattern of declining public approval through time is by no means assured. As observed by Edwards and Wayne (2006, 116), "Eisenhower maintained his standing with the public very well for two complete terms. Kennedy and Nixon held their public support for two years, as did Ford (after a sharp initial decline)." Further, President Reagan's approval fluctuated considerably through time. He entered office with public approval around 55 percent. It increased sharply with the assassination attempt. It declined during the

1982–83 recession and the Iran–Contra affair. However, he left office with public approval significantly higher than when he entered, at 63 percent. Similarly, President Clinton's approval rating upon assuming office was 58 percent. His approval dropped sharply during his first term as a result of multiple public relations debacles,[11] but increased steadily after 1995 to stabilize at around 60 percent for the remainder of his presidency. He left office with a much higher 67 percent public approval rating.

Do these fluctuations in public approval affect presidents' ability to persuade the mass public? We can address this question using the Gallup approval measure introduced and discussed in Chapter 4. The time series measure of the president's quarterly public approval rating is interacted with the presidential liberalism variable to evaluate whether there are variations in the success of presidential efforts at mass persuasion as a function of changing public approval. The interaction variable and its components are again entered into the same base statistical specifications as in Table 5.2. The public mood, approval, and presidential liberalism variables are again standardized to facilitate interpretation.

Results from the statistical analysis are reported in Table 5.3. Consider first the results for the lagged presidential liberalism variable. Given the interactive specification and standardization, this variable now represents the effect of presidential liberalism on public mood when public approval is at its average. Average public approval of presidential job performance for the period of analysis was 55.54 percent. The statistical results show that when public approval is at this level, each one-standard-deviation increase in presidential liberalism corresponds with a decline in public mood by 0.40 (column one) or 0.38 (column two) standard deviations in public mood. These results again confirm the general thermostatic relationship between presidential liberalism and public mood through time. When public

---

[11] The furor over Clinton's advocacy of gays openly serving in the military was the most prominent of these public relations debacles. However, there were others, including the White House Travel Office scandal, the suicide of Deputy Chief Counsel Vincent Foster, the Whitewater scandal, the Paula Jones allegations of sexual misconduct, and erroneous news reports that President Clinton halted air traffic at Los Angeles International Airport to get a haircut.

TABLE 5.3. *Public approval and presidential effects on public mood*

Model variable	Durr-like capacity model	EMS needs model
Conference Board Coincident Index	−0.40 (−0.95)	
Michigan Economic Expectations Index	0.01 (1.59)	
Δ Unemployment		0.56** (1.76)
Inflation		−0.11 (−2.67)*
Presidential liberalism$_{t-1}$	−0.40* (−5.75)	−0.38* (−6.00)
Public approval$_{t-1}$	0.19** (1.99)	0.13 (1.29)
Public approval$_{t-1}$ *presidential liberalism$_{t-1}$	0.21** (2.12)	0.21** (2.04)
Constant	−1.18 (−1.58)	0.44** (2.31)
Diagnostics		
N	180	184
$p(F)$	0.00	0.00

Note: The numbers in the table are coefficients and *t*-statistics (in parentheses). The *t*-statistics are calculated using Newey–West (1987) autocorrelation- and heteroskedasticity-consistent standard errors. N is the number of observations. $p(F)$ is the probability for the overall model F statistic. Public mood, presidential liberalism, and public approval are standardized to facilitate interpretation.
* Statistical significance at the 0.01 level.
** Statistical significance at the 0.05 level.

approval is at its average, people not only fail to respond to presidential efforts at persuasion, but also react in a manner opposite from what would be predicted from the president's relative liberalism. Perceiving presidential issue stances as too partisan relative to the centrist-leaning public thermostat, they move away from the president.[12]

[12] The coefficient for lagged presidential approval is positive and statistically significant in the Durr-like specification, and positive but not statistically significant in the EMS specification. This small positive relationship between public approval and public mood suggests that when the public approves of the president's job performance, they are also more likely to have a more liberal perspective on government policy. This result may be due to common optimism affecting both the president and public attitudes toward government expansion (e.g., see Wood 2007, Chapter 5).

Consider second the coefficients for the approval–presidential liberalism interaction variables. They are positive and statistically significant in both specifications. The positive relationship shows that when public approval is above average, the public responds more favorably to presidential efforts at persuasion. When public approval is below average, the public responds less favorably, moving even further in the opposite direction from the president's position.

Specifically, each one standard deviation that public approval moves above its average produces about a 0.21-standard-deviation increase in public mood for a president who is one standard deviation more liberal than usual. For the same president with the same relative liberalism, each one standard deviation that public approval moves below its average reduces the impact of presidential liberalism on public mood by about 0.21 standard deviation. A similar interpretation in the opposite direction can be applied to conservative presidents who are more or less popular simply by reversing the signs from the preceding.

Further, the coefficients are additive within the two specifications. For example, in the Durr-like specification, presidents who are one standard deviation more popular than average have effect coefficients of about -0.19 (i.e., $-0.40 + 0.21 = -0.19$). Presidents who are one standard deviation less popular than average have effect coefficients of about -0.61 (i.e., $-0.40 - 0.21 = -0.61$). These statistical estimates mean that presidents need very high public approval ratings to overcome the negative thermostatic effect fully. Roughly, they show that it requires public approval that is two standard deviations above average (78 percent) to nullify the persistent movement of the public away from the president's partisan position.

Of course, this dependence of presidential persuasion on public approval is a reason for presidents to pursue the permanent campaign. Presidents know that if they do not maintain high approval ratings, then there is no possibility at all of achieving their partisan agendas. Without high public approval ratings, their persuasive abilities for partisan issue stances continue to decline over time.

Presidential Allies and Public Persuasion
Another presidential resource that can facilitate efforts to persuade the mass public is the presence of institutional allies. As observed in

Chapter 4, presidents become more liberal when they have liberal allies in Congress. Here the argument is that the public also becomes more liberal when there is a perception that the president has liberal allies in Congress. An appearance of partisan consensus across institutions invites bandwagon effects, and should produce increasing public support for presidential issue stances through time.

In contrast, an appearance of institutional opposition to presidential issue stances invites criticism, raising questions about presidential leadership. As conflict emerges and grows, polarization develops across partisans, which reduces the president's persuasive abilities. These effects should be most strongly felt among those near the political center who are more loosely attached and persuadable. Those near the political center tend to be torn between the two partisan extremes. Presidential support declines in direct proportion to the emerging opposition and conflict.

In accordance with this argument, the presence of strong supportive allies in Congress should result in more successful presidential persuasion of the public, whereas enemies should diminish presidential persuasion. We can evaluate these hypotheses using a variable introduced in Chapter 4, labeled president's party percent seats in Congress.[13] Again, this variable gauges the relative dominance of the president's party in Congress. As the president's party becomes more dominant in Congress, we should expect the public to be more supportive of presidential issue stances. In contrast, as the opposition party increases relative to the president's party, we should see more challenges to presidential issue stances, which should result in less support for presidential issue stances.

Again, the time series measure of the president's party's dominance in Congress is interacted with the presidential liberalism variable to evaluate whether there are variations in the success of presidential efforts at mass persuasion as a function of presidential allies. The

---

[13] We could also use various degrees of unified/divided government indicator variables such as were reported in Chapter 4 (first column of Table 4.6). However, the interactive approach used here would result in a total of eight new variables, four of which would be collinear due to interaction effects. This would be problematic in producing multicollinearity. Therefore, the cleaner approach of using a single variable to represent presidential allies in Congress is preferred.

TABLE 5.4. *Presidential allies and presidential effects on public mood*

Model variable	Durr-like capacity model	EMS needs model
Conference Board Coincident Index	−0.36	
	(−0.97)	
Michigan Economic Expectations Index	0.02*	
	(3.60)	
Δ Unemployment		0.51**
		(1.77)
Inflation		−0.13*
		(−4.22)
Presidential liberalism$_{t-1}$	−0.30*	−0.24*
	(−3.80)	(−3.04)
President's party percent seats in Congress$_{t-1}$	−0.23*	−0.20*
	(−2.78)	(−2.63)
President's party percent seats in Congress$_{t-1}$ *presidential liberalism$_{t-1}$	0.20**	0.24**
	(1.73)	(2.25)
Constant	−1.99*	0.48*
	(−3.69)	(2.94)
Diagnostics		
N	180	184
p(F)	0.00	0.00

Note: The numbers in the table are coefficients and *t*-statistics (in parentheses). The *t*-statistics are calculated using Newey–West (1987) autocorrelation- and heteroskedasticity-consistent standard errors. N is the number of observations. $p(F)$ is the probability for the overall model F statistic. Public mood, presidential liberalism, and the president's party percent seats in Congress are standardized to facilitate interpretation.

 * Statistical significance at the 0.01 level.
** Statistical significance at the 0.05 level.

interaction variable and its components are again entered into the same base statistical specifications as those reported above. The relevant variables are again standardized to facilitate interpretation.

Results from the statistical analysis are reported in Table 5.4. Consider first the results for the lagged presidential liberalism variable. The coefficients for this variable now represent the case where the president's party is at the average of percent seats held in Congress over the entire time frame. Interestingly, this occurs empirically when the president's party holds almost exactly half the seats in each of the two chambers. This descriptive statistic suggests that on average through time presidents have not been able to count on strong allies in Congress. Given this lack of institutional dominance, presidential efforts at public persuasion that depend on institutional alliances should have been limited.

Consistent with this argument, the coefficient for presidential liberalism remains negative and statistically significant. This result again confirms the general thermostatic reaction among the public to the president's too partisan issue stances.[14] When the president's party is at its average in Congress, presidents are unsuccessful at persuading the mass public.

The relation of primary interest is the interaction effect of the president's party's percent seats in Congress with presidential liberalism. Confirming the hypothesis that presidential allies are important to presidential persuasion, the interaction coefficients are positive and statistically significant in both specifications. The positive relationship shows that when presidential support in Congress is above average, the public is more likely to respond favorably to presidential efforts at persuasion. When the president's party is weaker in Congress, the public is less likely to respond.

Specifically, each one-standard-deviation increase in the president's party's percent seats in Congress (i.e., a movement from 50 to 59 percent) corresponds with about a 0.20 (column one)- or 0.24 (column 2)-standard-deviation increase in the persuasion effect for a president who is one standard deviation more liberal/conservative than usual. For the same president with the same relative liberalism/ conservatism, each one standard deviation that presidential support moves below its average reduces the impact of presidential liberalism on public liberalism by the same amount.

Note again that the coefficients for presidential liberalism and its interaction with presidential support in Congress are additive. Summing the coefficients (for the Durr-like specification $-0.23 + 0.20 = -0.03$; for the EMS specification $-0.20 + 0.24 = 0.04$) suggests that if the president's party is dominant by about one standard deviation,

---

[14] The coefficient for the lagged president's party's percent in Congress variable is negative and statistically significant in both specifications. Each one-standard-deviation increase in the president's party's percent seats in Congress corresponds with a decline of about 0.23 (column one) or 0.20 (column two) standard deviation in public mood. This is merely a descriptive result, which shows that periods of stronger public conservatism have tended to correspond negatively with periods when the president's party is stronger in Congress.

then the president can roughly offset any negative thermostatic reaction by the public.

However, a shift of this magnitude in seats held by the president's party is rare, given the much lower average percent seats held by the president's party through time. Indeed, a movement from 50 to 59 percent seats held by the president's party would be a landslide election of historic proportions. Regardless, the statistical results show that presidents can count on some boost in their persuasive abilities due to the increased presence of institutional allies.

EVALUATING PARTISAN MODEL EXPECTATIONS ABOUT PRESIDENTIAL PERSUASION

The preceding statistical analyses show that presidential honeymoons, high public approval ratings, and institutional allies are important resources that presidents can use to enhance their ability to persuade the mass public. However, the theoretical discussion of the partisan model in Chapter 2 also suggests that the partisan setting facing each president may affect presidential efforts at persuasion.

Specifically, periods during which more of the electorate is persuadable should correspond to increased incentives for the president to seek additional support, either through centrist movement or through public persuasion. In Chapter 4 we evaluated empirically how presidents respond to the changing size of the persuadable region in Figures 2.2 through 2.4. The results reported there showed that presidents move slightly toward the median voter during periods when a larger percentage of the electorate is persuadable. However, given the small movement toward the political center, we can also assume that presidents make more efforts at political persuasion.

Along similar lines, the arguments in Chapter 2 also suggest that presidents might be more successful at public persuasion as the size of the persuadable region in Figures 2.2 through 2.4 increases. Again, we can evaluate this hypothesis using a variable introduced in Chapter 4, which was labeled *electoral percent persuadable*. Again, this variable gauges the propensity of partisans of either political party to defect from their own political party to vote for candidates from the opposing political party.

TABLE 5.5. *Electoral persuadability and presidential effects on public mood*

Model variable	Durr-like capacity model	EMS needs model
Conference Board Coincident Index	−0.26	
	(−0.79)	
Michigan Economic Expectations Index	0.01	
	(0.99)	
Δ Unemployment		0.44
		(1.61)
Inflation		−0.06**
		(−1.98)
Presidential liberalism$_{t-1}$	−0.35*	−0.34*
	(−5.02)	(−5.32)
Electoral percent persuadable$_{t-1}$	−0.42*	−0.37*
	(−4.94)	(−5.22)
Electoral percent persuadable$_{t-1}$ *presidential liberalism$_{t-1}$	0.12	0.12**
	(1.51)	(1.75)
Constant	−047	0.25**
	(−0.88)	(1.67)
Diagnostics		
N	180	184
$p(F)$	0.00	0.00

Note: The numbers in the table are coefficients and *t*-statistics (in parentheses). The *t*-statistics are calculated using Newey–West (1987) autocorrelation- and heteroskedasticity-consistent standard errors. N is the number of observations. $p(F)$ is the probability for the overall model F statistic. Public mood, presidential liberalism, and electoral percent persuadable are standardized to facilitate interpretation.

 * Statistical significance at the 0.01 level.
** Statistical significance at the 0.05 level.

This time series measure of electoral persuadability is again inter-acted with the presidential liberalism variable to evaluate whether there are variations in the success of presidential efforts at mass per-suasion as a function of the size of the persuadable region in Fig-ures 2.2 through 2.5. The interaction variable and its components are again entered into the same base statistical specifications as reported above. The relevant variables are again standardized to facilitate inter-pretation.

Results from the statistical analysis are reported in Table 5.5. Con-sider first the results for the lagged presidential liberalism variable. The coefficient for presidential liberalism now represents the presi-dent's effect on public mood when the electoral percent persuadable is at its average. Using the cross-party voting measure, the average percentage of persuadable citizens from 1958 through 2004 has been about 18.1 percent, with standard deviation about 3.47 percent. Thus, the coefficient for the presidential liberalism variable shows that when the percentage persuadable is at this level, each one-standard-deviation increase in presidential liberalism corresponds with a decrease in public liberalism of about 0.35 (column one) or 0.34 (column two) standard deviation. These results are statistically quite close to the results reported in Tables 5.2 through 5.4. Once again, they confirm the general thermostatic relationship between presidential liberalism and public mood through time.[15]

Consider now the coefficient for the electoral percent persuadable–presidential liberalism interaction variable. It is positive and near-significant or significant in both specifications.[16] The positive relationship shows that when the electoral percent persuadable is above average, the public is more likely to respond favorably to presidential efforts at persuasion. When the electoral percent persuadable is below average, the public is less likely to respond.

Each one-standard-deviation increase in electoral percent persuadable corresponds with about a 0.12-standard-deviation increase in the persuasion effect for a president who is one standard deviation more liberal/conservative than usual. For the same president with the same relative liberalism/conservatism, each one standard deviation that electoral persuadability moves below its average reduces the impact of presidential liberalism on public mood by about 0.12 standard deviation.

Note once again that these movements due to electoral persuadability do not fully offset the negative thermostatic reaction to presidential liberalism. For a president who is one standard deviation more liberal

[15] The coefficient for the lagged electoral percent persuadable variable is negative and statistically significant in both specifications. Each one standard deviation in the electoral percent persuadable corresponds with a decline of about 0.42 (column one) or 0.37 (column two) standard deviation in public mood. Again, this is merely a descriptive result, which shows that periods of looser partisan attachment have occurred mainly when public mood is in the conservative direction.

[16] Using a one-tailed test, the coefficient in the Durr-like specification is significant at the 0.07 level. The coefficient in the EMS specification is significant at the 0.04 level.

than the average facing an electorate with 21.5 percent persuadable citizens, the effect of presidential liberalism on public mood is still about −0.23 (column one) or −0.24 (column two). This is significantly less than would be expected for the average electorate, but does not come close to enabling presidential persuasion of the mass public in the more general case. Nevertheless, the statistical results show that the character of the electorate is a factor that presidents must consider when attempting the strategy of partisan persuasion.

CONCLUSIONS

Presidents are partisans who take issue stances that are either to the left or to the right of the political center. They do so because they are natural representatives of their own parties. As a result, presidents rarely move generically toward the political center. Instead, they appear oblivious in their public issue stances to dynamic movements of the mass public through time. Yet presidents need strong public support to maintain their standing and achieve policy success. The permanent campaigns of modern presidents are a manifestation of this constant need by presidents to persuade the persuadable.

Of course, there is a cost associated with presidents using the strategy of partisan persuasion. Those near the political center generally recognize that presidential issue stances are to the left or right of their own positions. Initially, they may not care much about this disparity. After all, many near the political center will have voted for the president over the opposing party, and may be reluctant to revoke their support. Yet, through time, as opposition emerges and presidential issue stances undergo greater scrutiny, those near the political center become less persuadable. There is a thermostatic reaction to the perception that presidential issue stances are too far to the left or right. As time passes, more effort and resources are required for presidents wanting to persuade those near the political center.

Accordingly, this chapter has shown that presidential efforts at public persuasion are generally unsuccessful. The graphical evidence in Figure 5.1 shows a clear pattern within presidencies of movement by the mass public away from presidential issue stances. The simple correlation between presidential and public liberalism is negative, and the null hypothesis of Granger independence between the two time series cannot be rejected. Furthermore, every multivariate statistical analysis reported in this chapter shows a negative relationship between presidential and public liberalism. The public systematically moves away from, rather than toward, the president.

However, the partisan model developed in Chapter 2 shows that presidents don't have to be hypersuccessful at public persuasion to maintain their majoritarian status. They only need to be marginally successful. Presidents can generally count on *PotentialSupport* that is more than a majority. Under most conditions, even minority party presidents need to persuade less than half of persuadable citizens to achieve majoritarian status. Thus, neither majority nor minority party presidents have to be overwhelmingly successful at public persuasion.

Do presidents have reason to believe that they can be at least marginally successful using the strategy of partisan persuasion? Presidents obviously need political resources to overcome or at least quell the persistent outgoing tide of public support. The evidence presented in this chapter suggests the conditions under which presidents can expect to be more or less successful.

During the early part of a presidential administration, presidential resources for public persuasion are at a maximum. Their recent electoral validation and the symbolism of changing democratic leadership provide an aura of democratic legitimacy. There is typically a surge in popular support following the election of a new president. The presidential election may also have swept allies into office in other institutions, which can engender greater loyalty and prospects for policy change. All of these factors suggest that presidents can be most successful at public persuasion early in a new administration. The empirical evidence reported in this chapter supports this assertion.

Later in an administration, certain political resources can help presidents be more successful, or at least less unsuccessful at public persuasion. Presidents are better at public persuasion when their public approval ratings are high. The empirical evidence presented in this chapter shows that if presidents can maintain very high public approval ratings through time, they can nullify the observed thermostatic reaction. Of course, we also know empirically that most presidents do not maintain such high approval ratings over their entire times in office. So they must continually attempt to bolster their public support through the permanent campaign.

Presidents are also better at public persuasion when they have allies in other political institutions. The empirical evidence in this chapter shows that as presidential support in Congress increases, the president's message becomes more persuasive to the public. This may be due to a bandwagon effect, or simply a stronger prospect of policy success. However, again the empirical evidence shows that support in Congress is a scarce presidential resource. Very large majorities in Congress are required to fully offset the thermostatic reaction against the president's partisan message. Initial elections rarely provide such majorities, and presidents generally lose congressional allies at midterm elections. So, again, this is not a political resource that presidents can count on.

Beyond political resources, presidential efforts at public persuasion are more successful during periods when more of the electorate is persuadable. As the percentage of persuadable citizens increases, presidents become more successful. However, again, this factor would rarely offset the persistent negative reaction against the president's partisan issue stances.

Presidents are not very successful at partisan persuasion over the long term. Nevertheless, they have strong reason to continue using this strategy in the future. They are natural representatives of their political parties. As self-interested politicians, they seek rewards for themselves and their political supporters. Presidents may also genuinely consider their partisan issue positions more appropriate to represent the national interest. Further, given the bimodal partisan nature of the American system, presidents do not need to move the public very far to maintain majoritarian status. Given these facts, presidents have every reason to continue the strategy of partisan persuasion. The generally unsuccessful permanent campaign will likely continue in the future.

What are the implications of this chapter for understanding presidential representation? Presidents are elected both to follow and to

lead. The previous chapter showed that presidents don't do much following. This chapter shows that presidents also don't do a very good
job of leading. The next chapter evaluates whether presidents are punished for failed representation and leadership in terms of changing
public support through time.

CHAPTER 6

Centrism, Partisanship, and Public Approval of the President's Job Performance

If presidents are partisans who neither cater to nor successfully persuade the mass public toward their own positions, then there may be costs associated with these failures. As observed in the introductory chapter, people expect presidents to be centrists in their manner of political representation. They generally abhor partisanship and prefer presidents to represent the nation as a whole, not simply those responsible for their election. Citizens have a common understanding that presidents are the only elected officials in the United States with a single constituency. They are taught the efficacy of the centrist model through their civics training. Many scholars of the American presidency also promote centrist views of the presidency. More generally, the belief that presidents should and do represent the broader public is strongly embedded in American political culture.

Given this orientation, if presidents are partisans rather than centrists in their manner of political representation, then people may punish them by withholding their support. The previous chapter contained some evidence of this effect. A negative reaction occurs during most presidencies, in which the public systematically moves away from the president's issue stances. After the honeymoon period, people increasingly fail to support the president's positions. Presidents can partially offset this negative reaction by attempting to maintain high approval ratings and allies in Congress. As a result, they have increasingly pursued the permanent campaign. However, past research suggests that these factors are largely beyond presidential control (Bond and Fleisher 1990; Bond, Fleisher, and Wood 2003; Edwards 1989, 2003). Thus, the evidence suggests that most presidents pay a price for their partisan issue stances in declining public support.

Of course, the question of whether presidents pay a price for being too liberal or too conservative relates directly to the centrist and partisan models discussed in Chapter 2. The centrist model clearly predicts that presidents must move strategically toward the political center to maintain their political support. Under a unimodal distribution of citizen preferences there is an enforced equilibrium between presidential issue stances and the public. If presidents do not reflect the political center, then people always shift their support away from the president. This predicted movement implies that presidents are punished for being too liberal or too conservative.

On the other hand, at least some of the electorate may not care much about policy. Those near the political center tend not to be strongly attached to ideological principles. Their emphasis may be on symbols, images, and perceptions of leadership. As presidents campaign to persuade the public, images of principled leadership may emerge. Strong leadership images, in turn, should result in stronger support for the president. Thus, in contrast to the centrist model, the partisan model might predict that presidents are not punished for partisan behavior.

The preceding chapter suggests that the centrist model is correct on the question of whether presidents are punished for being too liberal or conservative. Presidents generally lose public support for their partisan issue stances after their honeymoon periods. Do presidents also lose support in terms of lower public approval ratings? Further, does public approval of presidents' job performance vary systematically with the different strategies presidents use, whether centrist or partisan? How, if at all, does the president's permanent campaign affect public support for the president? If it does affect public support, then which strategy should presidents use: centrist or partisan persuasion?

This chapter addresses these questions by exploring statistical relationships among the president's issue liberalism, the public mood, and public approval of the president's job performance.

PAST RESEARCH ON PRESIDENTIAL APPROVAL

Political Behavior Scholarship

Scholars of mass political behavior have contributed greatly toward understanding the determinants of the president's job approval ratings. This research has typically explained presidential approval as a function of inertia, the president's core support, political drama, and the economy. Interestingly, many of these studies have ignored the president as important to determining presidential approval. This seems strange, given that the president is central to the concept of presidential approval.

A major focus of past political behavior research has been on how presidential approval ratings respond to the changing economy. Following Mueller's (1970) classic study, numerous studies revolved around this topic. Early work concluded that objective indicators of economic performance are important to the public's assessment of the president. When the economy does poorly, the president receives much of the blame; when it does well, the president receives much of the credit. Mueller's correlational analysis found a strong relationship between unemployment and presidential approval. However, Hibbs's (1974) reanalysis of Mueller's data found no statistically significant relationship between unemployment and presidential approval after accounting for autocorrelation. Kernell (1978) found that unemployment is not a key determinant of presidential approval, but Kenski (1977) concluded that inflation is important. The consensus that emerged from this early work was muddled on how objective economic conditions affect presidential approval ratings (Monroe 1978, 1979).

A refinement of the economic models of presidential approval concerned whether the public is retrospective or prospective in forming attitudes about the president. Following the lead of Key (1968), early scholars concluded that people look backward to past economic performance in forming their evaluations. Challenging this perspective, Chappell and Keech (1985) found that people are more sophisticated when allocating political support based on economic performance. Their empirical results showed that a model where citizens look to the future when evaluating a president's job performance works as well as or better than models based on current economic indicators or retrospective judgments.

Building on this perspective, MacKuen, Erikson, and Stimson (1992, 603) concluded that "controlling for business expectations, no other measure of economic sentiment directly affects approval. Economic conditions affect presidential popularity only to the extent that economic conditions alter expectations of the economic future." MacKuen, Erikson, and Stimson showed that the effects of unemployment and inflation on presidential approval disappear once citizens' expectations about the future state of the economy are included in the statistical analysis (see also Erikson, MacKuen, and Stimson 2002; but see Norpoth 1996).

Various scholars have questioned the MacKuen, Erikson, and Stimson (1992) study. Some suggested that their statistical analysis was flawed, because it failed to consider the stationarity properties of the approval time series.[1] For example, Clarke and Stewart (1994) attempted to strike a middle ground by estimating an error-correction model (Bannerjee et al. 1993; Davidson et al. 1978; Engle and Granger 1987) that treats presidential approval as nonstationary, but in a long-term equilibrium relationship with economic evaluations. Using this approach, they found that presidential approval responds to both retrospective and prospective economic evaluations.

Of course, all of these analyses assume that the relationship between people's economic evaluations and the president's job approval is stable through time. However, Edwards, Mitchell, and Welch (1995) showed that changing issue salience is important in determining how the economy and international relations affect presidential approval. As issues become more salient to the public through time, their impact on presidential approval increases; as they become less salient, their impact decreases.

Similarly, Hetherington (1996) showed that the economic news people hear is important to their economic evaluations, which in turn affect presidential approval. Indeed, the news can significantly alter people's perceptions of objective economic conditions, and there can

---

[1]   See footnote 6 in Chapter 4 for a discussion of the importance of time series stationarity.

be a large disparity between objective conditions and citizen perceptions.

All of this research has contributed greatly to understanding the
public's approval of the president's job performance. However, much
of this research is limited in that it has ignored the potential role of the
president in affecting people's evaluations. Implicit in much of this
work is the assumption that presidents are passive actors who cannot
alter the dynamics of their own public approval. Again, this approach
seems strange, given that the central character in the presidential
approval drama is the presidency itself.

The White House transmits a continuous stream of messages
intended to shape public opinion and media coverage. The president is arguably the most important political actor in the U.S. system.
The media consistently cover presidential messages, and may also have
independent effects. News about the president is omnipresent and a
topic of daily attention for most Americans. Thus, to ignore this component in explaining presidential approval is to omit a profoundly
important influence.

Presidency Scholarship

Presidency scholars have also been concerned with explaining the
president's job approval ratings. In contrast with much political behavior research, they have generally placed the presidency center stage
in the presidential approval drama. For example, a literature exists
on the ability of presidents to alter their own public approval ratings
through strategically timed military interventions, sanctions, travel,
or other activities (Brody and Page 1975; DeRouen 1995; Fordham
1998; James and Oneal 1991; Kernell 1978; MacKuen 1983; Mueller
1973; Ostrom and Job 1986;). In general, this research has found that
presidents can successfully affect their own approval ratings through
these tools. However, the effects tend to be small and short-lived.

Of course, a more direct approach for presidents wanting to affect
their own public approval is through persuasion and rhetoric. Most
presidency scholars studying presidential persuasion and rhetoric have
focused on changes in public approval after major speeches. For example, Ragsdale (1984, 1987) found that major presidential speeches
typically produce a small increase in public approval. Similarly, Brace

and Hinckley (1992) found that major speeches during a president's first term boost public approval briefly by about 6 percentage points, but have no impact during a president's second term. Various work by Ostrom and Simon (1985, 1989; see also Simon and Ostrom 1985, 1989) also suggested that presidential speeches produce higher public approval, but only when accompanied by an approval-enhancing event.

Other presidency scholars have cast serious doubt on the president's ability to alter public approval ratings through rhetoric (Brody and Shapiro 1989; Edwards 1983; Kernell 1997; Mondak 1993; Rosen 1973; Sigelman 1980a; Sigelman and Sigelman 1981; Thomas and Sigelman 1985). Variously, their studies found small effects, no effects, and even negative effects of presidential rhetoric on public opinion.

In the most recent and comprehensive analysis, Edwards (2003) examined public approval immediately before and after major speeches from Presidents Reagan through George W. Bush. Based on a pretest/post-test research design, he concluded that presidents are not regularly able to affect their own public approval through speeches. Additionally, when presidents do garner public support through speeches, the effects tend to be brief. Thus, the current understanding among presidency scholars is that presidents are not very successful at manipulating their own public approval ratings through persuasion.

Reconsidering the President's Effect on Presidential Approval

However, Druckman and Holmes (2004) provide experimental and survey evidence that presidents can impact their approval ratings by altering the criteria upon which people make their decisions to approve or disapprove of the president. If the economy is doing well or foreign policy is successful, then presidents can lead public attention toward these issue domains. Thus, they argue that presidents do not directly persuade the public, but prime the public to consider those issues most advantageous to the presidency.

Similarly, Erikson, MacKuen, and Stimson (2002, 31–61) frame some of their more recent work in terms of presidential images. They argue that images of presidential competence should result in higher public approval ratings. When presidents are perceived by the public as more adept at handling the major tasks of the office, they are evaluated more favorably. Presidents are expected to be most adept at foreign policy and economic management. As a result, when presidents fail at these tasks, they are evaluated negatively; when they succeed, they are evaluated positively. The mass media contribute to images of successful or failed presidential leadership in these areas through the manner in which they report on the presidency. Media coverage holding the implication that presidents are "in control" results in more favorable images than stories suggesting a lack of control.

These arguments are also consistent with Wood (2007), who shows that presidents can inspire economic confidence in the public by projecting an image of strong economic leadership. Images of presidential optimism about the economy also affect the president's public approval ratings (Wood 2007, Chapter 5). Controlling for objective economic indicators and the economic news, more presidential optimism about the economy produces higher public approval ratings. Thus, some past research suggests that images of strong presidential leadership are important to presidential approval.

PRESIDENTIAL LIBERALISM, PUBLIC LIBERALISM, AND PUBLIC APPROVAL

The Paradox of Approval-Enabled Partisanship

Past research suggests that images of strong presidential leadership may offset to some extent a negative reaction by the public to presidential partisanship. However, if the centrist model is correct, and presidents do pay a price for their partisanship, then there is a potential paradox associated with relationships among presidential liberalism, public liberalism, and presidential approval.

Under the centrist model, presidential policy choices, whether moderate or partisan, should make a difference to presidential approval. Policy choices that are moderate should do more to bolster presidential approval ratings than choices that are not moderate. As argued in the introductory chapter, the public strongly prefers presidential centrism to partisanship.

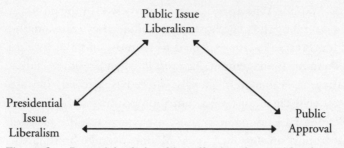

Figure 6.1. Potential relationships affecting the president's permanent campaign.

However, when presidents are more popular, they should also have greater leeway to take more partisan issue stances (see also Canes-Wrone, Herron, and Shotts 2001; Canes-Wrone and Shotts 2004; Hibbs 1987; Hicks 1984; Manza and Cook 2002). In this circumstance they have support to burn. Of course, under the centrist model, being more partisan is then more likely to drive public approval ratings down. Do presidents then become more centrist to move their approval ratings up? Erikson, MacKuen, and Stimson (2002, Chapter 2) recognize this potential paradox, but do not find statistical evidence of these effects. We shall attempt to resolve this potential paradox in the analyses below.

Theories of Presidential Centrism, Partisanship, and Public Approval

Figure 6.1 depicts potential relationships among presidential liberalism, public liberalism, and public approval of the president's job performance. As suggested by the multiheaded arrows, all relationships can be multidirectional. Theoretically, presidents may strategically adjust their issue stances in response to perceived mass preferences and public support. Public issue liberalism and public approval of the president's job performance can also change in response to presidential issue stances. The public may at times prefer liberal or conservative issue stances, and depending on whether the president is in synch with these preferences, may approve or disapprove of the president's job performance.

Under a centrist interpretation, when presidential issue stances are congruent with the preferences of the mass public, public approval should be higher. In contrast, a lack of congruence should result in a loss of presidential support due to competition with the other party. Of course, we know from the graphical evidence in Chapters 4 and 5 that presidential congruence with the mass public occurs only intermittently. Nevertheless, when it does occur, the centrist model predicts that people should reward or punish presidential behavior that conforms or fails to conform to their issue preferences.

In contrast, under a partisan interpretation, presidents can deviate from public issue preferences and still remain powerful. As leaders, presidents commonly attempt to persuade the mass public toward their own issue stances. If presidents are unsuccessful at public persuasion, as suggested by much of the evidence in Chapter 5, then they may still be punished through lower public approval ratings. Of course, the analyses in Chapters 2 and 4 suggest that presidents generally care more about partisan goals, and may not care much about losing some support if there is a sufficient reserve to remain powerful. Further, if presidential persuasion is successful, then presidents may actually be rewarded for deviating from public preferences. Some citizens may prize presidential leadership over policy in their evaluations of the president, thereby offsetting any potential decline in public approval.

The next few sections attempt to sort out these complex relationships using statistical methods that account for the multidirectional causalities depicted in Figure 6.1. The particular questions to be answered are the following: (1) Do presidents strategically adjust their public issue stances in response to changing public issue positions and approval ratings? (2) Do such adjustments in presidential issue stances produce changing public issue positions or affect their public approval ratings?

To be perfectly clear about what the centrist and partisan models predict for Figure 6.1, the expectations for each model are stated formally below in hypothesis form. In words, centrist theory predicts that presidents *always* attempt to mirror the median voter in order to build and maintain their public support. Presidential liberalism should therefore respond to declining public approval with movements toward the mass public. When presidents experience high public approval, resulting from their congruent policy choices, they have greater leeway to pursue partisan issue stances. However, strategic presidents should not exercise this leeway. The equilibrating force associated with the median voter incentive should restrict such movements. Presidents lose support when they are perceived as too partisan. With rational anticipation, high approval presidents should therefore choose to moderate their issue stances in anticipation that declining approval will result if they do not. Thus, under the centrist model, presidents should always follow the public, to maximize their public approval ratings. These arguments can be stated formally as follows.

Hypothesis 1a. Presidential issue liberalism should follow that of the mass public.

Hypothesis 2a. Presidents should seek to move even closer to the mass public as public approval declines. They should also remain close to the mass public under high-approval conditions due to rational anticipation. Given congruence under both low- and high-approval conditions, there should be no statistical relationship between changing public approval and presidential liberalism.

Hypothesis 3a. Public issue stances should be unresponsive to presidential issue stances. This is because the president mirrors the public (Hypothesis 1a), rather than attempting to change it.

Hypothesis 4a. Presidential issue stances that are congruent with the mass public should result in higher public approval.

In contrast, partisan theory predicts that presidents should generally be independent of the median voter and attempt to lead mass preferences toward their own issue preferences. As suggested by the evidence in Chapter 5, presidents may not be successful at leading the mass public. If they are unsuccessful, then they may be punished through lower public approval ratings. However, images of principled leadership may also increase their public approval ratings when they diverge from public issue stances. When public approval of the president's job performance is high, the president should have more leeway to pursue partisan issue stances. However, presidents may not moderate their partisan stances when public approval is low if they think they have a sufficient reserve of support or believe they can project an image of principled leadership. These theoretical expectations can be stated formally as follows.

> *Hypothesis 1b.* Presidential issue liberalism should either lead or be statistically independent of the liberalism of the mass public.
>
> *Hypothesis 2b.* Presidents should be partisans whether or not they have high or low approval ratings. Therefore, there should again be no statistical relationship between changing public approval and presidential liberalism.
>
> *Hypothesis 3b.* Public issue liberalism may (or may not) be responsive to presidential liberalism (depending on the success of presidential persuasion).
>
> *Hypothesis 4b.* Presidential issue stances that are independent of the mass public should produce either unchanged or higher public approval ratings (i.e., the public may reward the president for persuasion and/or perceived leadership).

Of course, the preceding chapters provide some evidence of what we are likely to find for these hypotheses. The analyses in Chapter 4 suggest that presidents are consistently partisans, rather than centrists, in their manner of political representation. The analyses in Chapter 5 suggest that presidents don't do a very good job of persuading the mass public toward their own issue positions. Failed presidential leadership results in a thermostatic reaction, with the president suffering a lack of public issue support after the honeymoon period. There is also some evidence in Chapter 5 that public approval of the president's job performance may enhance the president's ability to persuade the mass public. However, previous chapters provide no evidence about whether the president is punished through lower public approval ratings for a lack of issue congruence with the public.

Although we have some preliminary intuition about what we are likely to find in this analysis, it is useful to validate the results in earlier chapters with time series methods that take into account possible multidirectional causality. We also need to answer questions about

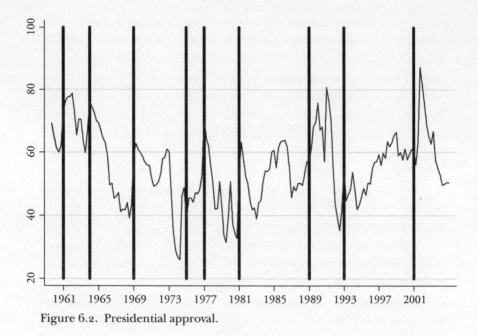

Figure 6.2. Presidential approval.

whether presidential partisanship results in declining or increasing public approval ratings. The next few sections turn toward disentangling the complex and multidirectional relationships depicted in Figure 6.1.

Measuring the Core Concepts

The core measures for the preceding hypotheses are presidential liberalism, public mood, and public approval of the president's job performance. The measures for presidential liberalism and public mood were discussed at length in Chapter 3 and graphed in Chapters 4 and 5. The measure for public approval of the president's job performance was introduced in Chapter 4 and used again in Chapter 5. However, it was not graphed.

It is of some probative value to graph the public approval measure. Figure 6.2 plots the president's Gallup approval ratings from the Eisenhower through the first George W. Bush administration. The figure also contains markers for the first quarter of each new presidential administration.

Figure 6.2 shows that presidents have differed greatly in their ability to attain and maintain high public approval ratings. Presidents Eisenhower, Reagan, and Clinton were relatively successful in maintaining strong approval ratings through time. However, there is a persistent pattern of declining approval for other presidents. President Kennedy had the highest average approval at 71 percent, but this masks a significant decline after his first year in office. Presidents Johnson, Nixon, and Carter started their presidencies with approval of 78, 65, and 75 percent, respectively, but left office with approval of only 44, 24, and 34 percent. Similarly, President George H.W. Bush had an approval rating of 89 percent at the start of the Persian Gulf War, but this fell to only 34 percent the month before the 1992 election. President George W. Bush had the highest single-poll rating of 90 percent shortly after the September 11 attacks, but his approval dropped as low as 22 percent late in his second term.

This pattern of declining public approval for most presidents suggests effects similar to those discussed in Chapter 5 for public responsiveness to presidential liberalism. Presidents typically enter office under the euphoria and symbolism of election, inauguration, and the honeymoon. As a result, during the early parts of presidential administrations, public approval tends to be artificially high. However, the public soon realize that presidents are partisans who are out of synch with their moderate issue stances. Subsequently, the public becomes less supportive of presidential job performance through time. This logic potentially explains the persistent decline in public approval observed in Figure 6.2 for most presidencies.

Although this graphical evidence is suggestive, it is not definitive. A more rigorous statistical analysis requires multivariate statistical methods with appropriate statistical controls. We must also use estimation techniques that account for interdependent responses among presidential liberalism, public mood, and public approval, as suggested by Figure 6.1.

Statistical Methods and Control Variables

The relationships among presidential liberalism, public liberalism, and public approval are potentially multidirectional. Presidential liberalism may affect public mood and approval. Public mood may affect presidential liberalism and approval. Changing public approval may cause presidents to adjust their issue liberalism strategically relative to the public. Changing public approval may also affect the public's relative liberalism due to positive perceptions of presidential leadership. If we are to disentangle these potentially multidirectional relationships, then we need statistical methods that account for the possibility of positive or negative feedback between variables.

Vector autoregression (VAR) methods (Freeman, Williams, and Lin 1989; Sims 1980; Freeman et al. 1998) are used in this chapter to evaluate the direction of causal relationships and track the temporal dynamics among the variables in the system depicted in Figure 6.1.[2] The VAR dependent variables are presidential liberalism, public mood, and public approval.

VAR methods were chosen to estimate the relationships in Figure 6.1 for several reasons. First, there is a strong possibility of multidirectional causal relations between these variables. Yet there is no firm theoretical or empirical basis for specifying a direction of causality for any of the possible relationships.[3] VAR methods make it possible to ascertain the direction of causal relations from the empirical analysis. The direction of causality is a major concern since this is what should enable us to evaluate the competing hypotheses above.

Second, the VAR approach enables strong controls for inertia. The core research concepts are all subject to inertia. Past presidential liberalism should predict current presidential liberalism. Past public mood should predict current public mood. And past public approval should predict current public approval. When VAR is used, each dependent

[2] VAR is a statistical technique in which each endogenous variable in a system is regressed on lags of itself, as well as lags of the other variables. If there are three endogenous variables, as in Figure 6.1, then there are three regression equations. Typically, such systems are symmetrical, with the same number of lags applied to each variable in each equation. Analysts must include a sufficient number of lags to preclude autocorrelation in the regression residuals, which can result in inconsistent estimates.

[3] An alternative approach to modeling relations such as those shown in Figure 6.1 is structural equation modeling. However, this approach requires that one use theory to impose restrictions on the system to achieve mathematical identification of the implied simultaneous relationships. We have no strong theory here, so VAR is more appropriate.

variable is regressed on multiple lagged values of itself, as well as on the other variables in the system.[4]

Including multiple lags of each variable typically makes estimation of individual regression parameters imprecise.[5] For this reason, VAR analysts typically ignore the regression coefficients and use alternative tools for interpretation. Granger (1969) tests are performed that evaluate joint hypothesis tests for blocks of coefficients associated with each variable.[6] A statistically significant block of coefficients implies a Granger causal relationship from the independent variable to the corresponding dependent variable. However, as proven by Lutkepohl (1993, 41–42), "the lack of a Granger-causal relationship from one group of variables to the remaining variables cannot necessarily be interpreted as a lack of a cause and effect relationship."

Another tool for determining the direction of causal relations is performing dynamic simulations based on the estimated system. This approach is called the moving average response (MAR) approach. Unlike Granger tests, the dynamic simulations take into account feedback across variables that can either suppress or accentuate relationships. Granger tests also contain no evidence about the magnitude or polarity of relationships (positive/negative sign). Using the MAR

[4] Based on Akaike's Information Criterion (Akaike 1973), four quarterly lags of all variables were included in the analysis. This may seem like a short lag length. However, it is consistent with the seasonal periodicity of the quarterly data. Sensitivity testing was also done to evaluate the effects of including additional lags up to eight. The relationships were stable and unchanged for longer lag lengths. Residuals from final analyses were nonautocorrelated and nonheteroskedastic.

[5] This is due to multicollinearity.

[6] Granger tests evaluate the null hypothesis that entire blocks of coefficients do not enter into the equation, using either F or Wald statistics. Some past literature has suggested that Granger tests may be suspect when there are cointegrating relationships among variables in a VAR (Freeman et al. 1998; Phillips 1992, 1995). Cointegration occurs when a set of variables share a common trend through time. The graphical and statistical evidence from Chapters 4 and 5 suggests definitively that presidential liberalism and public mood do not trend together. Further, the simple correlation of presidential approval and presidential liberalism is zero. Given these incongruent trends, it is doubtful that cointegration can exist in this system. Nevertheless, a set of augmented Dickey–Fuller(1979) and KPSS (Kwiatkowski et al. 1992) tests were performed to evaluate stationarity conditions and Engle–Granger (1987) tests were done to assess cointegration. All three variables are stationary. Therefore, cointegration cannot exist and the Granger tests are reported below using standard VAR.

approach one can observe the direction, magnitude, polarity, and time path of each relationship. Simulations are accomplished by shocking each variable mathematically to produce an implied response in the other variables in the system.[7] Results of the simulations are reported in matrices of graphs to make possible viewing all relationships at the same time.

The VAR approach permits modeling the possible multidirectional relationships among the variables in Figure 6.1. However, there are also exogenous variables that should be included in the three regressions for statistical control.[8] One exogenous factor that should affect all three dependent variables is the economy. Economic variables have been posited in numerous studies as key to understanding public approval (Beck 1991; Chappell and Keech 1985; Clarke and Stewart 1994; Erikson, MacKuen, and Stimson 2002; Kenski 1977; Kernell 1978; Key 1968; MacKuen 1983; MacKuen, Erikson, and Stimson 1992; Monroe 1978; Mueller 1970; Norpoth 1996; Wood 2000, 2007). Economic variables were also shown in Chapter 4 to affect presidential liberalism, and in Chapter 5 to affect public mood.

Based on these prior analyses, four economic variables are included to reflect the potential sensitivity of the dependent variables to economic performance. The included economic variables are once again the Conference Board's Index of Coincident Indicators, the University of Michigan's Index of Consumer Expectations, change in the quarterly unemployment rate, and the annualized quarterly inflation rate. These variables were discussed at length in Chapters 4 and 5.

An indicator variable for the president's honeymoon period is also included in each of the three equations. This measure was discussed in Chapter 5. There we observed that public mood is more responsive to presidential persuasion during honeymoon periods. Presidential

---

[7] The resulting innovations are orthogonalized using Choleski factorization, because such innovations have the convenient property that they are uncorrelated across both time and equations. In this study, confidence intervals for the moving average responses are calculated using Monte Carlo integration and the fractile method recommended by Sims and Zha (1999).

[8] Accordingly, the VAR-X approach is used to enable inclusion of exogenous variables that impinge on presidential liberalism, public mood, and public approval.

liberalism may also change during honeymoon periods as presidents push their particular political agendas. Public approval should also be higher during honeymoon periods, for reasons discussed at length in Chapter 5. Therefore, the honeymoon indicator is appropriate for all three VAR equations.

An indicator variable for election years is also included in each equation. This measure was introduced in Chapter 4. Past research has argued that presidents are more responsive to public opinion during election years. We found no evidence of this effect in Chapter 4. Nevertheless, given this assertion, It seems logical to include the election year variable to reflect possible changes in presidential liberalism. The public may also be more liberal during election years as candidates push new programs. They may also approve or disapprove of the current president more or less during election years, based on candidate attacks and position taking. Therefore, the election year indicator seems a reasonable statistical control variable for inclusion in each of the three VAR equations.

Finally, a time series to reflect political drama is included in each equation. Political drama refers to dramatic events that push presidential approval either up or down. This variable is constructed as an indicator variable for the presence or absence of events known to have increased or decreased public approval through time. For example, the Reagan assassination attempt substantially increased President Reagan's public approval ratings. In contrast, the Iran–Contra scandal substantially decreased them. In both cases the changes were only temporary. Similarly, various other events either increased or decreased short-term public approval through time. The events series used in constructing the political drama time series is drawn from Erikson, MacKuen, and Stimson (2002, 52) and updated to the present.[9] Given that these events are known to affect public approval, and given that public approval may affect presidential liberalism and public mood, they are also appropriate for inclusion in all three VAR equations.

[9] The events included the Reagan assassination attempt (April 1981), the Grenada invasion (November 1983), the Iran–Contra scandal (November 1986), the Bush–Gorbachev summit (December 1989), Iraq invading Kuwait (August 1990), the budget summit (October 1990), the Persian Gulf War (January 1991), the September 11 tragedy (September 2001), and the United States invading Iraq (April 2003).

TABLE 6.1. *Granger tests for presidential liberalism, mood, and approval system*

Independent variable		Dependent variable	*p*-value
Public mood	→	Public mood	0.00
Public approval			0.46
Presidential liberalism			0.20
Public mood		Public approval	0.83
Public approval	→		0.00
Presidential liberalism			0.11
Public mood		Presidential liberalism	0.63
Public approval			0.51
Presidential liberalism	→		0.00

Note: The arrows indicate Granger causality from the block of coefficients for the independent variable to the dependent variable based on 0.10 significance levels. The analyses also contained control variables, including change in unemployment, inflation, the Conference Board Index of Coincident Indicators, the Survey of Consumers Index of Consumer Expectations, presidential honeymoon indicators, election years, and the critical events described in footnote 2.

Statistical Results for the Presidential Liberalism, Public Mood, and Public Approval System

Do presidents strategically adjust their relative liberalism in response to changing public mood and/or approval, as might be suggested by centrist theory (Hypotheses 1a and 2a)? Or does presidential liberalism tend to lead or be independent of public mood and/or approval, as might be suggested by partisan theory (Hypotheses 1b and 2b)? Do the mass public generally fail to respond to changing presidential liberalism, as suggested by centrist theory (Hypothesis 3a)? Or do public responses to the president's permanent campaign depend on the effectiveness of presidential persuasion, as suggested by partisan theory (Hypothesis 3b)? Do movements in presidential liberalism toward the mass public produce higher public approval, as might be suggested by centrist theory (Hypothesis 4a)? Or do presidential independence and efforts to lead produce higher approval for the president (Hypothesis 4b)? Statistical results from a VAR system for partially answering these questions are reported in Table 6.1 and Figure 6.3.

Note first that the Granger tests in Table 6.1 show that each of the dependent variables is highly inertial, with the blocks of coefficients associated with each being strongly significant (*p*-value = 0.00). This inertial effect captures the dynamic history of each dependent

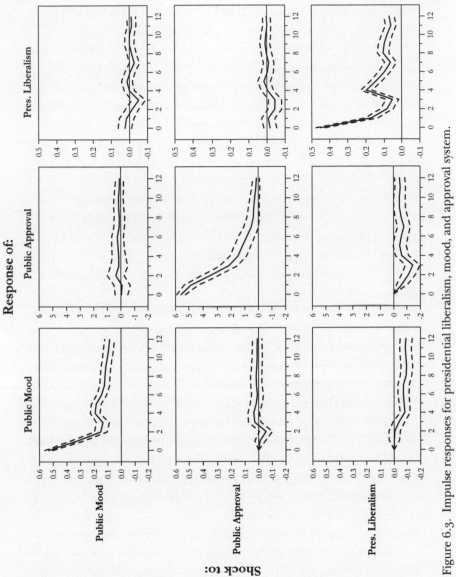

Figure 6.3. Impulse responses for presidential liberalism, mood, and approval system.

variable. Modeling this historical effect provides a strong statistical control for the possibility that relationships are due to chance.

The Granger tests for effects running from public mood and approval to presidential liberalism are shown in the third panel of Table 6.1. Neither variable Granger-causes presidential liberalism. The absence of Granger causal relationships from mood and approval to presidential liberalism once again suggests that presidents are oblivious to changing public issue preferences and support. Presidents are partisans, rather than strategic actors who respond to changing public opinion. This result mirrors with a different methodology the extensive analysis of the centrist versus partisan models in Chapter 4. The lack of presidential responsiveness to the mass public confirms once again that the partisan theory is a more appropriate explanation for presidential issue stances through time.

In the opposite direction, the Granger test in the first panel of Table 6.1 at the third row shows that presidents are not very effective in moving the public toward their own issue positions. Presidents persistently attempt the partisan persuasion strategy, but they generally fail at persuading the mass public. This result mirrors the statistical results in Chapter 5, which also show that presidential efforts at public persuasion are generally unsuccessful.

However, the Granger tests in the second panel of Table 6.1 contain a result suggesting that presidential liberalism may affect public approval. The Granger test from presidential liberalism to public approval has p-value 0.11. This test is not statistically significant at conventional levels, but may imply that presidents affect their own approval ratings through strategic adjustment of their issue positions through time.

Of course, Granger causality tests tell us nothing about the polarity (i.e., whether relations are positive or negative) or magnitude of potential causal relationships. Furthermore, as proved by Lutkepohl (1993, 42), the absence of a Granger causal relation cannot be interpreted as a lack of a cause and effect relationship. Simultaneous feedback can mask causal relationships. Therefore, we must also examine the moving average responses in Figure 6.3 to fully understand the VAR results.

The variables being shocked in the moving average response simulations are on the diagonal of Figure 6.3. The responses to the shocks are read horizontally across the rows. Consider first again the question of whether presidents strategically adjust their positions in response to changing public mood and approval. The first two panels of Figure 6.3 provide definitive answers to these questions. The first panel shows that a one-standard-error shock to public mood (row one, column one) produces no statistically significant increase in presidential liberalism (row one, column three). In fact, after a liberal shock to public mood, there is a marginally significant conservative movement in presidential liberalism three temporal quarters later. In other words, presidents do not adjust their issue positions strategically through time to mirror those of the mass public as would be predicted by the centrist model. Rather, they become even more partisan in the opposite direction when public liberalism changes.

The second panel of Figure 6.3 shows that a one-standard-error shock to public approval (row two, column two) produces a marginally significant conservative movement in presidential liberalism during the second and third quarters after the shock (row two, column three). The same shock to approval also drives the public in a slightly more conservative direction two quarters later (row two, column one). These coincident movements show that as public approval increases, the president and the public both move in the same direction. Presidents do not move away from the public as their public approval increases, or toward the public as it declines. Rather, changing public approval produces consistent movements from both the president and public. This result is inconsistent with the notion posited by earlier research (Erikson, MacKuen, and Stimson 2002, 31–61; see also Canes-Wrone, Herron, and Shotts 2001; Canes-Wrone and Shotts 2004; Hibbs 1987; Hicks 1984; Manza and Cook 2002) that higher public approval gives the president more leeway for divergent issue stances. If presidents respond strategically to such leeway, then we should see movements of the president and public in opposite directions. We see no such movement. Therefore, we must conclude that presidents are partisans, rather than strategic actors, in responding to changing public approval.

Of course, Hypotheses 2a and 2b above suggest alternative reasons for this nonfinding. Both the centrist and partisan models predict a lack of responsiveness by the president to changing public approval. Under the centrist model, presidents do not become more partisan when their approval ratings are high, because they anticipate that this might drive their approval ratings down. Under the partisan model, presidents do not become less partisan when their approval ratings are low, because they are self-interested actors pursuing partisan goals and believe in their own powers of persuasion. Thus, this nonfinding can be explained using either the centrist or partisan model.

Consider now how changing presidential liberalism affects public liberalism and public approval. These questions are addressed in the third panel of Figure 6.3. The results show that a one-standard-error increase in presidential liberalism (row three, column three) produces a decline in public liberalism (row three, column one). Again, this opposite movement confirms the thermostatic reaction to presidential liberalism discussed in Chapter 5. It also shows definitively that presidents are not very successful in leading the mass public. In fact, the public is reactionary against strong presidential issue stances. The likely reason is that people perceive the president as too liberal relative to the moderate public thermostat. As a result, they move away from presidential issue stances when the president is perceived as too partisan.

In the third panel of Figure 6.3, the same increase in presidential liberalism produces a decline in public approval (row three, column two). In other words, as the president is perceived as being more liberal, the public punishes the president's partisan issue stance through declining public support. We should not, however, draw strong conclusions from this result. As it stands, this is merely a descriptive result showing that the public approves less of presidential liberalism than it does of presidential conservatism.

The Presidential Congruence and Public Approval System

What we need if we are to move further in answering the research questions of this chapter is an analysis that considers the absolute distance between the president and the public on a liberal–conservative continuum. This distance is labeled "congruence" for the discussions that follow.

Does presidential congruence with the mass public lead to higher public approval ratings? Are presidents punished for their lack of congruence (i.e., partisanship) through lower approval ratings? Do presidents respond to lower approval ratings with more congruence? Do they respond to higher public approval with more partisanship?

We must measure "congruence" to answer these questions. The measure used here defines congruence as the absolute value of the distance between presidential and public issue stances, whether or not the president diverges from the public in a liberal or conservative direction. This measure is accomplished by first regressing standardized presidential liberalism on standardized public mood.[10] Given that both measures are standardized, the regression intercept is zero. The regression slope coefficient adjusts any difference in scale between the two variables.

The residuals from this regression are then saved and transformed. The transformation takes the negative of the absolute value of the residuals. This procedure results in a measure that captures the absolute distance from the president to the public in values that range from zero to negative. Values of zero indicate perfect presidential congruence with the public. More negative values indicate less presidential congruence.

One can think of this measure as capturing the centrist disequilibrium between the president and the public through time. If the president and the public are in equilibrium the value of the residual is zero. If the president is to the left or right of the public, the value of the residual is negative.[11]

Using this new dependent variable, a second VAR was estimated between presidential congruence and public approval. The system remains the same as above, except that presidential issue liberalism and public mood are now collapsed into a single variable capturing presidential congruence and partisanship.

[10] Regression is an accepted mathematical technique for placing variables in the same vector space. See, for example, Kolman and Hill (1996, Section 8.4).

[11] This approach to measurement is similar to the approach sometimes taken in constructing two-stage error-correction models (Engle and Granger 1987). However, in this case, we are making the disequilibrium measure negative for both liberal and conservative periods. Of course, we already know from earlier graphical evidence (Figures 4.1 and 5.1) that the two variables are more often in a state of disequilibrium. So values that are precisely zero are uncommon.

TABLE 6.2. *Granger tests for presidential congruence–approval system*

Independent variable		Dependent variable	p-value
Congruence	→	Congruence	0.00
Public approval			0.99
Congruence		Public approval	0.53
Public approval	→		0.00

Note: The arrows indicate Granger causality from the block of coefficients for the independent variable to the dependent variable based on 0.10 significance levels. The analyses also contain control variables, including change in unemployment, inflation, the Conference Board Index of Coincident Indicators, the Survey of Consumers Index of Consumer Expectations, presidential honeymoon indicators, election years, and the critical events described in footnote 9.

The Granger tests for this analysis are reported in Table 6.2. They show that both dependent variables are again highly inertial. Each dependent variable Granger-causes itself. However, there is an absence of Granger causality between congruence and approval in either direction. In other words, the Granger tests again suggest a lack of presidential responsiveness to changing public approval. The results also suggest that public support for the president is unresponsive to congruence between presidential and public issue stances.

However, as mentioned above "the lack of a Granger-causal relationship from one group of variables to the remaining variables cannot necessarily be interpreted as a lack of a cause and effect relationship" (Lutkepohl 1993, 42). Thus, we must also examine the moving average response simulations to fully understand the mutual dynamics of congruence and public approval. These are contained in Figure 6.4.

The simulations show a statistically significant dynamic response running from congruence to public approval. A one-standard-error increase in presidential congruence with the public (row one, column one) produces consistently higher public approval ratings (row one, column two) for about two temporal quarters. In other words, presidents are rewarded through increased public approval for expressing issue stances that are congruent with the mass public. Conversely, they are punished for issue stances that diverge from the mass public. Presumably, this is because the public disapproves of presidential

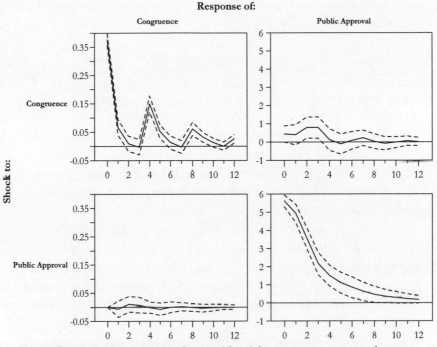

Figure 6.4. Impulse responses for presidential congruence–approval system.

issue stances that are either "too liberal" or "too conservative" when compared to the more moderate public thermostat.

In the other direction, the simulations show that congruence does not respond to changing public approval. A one-standard-error positive shock in public approval produces no change in presidential congruence with the public (row two, column one). Presidents experiencing high public approval do not move away from the public. Rather, they remain consistently divergent in their issue stances through time.

This result is consistent with that reported above for Figure 6.3. Again, this finding runs counter to earlier work, which argues that presidents have less incentive to follow the mass public when their public approval ratings are high (Erikson, MacKuen, and Stimson 2002, 31–61; see also Canes-Wrone, Herron, and Shotts 2001; Canes-Wrone and Shotts 2004; Hibbs 1987; Hicks 1984; Manza and Cook 2002. Instead, the analysis in this chapter finds that presidents remain consistently partisan when their approval ratings are either high and low. This is irrespective of whether they are rewarded or punished by the public through changing public support.

CONCLUSIONS

The permanent campaign of presidential rhetoric has altered the president's role in American government (Blumenthal 1982; Gergen 2000; Jones 2000; Ornstein and Mann 2000; Tenpas 2000). Presidents are continually espousing issue stances long after elections intended to appeal to their constituencies and bolster their public approval. Therefore, it is important to understand the causes and consequences of these presidential activities.

This chapter has focused on whether the permanent campaign is caused by efforts of presidents to bolster their public approval ratings through either centrist or partisan strategies. Additionally, it has focused on whether presidents are punished for taking issue stances that are perceived by the public as either too liberal or too conservative.

The statistical evidence again confirms that presidents are partisans who do not respond to changing public liberalism. They also do not respond strategically to changing public approval ratings. Whether public approval of the president's job performance is high or low, presidential issue stances remain consistently partisan.

However, the statistical results do not completely discredit the centrist model. Consistent with centrist predictions, the evidence shows that presidents benefit from greater issue congruence with the mass public. Their public approval ratings increase when they mirror mass issue preferences. Their public approval ratings also decline when they express issue stances that are incongruent with the public. Thus, the statistical evidence shows that presidents are punished for their partisan behavior through declining public support.

As an empirical regularity, the evidence in prior chapters has shown that presidents are generally "too liberal" or "too conservative" relative to the public. Thus, public reaction against their partisan issue stances is probably a key to solving the long-standing puzzle of why public approval declines systematically through time for most presidents. The regularity of declining public approval is part of the thermostatic reaction to public perceptions of presidential partisanship. The public is inherently moderate and prefers presidential representation that is also moderate. As the public perceives that the president is not the moderate representative they expected, public support is gradually withdrawn.

Why should presidents remain partisans even though they might know they will be punished for such behavior? Again, presidents are natural partisans who are innately inclined toward partisan solutions. Presidents also commonly believe in their powers of persuasion. Furthermore, presidents may sincerely believe, as Washington did during the 1795–96 Jay Treaty controversy, that their partisan view of the national interest is more appropriate than responding limply to the whims of a broader electorate.

Presidents may also be motivated by savvy calculations of their support among the electorate. Most presidents have a residue of popular support upon entering office. As a result, they can often afford to lose support and remain viable. The partisan strategy strengthens the commitment of core constituencies and may also appeal to a group of weakly committed citizens near the political center. Most presidents do not have to move very many people very far to maintain their majoritarian status.

Of course, the most obvious reason presidents pursue a partisan strategy is that they get to pursue their own personal and partisan goals. Therefore, it may be quite reasonable for presidents to pursue the partisan over the centrist strategy, even in the face of likely punishment.

For whatever reason presidents are partisans, we can only conclude from the evidence reported in this and earlier chapters that the centrist model is wrong as an explanation for presidential behavior. We turn in the concluding chapter toward discussing the implications of noncentrist, partisan presidential representation for American democracy.

CHAPTER 7

The Efficacy for American Democracy of Noncentrist, Partisan Presidential Representation

On the evening of September 24, 2008, President George W. Bush appeared on national television to persuade the American public of the need to "bail out" the U.S. financial sector. In that speech he implied that his plan was motivated by the national interest, rather than partisanship. He said, "I know that Americans sometimes get discouraged by the tone in Washington and the seemingly endless partisan struggles. Yet history has shown that in times of real trial, elected officials rise to the occasion" (*Weekly Compilation of Presidential Documents* 2008, 1254).

The U.S. financial sector was in deep trouble. A major reason was that banks and asset management firms had invested heavily in mortgage-backed securities, which were increasingly risky due to the high rate of mortgage defaults in 2007 and 2008. Investor panic ensued as housing prices declined, and it became apparent that many companies holding these securities were undercapitalized. In March, shares of Bear Sterns declined to near zero, and the Federal Reserve brokered its acquisition by J. P. Morgan Chase. In July, the fourth largest bank failure in U.S. history occurred, with the collapse of Indymac Bank. In early September, the federal government took over Fannie Mae and Freddie Mac, which owned or guaranteed about half of the $12 trillion U.S. mortgage market. In mid-September, a troubled Merrill Lynch was acquired by Bank of America. A day later, the largest bankruptcy in U.S. history occurred with the failure of Lehman Brothers. To prevent another large bankruptcy, the Federal Reserve injected $85 billion into American International Group to recapitalize a huge company that was also heavily invested in mortgage-backed securities.

Against this backdrop, President Bush's speech was notable in terms both of what it proposed, and of its relationship to standard partisan prescriptions. The president stated,

> ... our entire economy is in danger. So I proposed that the Federal Government reduce the risk posed by these troubled assets and supply urgently needed money so banks and other financial institutions can avoid collapse and resume lending.... I'm a strong believer in free enterprise, so my natural instinct is to oppose government intervention. I believe companies that make bad decisions should be allowed to go out of business. Under normal circumstances, I would have followed this course. But these are not normal circumstances. The market is not functioning properly. There's been a widespread loss of confidence, and major sectors of America's financial system are at risk of shutting down.... Under our proposal, the Federal Government would put up to $700 billion taxpayer dollars on the line to purchase troubled assets that are clogging the financial system. (*Weekly Compilation of Presidential Documents* 2008, 1252–53)

Remarkably, the president's proposal allowed the Treasury Department to buy shares in these troubled institutions, partially nationalizing the U.S. financial sector. Of course, the standard Republican prescription is free markets with minimal government intervention and regulation. Thus, the president's proposal ran strongly against partisan expectations for a Republican presidency.

Much of the American public was skeptical about the president's plan. A week after the president's speech, a Fox News poll (Paicopolos 2008) reported that a 53 percent majority of Americans were opposed to the "bailout" package. Even larger majorities among Republicans (57 percent) and independents (59 percent) were opposed the plan. Extraordinarily, public support for the "bailout" actually dropped following the president's speech. According to a report by the Pew Research Center (October 6, 2008), during the week of September 19–22 before the speech, support for a "bailout" was 57 percent, whereas for the same survey respondents during the week of September 27–29 after the speech, it was only 45 percent. Surprisingly, support dropped significantly more among Republicans than it did among Democrats and Independents. Further, according to a CBS News poll (October 1, 2008), the president's approval rating declined after the speech to only 22 percent, with only 15 percent approving of the president's handling of the economy.

This lack of public support obviously limited the president's powers of legislative persuasion. To be sure, the plan was unpopular among the president's fellow partisans in Congress. On September 29 the U.S. House of Representatives rejected the president's "bailout" plan by a vote of 228 to 205. The opposing votes included 133 Republicans, with only 65 members of the president's own party favoring the bill. Members of the president's party voted against it by more than two to one. The often-claimed reason for the Republican opposition was that House members had received a massive influx of constituent mail expressing anger and overwhelming opposition to the bill. Also, members claimed that a highly partisan speech by House Speaker Nancy Pelosi just prior to the vote poisoned the atmosphere in which the vote was taken (Calmes September 29, 2008; Fox News September 29, 2008). Needless to say, the failed House vote was a major political defeat for President Bush, who had tried to persuade the public through the televised address, and also intensely lobbied wavering Republican legislators through personal phone calls (Calmes September 29, 2008).

The president's failure to persuade the public and members of the House of Representatives sent a devastating signal to financial markets. The stock market declined dramatically. On the day of the failed House vote, the Dow Jones Industrial Average dropped by 778 points, or roughly 7 percent of its total value. The financial meltdown also continued after the failed House vote, with the collapse of Washington Mutual, the nation's largest savings and loan, and Wachovia, which was later acquired by Wells Fargo & Co. In the aftermath of this continuing turbulence in the financial sector, many banks quit lending to one another, and credit effectively dried up for many businesses and consumers. Consumers and businesses became increasingly uncertain about the economy and were often unable to make purchases due to tightened credit standards.

Continuing to seek passage, on October 1 the Senate approved a sweetened version of the president's "bailout" package by a vote of 74 to 25, with 15 Republicans in opposition. Finally, on October 3, a revised bill was passed by the House of Representatives. Among

Republicans, 91 House members voted for the final bill with 108 opposing. The president was still unable to muster a majority of his own party. Nevertheless, the president signed the financial "bailout" package on the same day it was passed.

Obviously, this period was one of great national stress. During such times Americans usually look to the White House for leadership and assurance. However, President Bush's attempts to provide it were largely unsuccessful, because he did not inspire trust. Trust in the president was exhausted due to Americans' recognition that his earlier partisan tax and regulatory policies had resulted in increasing inequality, had failed to support the middle class, and might have contributed to the financial crisis. Trust in the president was also exhausted due to the continuing unpopularity of the war in Iraq and the president's role in getting the nation into that war. President Bush's standing had sagged to record lows in the polls even before the financial meltdown, undermining his credibility for charting a way out of it. It was fear of financial collapse, not persuasion by the president, that enabled passage of the $700 billion "bailout" package.

Over the next five trading days after the bill was signed into law, the Dow Jones Industrial Average dropped by a larger percentage than during any comparable period in its 112-year history. It lost 22 percent of its total value (1,874 points) on the expectation that regardless of governmental action, the nation was possibly facing the most serious economic decline since the Great Depression. Investors were highly skeptical that the president's plan would work, and reacted accordingly.

During this period, the Treasury Department and Federal Reserve continued to work toward restoring confidence in U.S. financial institutions. On October 6, the Federal Reserve announced that it was providing up to $900 billion in short-term loans to banks. Given that credit markets were frozen, it moved the next day to make up to $1.3 trillion directly available to companies. On October 8, the central banks in the United States, the United Kingdom, China, Canada, Sweden, and Switzerland and the European Central Bank cut interest rates in a coordinated effort to aid the world economy. Finally, on October 14, Treasury Secretary Henry M. Paulson announced that the government was purchasing $250 billion in preferred stock from the largest banks in the nation, with the requirement that they resume normal lending activities. In effect, the U.S. banking industry was partially nationalized under a Republican administration.

Again, this was hardly the solution that would be expected from a partisan Republican president. Following these actions, Treasury Secretary Paulson called parts of the proposal "objectionable," saying that "today's actions are not what we ever wanted to do" (U.S. Treasury Department 2008). President Bush and his top economic policymakers strongly emphasized that the dramatic actions taken by government were not meant to undermine the nation's free market principles. But given the depth of the crisis and the risk that it would spark a broader economic downturn, the president and his economic team said they felt extraordinary steps were needed in the national interest.

THE FINANCIAL MELTDOWN AND PRESIDENTIAL REPRESENTATION

President Bush's response to the financial meltdown of 2008 provides an example of presidential representation complementary to the introductory case study of George Washington during the Jay Treaty crisis of 1795–96.

Both presidents faced an issue that was critical to the national interest. Both proposed decisive action to address the issue. Like Washington, President Bush was not a centrist in responding to the crisis. The public was largely opposed to the president's plan. As a result, the president was again in the position of needing to persuade the mass public. Faced with strong opposition in the U.S. House of Representatives, the president attempted to muster public and legislative support. However, for President Bush, the task of persuasion was not easy, given the lack of trust and approval of his past leadership by most citizens. Where Washington had potent political resources for persuading the public and legislators, Bush was abysmally weak in the resources needed for public and legislative persuasion. Accordingly, unlike Washington, Bush failed at persuading the public, as well as at securing loyalty from members of his own party in the House.

Presidents Washington and Bush brought different resources and perspectives to their respective tasks of presidential leadership.

Arguably, Washington spent his life serving the community at large. At great risk to his person and property, he served his country as commander-in-chief during the Revolutionary War. He did not overtly seek the presidency, but was selected by his fellow countrymen as best qualified to represent the nation at large. While occupying the presidency, Washington consistently behaved as a national caretaker, sometimes seeking the happiness of his fellow citizens and at others doing what he thought was best for the community regardless of public opinion. He worked hard to keep the nation out of a war that he believed would be harmful to national interests. Most analysts agree that Washington was a "statesman" president, rather than a partisan catering to narrow special interests.

In contrast, President George W. Bush spent the first 91 months of his administration strongly embracing partisan principles. Where Washington had clamored to keep the nation out of a war, Bush clamored to get the nation into a war. He consistently favored higher military spending in pursuit of the Iraq war. He advocated and achieved two of the three largest tax cuts in U.S. history. These tax cuts favored the wealthy, and generated greater economic inequality than had existed since the Great Depression (e.g., see Bartels 2008, Figure 2.2). To the pleasure of his conservative constituents, Bush proposed privatization of the Social Security system and school vouchers. He nominated pro-life justices to the Supreme Court. He opposed environmental regulation of greenhouse gases, which most physical scientists agree are a major cause of global climate change. His policy in many regulatory areas was reliance on "voluntary compliance," rather than the "command and control" approaches of earlier administrations. He advocated "free market" and deregulatory principles favoring the wealthy, which may have contributed to the excessive risk-taking of the financial industry (e.g., see Becker et al. 2008). Indeed, President Bush's record of adherence to Republican principles was very high prior to September 2008.[1]

---

[1] There are some exceptions. Republicans generally consider themselves fiscal guardians, but federal spending grew more under the George W. Bush administration than under any president since Lyndon Johnson. Also, President Bush secured passage of federal prescription drug coverage assistance for seniors, as well as an AIDS program for Third World countries.

The Bush presidency was a partisan presidency. Nevertheless, President Bush's response to the 2008 financial crisis clearly rejected partisan principles in favor of protecting the nation. The positions he advocated were inconsistent with Republican prescriptions, and were opposed by most of the president's fellow partisans. Therefore, contrary to the analyses in earlier chapters, the president did not behave as might be predicted by the median partisan. Instead, he finally took the broader perspective of doing what seemed right for the community at large.

An important lesson from both the Washington and Bush vignettes is that there are no absolutes with any theory of presidential representation, whether centrist or partisan. Modern presidents *generally* behave as partisan representatives, but they do not *always* do so. Modern presidents *generally* fail at political persuasion, but they do not *always* fail.

Consistent with partisan theory, neither Washington nor Bush was a centrist representative in responding to their respective crises. As a result, both needed to persuade the public and legislators. However, inconsistent with partisan theory, both presidents responded to their respective crises as "statesmen," rather than partisan representatives. With strong political resources, Washington succeeded at political persuasion. With weak political resources, Bush failed at political persuasion.

LIMITATIONS OF THE PARTISAN THEORY OF PRESIDENTIAL REPRESENTATION

These are obviously not the only cases where presidents have taken positions against their own parties either as "statesmen" representing community interests or as centrists. For example, Beschloss (2007) argues that President Kennedy was reluctant to vigorously pursue a civil rights agenda early in his administration due to the closeness of the 1960 presidential election and the fragility of his electoral coalition. However, as the civil rights movement became increasingly visible in 1962–63, he strongly pushed the issue, even when it diminished his prospects for reelection in 1964 and ran the risk of splintering his own party along regional lines. Beschloss describes this presidential behavior as courageous, because so many were opposed to racial integration.

Perhaps the most consistently nonpartisan president was Nixon, who quite often aligned himself with Democrats in opposition to his own party. As discussed in Chapter 3, Nixon proposed a multiplicity of environmental laws. By executive order, President Nixon created the Environmental Protection Agency and the National Oceanic and Atmospheric Administration. He signed legislation protecting worker health and safety. He signed the Equal Employment Opportunity Act of 1972, which expanded civil rights protections. President Nixon also used administrative tools to revitalize the Federal Trade Commission. He proposed expanding various welfare programs, and signed legislation increasing Social Security, Medicare, and Medicaid benefits. Clearly, Nixon was the most willing to compromise with the other party of any modern president.

One of the most memorable examples of a modern president going against his own party concerned President George H. W. Bush's "Read my lips! No new taxes!" promise at the 1988 Republican convention. The federal deficit had grown to unsustainable levels following the 1981 Reagan tax cut, and President Bush was saddled with the task of achieving fiscal control. He faced a Democratic Congress that would only agree to spending cuts if there were also tax increases that spread the pain across both Democratic and Republican constituencies. Bush broke his "Read my lips!" promise to fellow Republicans when he approved higher taxes through the 1990 budget agreement to reduce the federal deficit. This reversal caused great controversy, especially in the more conservative wing of the Republican Party. However, given the magnitude of the nation's fiscal problems, it was an action that was clearly in the best interests of the community.

President Clinton also went against his fellow partisans in 1993 by seeking ratification of the North American Free Trade Agreement (NAFTA). NAFTA had been negotiated and signed during the closing days of the George H. W. Bush administration. However, the agreement was subject to legislative approval.[2] President Clinton agreed

---

[2] The agreement was signed subject to approval by the legislative bodies of the three signatory countries, the United States, Canada, and Mexico. This process differed

with the principle of free trade and pressed for its ratification by Congress. Congress was controlled by Democrats, most of whom opposed the agreement as injurious to their labor constituents and the environment, and giving an unfair trade advantage to neighboring countries. The president prevailed on the issue by aligning himself more closely with Republicans than with Democrats. After intense political debate, the U.S. House of Representatives passed NAFTA by a vote of 234 to 200, with 132 Republicans favoring the agreement along with only 102 Democrats. In the Senate the legislation approving the agreement passed by a vote of 61 to 38, with 34 Republicans in favor along with 27 Democrats.

These and other examples suggest that presidents sometimes follow a course that runs against partisan principles. There are also specific instances historically when presidents may have followed a centrist strategy. For example, Canes-Wrone (2006, Chapter 6) identifies two cases where presidents allegedly "pandered" to the mass public. President Carter, during his first three years, favored and achieved expanding humanitarian aid to third world countries. This position was not popular among the broader public. According to survey evidence from the General Social Survey, roughly 65 percent of Americans thought the nation was spending too much on foreign aid. President Carter's popularity had declined by 1980 as a result of the Iran hostage crisis and the struggling economy. The president was facing a tough reelection campaign in 1980. Thus, Canes-Wrone (2006, 135) asserts, "he reversed his previous position and recommended that the United States cut economic assistance." According to Canes-Wrone, the president "pandered" to the mass public on this unpopular program during an election year.[3]

from the treaty-making process in that a majority of both chambers of Congress was required for approval, rather than the two-thirds of the Senate normally required for treaty ratification.

[3] There are alternative interpretations to that offered by Canes-Wrone, some of which she acknowledges. One that she does not acknowledge is that President Carter had already achieved increased humanitarian aid in earlier budgets, so that he may not have felt a need for an additional increase in this particular budget year. Related to this possibility, he may also have felt constrained by a tight budget during a year when it was clear that the economy was in decline.

Canes-Wrone (2006, Chapter 6) also reports a second case of presidential "pandering" during the George H. W. Bush presidency. The nation was in the midst of the 1991–92 recession, and the Democratic Congress sent the president a bill that would extend unemployment benefits for an additional 20 weeks to workers whose benefits were about to expire. The bill was very popular with the public. A *Los Angeles Times* poll taken soon after reported that more than 60 percent of survey respondents favored the legislation. However, programs that encourage people not to work are inconsistent with Republican principles. Republicans also generally favor minimal government interference in the market economy. President Bush also viewed the unemployment benefits extension as fiscally irresponsible, potentially running up the federal deficit. Accordingly, in October 1991 he vetoed the legislation. However, he signed a similar bill less than two months later as his public approval ratings were falling and the 1992 election was approaching. According to Canes-Wrone, the president switched positions on this popular legislation to bolster his public approval and his prospects for reelection.

These counterexamples, along with the Jay Treaty and 2008 financial crisis vignettes, demonstrate that presidents may sometimes act as nonpartisan or centrist representatives. However, the analyses in Chapters 4 through 6 suggest that they do not *generally* do so. Modern presidents have espoused issue positions based on partisan principles consistently through time and largely adhered to those positions throughout their administrations. Presidents are typically unresponsive to mass preferences in formulating their issue positions. They are also largely unsuccessful at persuading the mass public toward their own positions. Thus, modern presidents are *generally* noncentrist, partisan representatives.

The partisan theory of presidential representation is limited in that it cannot correctly predict every presidential issue stance through time. However, social science theories are not required to be complete explanations of the phenomena of interest. Rather, theories are simplifications of reality that enable better understanding. The purpose is to explain relationships between the concepts of interest systematically, but not necessarily completely. Thus, the partisan theory of presidential representation that was developed in Chapter 2 and validated in Chapters 4 through 6 *generally* explains presidential behavior. However, it cannot *completely* explain presidential behavior or why presidents sometimes deviate from partisan principles.

WHAT (IF ANYTHING) IS WRONG WITH PARTISAN PRESIDENTIAL REPRESENTATION?

To what extent is partisan presidential representation undesirable? To answer this question, it is important to note first that there may be nothing wrong with this mode of presidential representation so long as presidential behavior is guided by what truly is in the community's best interests.

For example, there are some issues for which there are multiple ways to address a public problem. Under these circumstances, it becomes difficult to say that a partisan solution is inferior to a centrist solution. Consider the case of how to address the nation's health care needs. Democrats favor a system of universal health care coverage sponsored by the federal government, similar to those in Canada and Europe. This approach is viewed by Republicans as socialistic and favoring big government over free markets. Republicans support a system under which health care remains private, but with federal tax incentives for individuals to purchase their own health insurance. Democrats view this approach as favoring the wealthy, who are the ones benefiting the most from tax incentives. A centrist solution might reach a compromise between the two extremes. Who is to say which of these three approaches is best? The two partisan approaches are rooted in their respective party ideologies, but neither approach can be said to run definitively against community interests. A compromise between the two approaches also has no rationale for claiming to better represent community interests.

Of course, such ambiguities exist for multiple issue domains, including education, crime, urban problems, welfare, and military spending. These ambiguities make it difficult to determine whether partisan solutions run contrary to community interests. Indeed, the question of whether there is anything wrong with partisan representation seems highly subjective in the short term.

However, over the long term, history may reveal the efficacy of partisan solutions through observable outcomes. For example, history has taught the lesson multiple times that partisan fervor for "free markets" and deregulation can lead to suboptimal outcomes for the community. The events and processes leading to the financial meltdown of 2008 hold striking similarities to those associated with the Great Depression. In both cases, the nation was led by partisan presidents favoring "free market" principles. Unregulated markets led to speculative investment by banks and financial firms. As these investments failed to pan out, business failures occurred with extraordinary frequency due to undercapitalization. There was a stock market collapse due to a loss of faith in the financial system. Credit froze with an ensuing reduction in investment, income, and employment. In both cases personal debt was high, with many unable to meet their financial obligations. Consumption declined sharply, to produce a macroeconomic decline. In the aftermath, government responded to move the financial system away from "free market" principles.

History tells us pretty definitively that "free markets" may not be optimal for the community in relation to banking and credit markets. History has also judged "free markets" to be suboptimal in other areas such as slavery, child labor, illegal drugs, drug safety, the environment, worker health and safety, automobile safety, consumer products, tobacco, discrimination, and prostitution. In all of these areas, unfettered markets benefit the few at a cost to the larger community. Thus, uncritical and unthinking partisan fervor for free markets seems inappropriate for modern presidents.

We can retrospectively judge partisan fervor for free markets as inappropriate. However, waiting for history to tell us whether partisan representation leads to suboptimal outcomes is itself suboptimal. So we should also ask whether certain aspects of partisan representation can result in suboptimal outcomes for the larger community. The answer to this question is clearly and unequivocally yes.

Representing community interests demands thoughtful deliberation, rational decision-making, and an abiding concern for the entire community. Partisan representation is not conducive to any of these features. Partisanship often tends to favor a subset of the community over the community at large. It is often grounded in ideological blindness and an incomplete analysis of data. Partisanship typically entails rigid and sightless adherence to a set of ideological principles. Strong partisans tend to adopt shortcuts, rather than clear reasoning, in determining their issue stances.

Shortcuts for Democrats tend to favor producing *equal results* within the community, such as through social welfare programs, or controlling and regulating markets to favor those disadvantaged by "free markets." Democratic shortcuts also tend to advantage those near the lower end of the economic ladder. There is generally a cost to the larger community from implementation of Democratic programs through higher taxes or imposed behavioral constraints.

For example, from the 1960s through the mid-1990s, Democrats clung stubbornly to a social welfare system that favored their poor constituents over the middle and upper classes. People who opposed Aid to Families with Dependent Children (AFDC) or food stamps were often demonized by Democrats as either racist or conservative ideologues. Yet, through time, it became increasingly obvious that the U.S. welfare system was not working either for the people on welfare or for the community at large.

The AFDC and Food Stamp programs fostered dependence and long-term helplessness among many recipients (Bane and Ellwood 1986; Blank 1991; Stevens 1994). These programs inhibited the development of children and fostered an inter-generational cycle of poverty (Antel 1992; Gottschalk 1990; Plant 1984). The AFDC program produced disincentives to work. Having fewer people working reduced the nation's productive capacity and drained resources. Welfare recipient behavior also produced anger among many citizens, who observed recipients in grocery store checkout lines buying alcohol, cigarettes, or other nonessential items. Therefore, these highly partisan programs, although supported with ideological fervor, were ultimately deemed not to be in the community's best interests. They were replaced in 1996 with Temporary Assistance for Needy Families, which encouraged recipients to work and diminished their long-term dependence on government assistance.

In contrast, Republicans often adopt ideological shortcuts promoting *equal treatment* within the community, such as advocating that all people retain an equal proportion of their incomes or reliance on "free" and unregulated markets. Republican shortcuts clearly favor those at the top of the economic ladder and promote an increasingly unequal distribution of wealth. The Republican preference for "free markets" also enables exploitation of those within the community who are disadvantaged by markets. All participants are free to compete equally, but in a system that is biased against success for some competitors. Thus, Republican shortcuts also promote partial interests at an expense to other parts of the community.

Like Democrats, Republicans have also clung stubbornly to ideas favoring the few over the broader community. Perhaps the most prominent example is their advocacy of tax cuts grounded in supply-side economics. Supply-side tax cuts operate under the principle that if we favor the wealthy through lower taxes, then the wealthy will save and invest their surplus to produce higher employment and benefits to the community. Ideological belief in this principle motivated the three largest tax cuts in U.S. history under Republican administrations: the 1981 Reagan tax cut and the 2001 and 2003 Bush tax cuts. Yet there was and is no convincing empirical evidence that tax cuts for the wealthy stimulate investment, employment, or economic growth or benefit the larger community. In fact, the empirical evidence runs contrary to the supply-side hypothesis. Controlling for other relevant factors, there was no statistically significant increase in savings, investment, employment, or economic growth following any of these tax cuts (Ettlinger and Irons 2008; Krugman 1995). There was, however, increased income inequality that can be attributed to supply-side economics (e.g., see Bartels 2008, Chapters 2 and 6). Thus, partisan decision-making resulted in outcomes favoring the few, which were suboptimal for the larger community.

In evaluating the desirability of noncentrist, partisan presidential representation, we should also recognize the admonitions of the intellectuals who founded our republic. The architects of our constitution recognized early on that partisan representation *by definition* favors the interests of the few over the broader interests of the community. This is why they were so opposed originally to a party-based democracy. Madison detailed the evils of faction in Federalist 10, but expressed skepticism that it could be avoided. He said,

> The latent causes of faction are thus sown in the nature of man; and
> we see them everywhere brought into different degrees of activity,

according to the different circumstances of civil society. A zeal for different opinions concerning religion, concerning government, and many other points. . . . But the most common and durable source of factions has been the various and unequal distribution of property. Those who hold and those who are without property have ever formed distinct interests in society. . . . A landed interest, a manufacturing interest, a mercantile interest, a moneyed interest, with many lesser interests, grow up of necessity in civilized nations, and divide them into different classes, actuated by different sentiments and views.

Washington, Madison, and other founders wanted to avoid government by faction through their original constitutional design. Regarding the presidency, they designed the selection process so that representatives of the community at large would occupy the office. Nevertheless, they anticipated that not all presidents would be nonpartisan centrists, and that those who were would not always be able to rein in the perceived evils of faction. As expressed by Madison in Federalist 10,

It is in vain to say that enlightened statesmen will be able to adjust these clashing interests, and render them all subservient to the public good. Enlightened statesmen will not always be at the helm. Nor, in many cases, can such an adjustment be made at all without taking into view indirect and remote considerations, which will rarely prevail over the immediate interest which one party may find in disregarding the rights of another or the good of the whole. . . . The inference to which we are brought is, that the *causes* of faction cannot be removed, and that relief is only to be sought in the means of controlling its *effects*.

The initial design of the presidency was intended to control the effects of faction. The founders wanted the presidency to be occupied by "statesmen," not partisans. The original constitution contained no provision for partisan presidential elections. The expectation was that men of good faith would come forward to represent the community at large.

However, the founders' effort to establish a "statesman" presidency was in vain, because partisanship developed quickly in the early American democracy. The Washington administration was the only true "statesman" presidency. Late in the Washington administration, the seeds of partisanship emerged during the Jay Treaty crisis, as supporters and detractors of the treaty divided themselves along Federalist and Democratic-Republican lines. Partisanship continued during the Adams administration, as the presidency and vice-presidency were occupied by representatives loyal to the competing parties. Finally, after the election debacle of 1800, the Twelfth Amendment was ratified, which enabled partisan presidential elections. The presidency has been a partisan institution since the election of 1804.

Although undesirable, partisan presidential representation seems inevitable under a constitutional system that selects presidents through partisan elections. Nevertheless, as suggested by Madison, we should attempt "controlling its *effects*." If the faction represents a minority, Madison suggested that the control is periodic elections. If the faction represents a majority, then the control must lie elsewhere in the constitution, perhaps through separation of powers or judicial review. In either case, we should recognize the presidency for what it is, a partisan institution, rather than continuing to perpetuate the myth of presidential representation.

THE MYTH OF PRESIDENTIAL REPRESENTATION

The presidency is central to the functioning of American democracy. Yet our vision of the presidency has often been blurred by misinformation promulgated by presidents, the public, and social scientists alike. What is the myth of presidential representation? It is that presidents continue to function in the same representational mode as originally intended by the founders.

The founders' intentions for the presidency were well summarized in the Preface and introductory chapter through Washington's letter to the Selectmen of Boston on July 28, 1795. This view is worth repeating here.

In every act of my administration, I have sought the happiness of my fellow citizens. My system for the attainment of this object has uniformly been to overlook all personal, local, and partial considerations; to contemplate the United States as one great whole;

to confide that sudden impressions, when erroneous, would lead to candid reflection; and to consult only the substantial and permanent interests of our country. (Fitzpatrick 1931)

Yet modern presidents do not uniformly "consider the happiness" of their fellow citizens "in every act" of their administrations. They do not overlook "all personal, local, and partial considerations." They do not typically "contemplate the United States as one great whole." They do not "consult only the substantial and permanent interests" of their country. Instead, they consistently promulgate policies directed at increasing the happiness of their fellow partisans. As partisans, presidents do not generally respond to the mass public, and they also fail to persuade the mass public toward their own positions. Modern presidents also tend to focus on short-term rewards, such as reelection, rather than long-term interests of the nation.

Indeed, one is led to question whether modern presidents and presidential candidates even understand what it means to be "enlightened statesmen" in the sense intended by Madison in Federalist 10. Rhetorically, they consistently claim to put the nation or "Country First!" At the same time, they consistently pursue policies directed at supporting the interests of the few, rather than the community as a whole. Thus, as noted in the introductory chapter, presidents and presidential candidates are some of the most prominent promulgators of the myth of presidential representation.

Presidents are not alone, however, in promulgating the myth. As noted in the introductory chapter, the founders' vision of presidential representation is also spread through our educational system. Citizens learn from elementary school through college that presidents are the only elected U.S. officials with a single constituency, the entire nation. The notion that presidents are centrist representatives permeates textbooks on American government and the presidency. Citizens are taught by our educational system and the media that presidents should and do represent the mass public. Indeed, belief in the founders' model of presidential representation pervades American political culture. Interestingly, however, citizens often react negatively to evidence of presidential pandering. Amidst this intellectual confusion, citizens continue to elect and reelect presidents who turn out to be partisans.

Perhaps the most egregious promulgators of the myth of presidential representation are scholars of the American presidency. The prevailing paradigm among many scholars has been that presidents are
rational actors who cater to the median voter (either conditionally
or unconditionally) to maximize their political support. According
to centrist theory, policies favoring the broad electorate should elicit
greater political support, and in order to achieve particular policies
they must have sufficient political support. As self-interested politicians, presidents also desire the public's approval of their policies and
job performance, and the resulting advantages for themselves and
their political party. As a result, advocates of the centrist paradigm
have argued that presidents do not stray too far from community
preferences.

Of course, the evidence in this book shows that the centrist paradigm
is wrong. The centrist paradigm is rooted in the assumption of a unimodal distribution of citizen preferences. This assumption would be
correct if the presidency still reflected the founders' original design.
However, the Twelfth Amendment created a partisan presidential election system. Under the winner-take-all system that has existed since
1804, citizen preferences are forced into a bimodal distribution. As
demonstrated in Chapters 2 through 6 of this book, the partisan
model, which assumes a bimodal distribution of citizen preferences,
is a more appropriate model for understanding presidential representation.

Washington, Madison, and other framers established the normative
standard for presidential representation. Consistent with their normative standard, our first president was a "statesman," elected through
a nonpartisan system, who attempted to diminish the effects of partisanship on government policies. However, the ensuing reality of presidential representation was established through the Twelfth Amendment. With this change, the presidency became a partisan institution,
because the system for electing presidents is partisan. Thus, the origins
of the myth of presidential representation lie in this often overlooked
modification to our system, which dramatically altered the framers'
intentions.

Of course, few would doubt that the framers' ideal for presidential representation is more desirable than the partisan presidency

we have today. A presidency that really does put the nation first for an entire presidency seems far more appropriate than a presidency that only claims to put the nation first, but actually serves partisan ends and only occasionally exhibits centrist or "statesman" tendencies.

Given our partisan electoral system, how might we move closer to the founders' ideal? As suggested by Madison, partisanship is inevitable, so we must somehow find ways of "controlling its *effects*." One way of enhancing such control is producing a stronger normative expectation that presidents be "statesmen," rather than partisans. The system should reward presidents who seemingly represent the community at large, and punish those who exhibit excessive partisanship.

As shown in Chapters 5 and 6, this already occurs to some extent through citizen responses to partisan efforts at persuasion and changing public approval. Citizens react negatively to partisan presidents and more sympathetically to presidents who exhibit less partisanship. However, producing better presidential representation of the community requires that we enhance this thermostatic reaction by enabling citizens to better forecast when presidents will be "statesmen" versus partisans. Forecasting such attributes beforehand should make possible electing better presidents, rather than punishing undesirable attributes after the fact.

Accomplishing better citizen forecasts requires a public and media better informed on the nature of modern presidential representation. An electorate that understands the natural and overriding tendency of presidents to be partisans can make presidential candidates and presidents more accountable. Citizens and the media need to be able to look past candidate rhetoric positing representation of the nation at large to expose policy stances that actually benefit the few at the expense of the many.

Scholars of the presidency have a special obligation to contribute toward producing the norm of a "statesman" president by reducing confusion about the actual nature of presidential representation. Future scholarly research should be guided by sound theoretical models, rather than the most convenient models. This book is intended to initiate this effort. However, the effort to better understand presidential representation also requires participation by the entire scholarly community. Thus, future research should continue the process of better understanding the nature of presidential representation. Such understanding will enhance scientific knowledge of the presidency, as well as enabling citizens to achieve presidential representation more consistent with the normative model embodied in the original constitution.

References

Akaike, Hirotogu. 1973. "Information Theory and the Extension of the Maximum Likelihood Principle." Paper read at the Second International Symposium on Information Theory, Budapest.

Aldrich, John. 1983. "A Downsian Spatial Model with Party Activism." *American Political Science Review*. Vol. 77 (No. 4): 974–90.

Angle, Paul M. 1991. *The Complete Lincoln–Douglas Debates of 1858*. Chicago: University of Chicago Press.

Antel, John J. 1992. "The Intergenerational Transfer of Welfare Dependency: Some Statistical Evidence." *Review of Economics and Statistics*. Vol. 74, No. 2: 467–73.

Austin-Smith, David, and Jeffrey Banks. 1988. "Elections, Coalitions, and Legislative Outcomes." *American Political Science Review*. Vol. 82 (No. 2: 405–22.

Bailey, Michael A. 2007. "Comparable Preference Estimates across Time and Institutions for the Court, Congress, and Presidency." *American Journal of Political Science*. Vol. 51, No. 3: 433–38.

Bane, Mary Jo, and David Ellwood. 1986. "Slipping into and out of Poverty." *Journal of Human Resources*. Vol. 21, No. 1: 1986. 1–23.

Bannerjee, Anindya, Juan Dolado, John W. Galbraith, and David E. Hendry. 1993. *Integration, Error Correction, and the Econometric Analysis of Non-stationary Data*. Oxford, UK: Oxford University Press.

Bartels, Larry M. 2008. *Unequal Democracy: The Political Economy of the New Gilded Age*. Princeton, NJ: Princeton University Press and Russell Sage Foundation.

Beck, Nathaniel. 1991. "The Economy and Presidential Approval: An Information Theoretic Perspective." In H. Norpoth, M. S. Lewis-Beck, and J.-D. Lafay, eds., *Economics and Politics: The Calculus of Support*. Ann Arbor, MI: University of Michigan Press. 85–101.

Becker, Jo, Sheryl Gay Stolberg, and Stepen Labaton. 2008. "White House Philosophy Stoked Mortgage Bonfire." *New York Times*, November 21. NYTimes.com. No page range. Electronic version.

Beschloss, Michael. 2007. *Presidential Courage: Brave Leaders and How They Changed America 1789–1989*. New York: Simon and Schuster.

Blank, Rebecca. 1991. "Why Were Poverty Rates So High in the 1980s?" ed. National Bureau of Economic Research. Cambridge, MA: U.S. Government Printing Office.

Blumenthal, Sidney. 1982. *The Permanent Campaign*. New York: Simon & Schuster.

Bond, Jon R., and Richard Fleisher. 1990. *The President in the Legislative Arena*. Chicago: University of Chicago Press.

Bond, Jon R., Richard Fleisher, and B. Dan Wood. 2003. "The Marginal and Time-Varying Effect of Public Approval on Presidential Success in Congress." *Journal of Politics*. Vol. 65, No. 1: 92–110.

Bond, Jon R., and Kevin B. Smith. 2008. *The Promise and Performance of American Democracy*. 8th ed. New York: Thomson–Wadsworth.

Box-Steffensmeier, Janet M., Suzanna De Boef, and Tse-Min Lin. 2004. "The Dynamics of the Partisan Gender Gap." *American Political Science Review*. Vol. 98, No. 3: 515–28.

Box-Steffensmeier, Janet M., David C. Kimball, Scott R. Meinke, and Katherine Tate. 2003. "The Effects of Political Representation on the Electoral Advantages of House Incumbents." *Political Research Quarterly*. Vol. 56, No. 3: 259–70.

Brace, Paul, and Barbara Hinckley. 1992. *Follow the Leader: Opinion Polls and Modern Presidencies*. New York: Basic Books.

Breusch, T. S. 1979. "Testing for Autocorrelation in Dynamic Linear Models." *Australian Economic Papers*. Vol. 17, No. 2: 334–55.

Brody, Richard A. 1991. *Assessing the President: The Media, Elite Opinion, and Public Support*. Stanford, CA: Stanford University Press.

Brody, Richard A., and Benjamin I. Page. 1975. "The Impact of Events on Presidential Popularity: The Johnson and Nixon Administrations." In A. Wildavsky, ed., *Perspectives on the Presidency*. Boston: Little, Brown. 136–148.

Brody, Richard A., and Catherine Shapiro. 1989. "Policy Failure and Public Support: The Iran Contra Affair and Public Assessments of President Reagan." *Political Behavior*. Vol. 11, No. 4: 353–69.

Brody, Richard A., and Lee Sigelman. 1983. "Presidential Popularity and Presidential Elections: An Update and Extension." *Public Opinion Quarterly*. Vol. 47 (No. 3): 325–28.

Bullion, John L. 2008. *Lyndon B. Johnson and the Transformation of American Politics,* ed. M. C. Carnes. New York: Pearson Longman.

Burns, James MacGregor, J. W. Peltason, and Thomas E. Cronin. 1990. *Government by the People*. Englewood Cliffs, NJ: Prentice Hall.

Bush, George W. 2000. "Why You Should Vote for *Me.*" *USA Today*, November 7.

Calmes, Jackie. 2008. "In Bailout Vote, a Leadership Breakdown." In *New York Times*, September 29.

Campbell, Angus, Philip Converse, Warren Miller, and Donald Stokes. 1960. *The American Voter.* New York: Wiley.

Canes-Wrone, Brandice. 2006. *Who Leads Whom? Presidents, Policy, and the Public.* Chicago: University of Chicago Press.

Canes-Wrone, Brandice, Michael C. Herron, and Kenneth W. Schotts. 2001. "Leadership and Pandering: A Theory of Executive Policymaking." *American Journal of Political Science.* Vol. 45 (July): 532–50.

Canes-Wrone, Brandice, and Kenneth W. Shotts. 2004. "The Conditional Nature of Presidential Responsiveness to Public Opinion." *American Journal of Political Science.* Vol. 48 (October): 690–706.

CBS News Polls. 2008. *Poll: U.S. Concerned but Split on Bailout: CBS News Survey Shows That Americans Fear Effects of Financial Crisis but Are Not Convinced Bailout Plan Is the Answer.* CBS News 2008. (Cited October 1 2008.)

Chappell, Henry W., and William R. Keech. 1985. "A New View of Political Accountability for Economic Performance." *American Political Science Review.* Vol. 79, No. 1: 10–27.

Clarke, Harold D., and Marianne C. Stewart. 1994. "Prospections, Retrospections, and Rationality: The 'Bankers' Model of Presidential Approval Reconsidered." *American Journal of Political Science.* Vol. 38, No. 4: 1104–23.

Cohen, J., and P. Cohen. 1983. *Applied Multiple Regression/Correlation Analysis for Behavioral Sciences.* Hillsdale, NJ: Lawrence Erlbaum Associates.

Cohen, Jeffrey E. 1995. "Presidential Rhetoric and the Public Agenda." *American Journal of Political Science.* Vol. 1 (February): 87–107.

Cohen, Jeffrey E. 1999. *Presidential Responsiveness and Public Policy-Making: The Public and the Policies That Presidents Choose.* Ann Arbor: University of Michigan Press.

Cohen, Jeffrey E., and David Nice. 2003. *The Presidency.* New York: McGraw-Hill.

Conference Board. 2001. *Business Cycle Indicators Handbook.* New York: The Conference Board.

Conover, Pamela Johnson, and Lee Sigelman. 1982. "Presidential Influence and Public Opinion: The Case of the Iranian Hostage Crisis." *Social Science Quarterly.* Vol. 63 (June): 249–64.

Cook, Timothy E., and Lyn Ragsdale. 2000. "The President and the Press: Negotiating News Worthiness at the White House." In M. Nelson, ed., *The Presidency and the Political System, 4th Edition.* Washington, DC: Congressional Quarterly Press. 297–331.

Cronin, Thomas E., and Michael A. Genovese. 2004. *Paradoxes of the American Presidency*. 2nd ed. New York: Oxford University Press.

Davidson, James E. H., David F. Hendry, Frank Srba, and Stephen Yeo. 1978. "Econometric Modeling of the Aggregate Time Series Relationship Between Consumer's Expenditure and Income in the United Kingdom." *The Economic Journal*. Vol. 88 (No. 3): 661–92.

Davis, O. A., and Melvin A. Hinich. 1966. "A Mathematical Model of Policy Formulation in a Democratic Society." In J. L. Bernd, ed., *Mathematical Applications in Political Science II*, ed. J. L. Bernd. Dallas, TX: Southern Methodist University Press. 175–208.

Davis, O. A., Melvin A. Hinich, and Peter Ordeshook. 1970. "An Expository Development of a Mathematical Model of the Electoral Process." *American Political Science Review*. Vol. 64 (No. 2): (426–448).

De Boef, Suzanna, and Luke Keele. 2008. "Taking Time Seriously." *American Journal of Political Science*. Vol. 52, No. 1: 184–200.

Delli Carpini, Michael X., and Scott Keeter. 1997. *What Americans Know about Politics*. New Haven, CT: Yale University Press.

DeRouen, Karl. 1995. "The Indirect Link: Politics, the Economy, and the Use of Force." *Journal of Conflict Resolution*. Vol. 39, No. 4: 671–95.

Dickey, David, and Wayne A. Fuller. 1979. "Distribution of the Estimates for Autoregressive Time Series with a Unit Root." *Journal of the American Statistical Association*. Vol. 74 (June): 427–31.

Downs, Anthony. 1957. *An Economic Theory of Democracy*. New York: Harper and Row.

Druckman, James N., and Justin W. Holmes. 2004. "Does Presidential Rhetoric Matter? Priming and Presidential Approval." *Presidential Studies Quarterly*. Vol. 34 (December): 755–78.

Durr, Robert H. 1993. "What Moves Policy Sentiment." *American Political Science Review*. Vol. 87 (March): 158–70.

Duverger, Maurice. 1951. *Les Partis Politique*. Paris: Librairie Armand Collin.

Edwards, George C. III. 1980. *Presidential Influence in Congress*. San Francisco: W. H. Freeman.

Edwards, George C. III. 1983. *The Public Presidency: The Pursuit of Popular Support*. New York: St. Martin's Press.

Edwards, George C. III. 1989. *At the Margins: Presidential Leadership of Congress*. New Haven, CT: Yale University Press.

Edwards, George C. III. 1997. "Aligning Tests with Theory: Presidential Approval as a Source of Influence in Congress." *Congress and the Presidency*. Vol. 24, No. 2: 113–30.

Edwards, George C. III. 2003. *On Deaf Ears: The Limits of the Bully Pulpit*. New Haven, CT: Yale University Press.

Edwards, George C. III. 2007. *Governing by Campaigning: The Politics of the Bush Presidency*. New York: Longman.

Edwards, George C. III, William Mitchell, and Reed Welch. 1995. "Explaining Presidential Approval: The Significance of Issue Salience." *American Journal of Political Science.* Vol. 39, No. 1: 108–34.

Edwards, George C. III, Martin P. Wattenberg, and Robert I. Lineberry. 2008. *Government in America: People, Politics, and Policy.* 13th ed. New York: Pearson–Longman.

Edwards, George C. III, and Steven J. Wayne. 2006. *Presidential Leadership: Politics and Policy Making.* 7th ed. Belmont, CA: Thompson/Wadsworth.

Edwards, George C. III, and B. Dan Wood. 1999. "Who Influences Whom? The President and the Public Agenda." *American Political Science Review.* Vol. 93, No. 2: 327–44.

Elkins, Stanley, and Eric McKitrick. 1993. *The Age of Federalism.* New York: Oxford University Press.

Ellis, Christopher, and James A. Stimson. 2007. "On Conservatism in America." Paper delivered at the annual meeting of the American Political Science Association. Chicago, IL.

Enelow, James M., and Melvin J. Hinich. 1981. "A New Approach to Voter Uncertainty in the Downsian Spatial Model." *American Journal of Political Science.* Vol. 25 (No. 3): 483–93.

Enelow, James M., and Melvin J. Hinich. 1982. "Ideology, Issues, and the Spatial Theory of Elections." *American Political Science Review.* Vol. 76 (No. 3): 493–501.

Enelow, James M., and Melvin J. Hinich. 1984. *The Spatial Theory of Voting: An Introduction.* New York: Cambridge University Press.

Engle, Robert F. III, and Clive W. J. Granger. 1987. "Co-integration and Error Correction: Representation, Estimation, and Testing." *Econometrica.* Vol. 55 (March): 251–76.

Erikson, Robert S., Michael B. MacKuen, and James A. Stimson. 2002. *The Macro Polity.* Boston: Cambridge University Press.

Erikson, Robert S., and Christopher Wlezien. 2004. "The Fundamentals, the Polls, and the Presidential Vote." *PS: Political Science and Politics.* Vol. 37 (October): 747–51.

Ettlinger, Michael, and John Irons. 2008. "Take a Walk on the Supply Side: Tax Cuts on Profits, Savings, and the Wealthy Fail to Spur Economic Growth." Washington, DC: Economic Policy Institute.

Fenno, Richard F. 1973. *Congressmen in Committees.* Boston: Little, Brown.

Finbow, Robert. 1998. "Presidential Leadership or Structural Constraints? The Failure of President Carter's Health Care Proposals." *Presidential Studies Quarterly.* Vol. 28, No. 1: 169–88.

Fitzpatrick, John C., ed. 1931. *The Writings of George Washington from the Original Manuscript Sources, 1745–1799.* Vol. 34. Washington, DC: U.S. Government Printing Office.

Flemming, Roy B., and B. Dan Wood. 1997. "The Public and the Supreme Court: A Pooled Time Series Analysis of Individual Justice

Responsiveness to American Policy Moods." *American Journal of Political Science.* Vol. 41 (April): 468–98.

Fordham, Benjamin. 1998. "Partisanship, Macroeconomic Policy, and U.S. Uses of Force, 1949–1994." *Journal of Conflict Resolution.* Vol. 42, No. 4: 418–39.

Fox News. 2008. "Lawmakers Blame Partisanship for Failed House Bill." FoxNews.com, September 29.

Free, Lloyd A., and Hadley Cantril. 1967. *The Political Beliefs of Americans.* New Brunswick, NJ: Rutgers University Press.

Freeman, John R., Daniel Hauser, Paul Kellstedt, and John Williams. 1998. "Long-Memoried Processes, Unit Roots, and Causal Inference in Political Science." *American Journal of Political Science.* Vol. 42, No. 4: 1289–1327.

Freeman, John R., John T. Williams, and Tse-min Lin. 1989. "Vector Autoregression and the Study of Politics." *American Journal of Political Science.* Vol. 33 (November): 842–77.

Gergen, David. 2000. *Eyewitness to Power: The Essence of Leadership.* New York: Simon & Schuster.

Godfrey, L.G. 1978. "Testing Against the General Autoregressive and Moving Average Error Models when the Regressors include Lagged Dependent Variables." *Econometrica.* Vol. 46 (No. 4): 1293–1302.

Gottschalk, Peter. 1990. "AFDC Participation across Generations." *American Economic Review.* Vol. 80, No. 2: 367–71.

Granger, Clive W. J. 1969. "Investigating Causal Relations by Econometric Models and Cross-Spectral Models." *Econometrica.* Vol. 37 (July): 424–38.

Granger, Clive W. J., and Paul Newbold. 1974. "Spurious Regressions in Econometrics." *Journal of Econometrics.* Vol. 2, No. 2: 111–20.

Greenstein, Fred I. 2004. *The Presidential Difference: Leadership Style from FDR to George W. Bush.* 2nd ed. Princeton, NJ: Princeton University Press.

Groseclose, Tim, Steven D. Levitt, and James M. Snyder Jr. 1999. "Comparing Interest Group Scores across Time and Chambers: Adjusted ADA Scores for the U.S. Congress." *American Political Science Review.* Vol. 93, No. 1: 33–50.

Grossman, Michael B., and Martha J. Kumar. 1981. *Portraying the President.* Baltimore: Johns Hopkins University Press.

Grossman, Michael B., and Martha Joynt Kumar. 1979. "The White House and the News Media: The Phases of Their Relationship." *Political Science Quarterly.* Vol. 94, No. 1: 37–53.

Hart, Roderick P. 1989. *The Sound of Leadership: Presidential Communication in the Modern Age.* Chicago: University of Chicago Press.

Healey, Joseph F. 2008. *Statistics: A Tool for Social Research.* 8th ed. New York: Wadsworth.

Heclo, Hugh. 2000. "Campaigning and Governing: A Conspectus." In N. Ornstein and T. Mann, eds., *The Permanent Campaign and Its Future*, ed. N. Ornstein and T. Mann. Washington, D.C.: American Enterprise Institute and The Brookings Institution. 1–37.

Hetherington, Marc J. 1996. "The Media's Role in Forming Voters' National Economic Evaluations in 1992." *American Journal of Political Science*. Vol. 40 (May): 372–95.

Hibbs, Douglas A. Jr. 1974. "Problems of Statistical Estimation and Causal Inference in Time Series Regression Models." In H. L. Costner, ed., *Sociological Methodology, 1973–74*. San Francisco: Jossey–Bass. 252–308.

Hibbs, Douglas A. Jr. 1987. *The American Political Economy: Macroeconomics and Electoral Politics*. Cambridge, MA: Harvard University Press.

Hicks, Alexander. 1984. "Elections, Keynes, Bureaucracy, and Class: Explaining United States Budget Deficits, 1961–1978." *American Sociological Review*. Vol. 49 (April): 165–82.

Hill, Kim Quaile. 1998. "The Policy Agendas of the President and the Mass Public: A Research Validation and Extension." *American Journal of Political Science*. Vol. 42 (October): 1328–34.

Hill, Kim Quaile, and Patricia A. Hurley. 1999. "Dyadic Representation Reappraised." *American Journal of Political Science*. Vol. 43, No. 1: 109–37.

Hinckley, Barbara. 1990. *The Symbolic Presidency: How Presidents Portray Themselves*. New York: Routledge.

Holbrook, Thomas M. 2004. "Good News for Bush? Economic News, Personal Finances, and the 2004 Election." *PS: Political Science and Politics*. Vol. 37 (October): 759–61.

Jackson, John E. 1974. *Constituencies and Leaders in Congress*. Cambridge, MA: Harvard University Press.

Jacobs, Lawrence R., and Robert Y. Shapiro. 2000. *Politicians Don't Pander*. Chicago: University of Chicago Press.

Jacobson, Gary C. 2007. *A Divider, Not a Uniter: George W. Bush and the American People*. New York: Pearson Longman.

James, Patrick, and James Oneal. 1991. "The Influence of Domestic and International Politics on the President's Use of Force." *Journal of Conflict Resolution*. Vol. 35, No. 2: 307–32.

Jones, Charles O. 2000. "Preparing to Govern in 2001: Lessons from the Clinton Presidency." In N. Ornstein and T. Mann, eds., *The Permanent Campaign and Its Future*. Washington, DC: American Enterprise Press and The Brookings Institution. 185–218.

Kenski, Henry C. 1977. "The Impact of Economic Conditions on Presidential Popularity." *Journal of Politics*. Vol. 39 (August): 764–73.

Kernell, Samuel J. 1978. "Explaining Presidential Popularity: How Ad Hoc Theorizing, Misplaced Emphasis, and Insufficient Care in Measuring One's Variables Refuted Common Sense and Led Conventional

Wisdom down the Path of Anomalies." *American Political Science Review.* Vol. 72 (June): 506–22.

Kernell, Samuel J. 1984. "The Presidency and the People: The Modern Paradox." In M. Nelson, ed., *The Presidency and the Political System.* Washington, DC: Congressional Quarterly Press.

Kernell, Samuel J. 1997. *Going Public: New Strategies of Presidential Leadership, Third Edition.* Washington, DC: Congressional Quarterly Press.

Key, V. O. 1968. *The Responsible Electorate: Rationality in Presidential Voting 1936–1960.* New York: Vintage Books.

Kiewiet, D. Roderick, and Mathew D. McCubbins. 1988. "Presidential Influence on Congressional Appropriations Decisions." *American Journal of Political Science.* Vol. 32, No. 3: 713–36.

Kingdon, John W. 1989. *Congressmen's Voting Decisions.* 3rd ed. Ann Arbor, MI: University of Michigan Press.

Koch, Doro Bush. 2008. "Interview Excerpts of President Bush and the First Lady." ed. T. N. O. H. I. StoryCorps. Washington, DC: White House, Office of the Press Secretary.

Koenig, Lewis W. 1996. *The Chief Executive.* 6th ed. New York: Harcourt Brace.

Kolman, Bernard, and David R. Hill. 1996. *Introductory Linear Algebra with Applications.* New York: Prentice–Hall.

Krause, George. 2000. "Partisan and Ideological Sources of Fiscal Deficits in the United States." *American Journal of Political Science.* Vol. 44, No. 3: 541–59.

Krugman, Paul. 1995. *Peddling Prosperity.* New York: Norton.

Kumar, Martha J. 2007. *Managing the President's Message: The White House Communications Operation.* Baltimore, MD: Johns Hopkins University Press.

Kwiatkowski, D., Peter Phillips, Peter Schmidt, and Y. Shin. 1992. "Testing the Null Hypothesis of Stationarity against the Alternative of a Unit Root." *Journal of Econometrics.* Vol. 54 (Nos. 1–3): 159–78.

Lewis-Beck, Michael S., and Tom W. Rice. 1992. *Forecasting Elections.* Washington, DC: Congressional Quarterly Press.

Lewis-Beck, Michael S., and Charles Tien. 2004. "Jobs and the Job of the President: A Forecast for 2004." *PS: Political Science and Politics.* Vol. 37 (October): 753–58.

Lipscomb, Andrew Adgate, and Albert Ellery Bergh, eds. 1904a. *The Writings of Thomas Jefferson.* Vol. 7. Washington, DC: Thomas Jefferson Memorial Association.

Lipscomb, Andrew Adgate, and Albert Ellery Bergh, eds. 1904b. *The Writings of Thomas Jefferson.* Vol. 13. Washington, DC: Thomas Jefferson Memorial Association.

Lowi, Theodore J. 1985. *The Personal President.* Ithaca, NY: Cornell University Press.

Lutkepohl, Helmut. 1993. *Introduction to Multiple Time Series Analysis.* Berlin: Springer-Verlag.

MacKuen, Michael B. 1983. "Political Drama, Economic Conditions, and the Dynamics of Presidential Popularity." *American Journal of Political Science.* Vol. 27, No. 2: 165–92.

MacKuen, Michael B., Robert S. Erikson, and James A. Stimson. 1992. "Peasants or Bankers? The American Electorate and the U.S. Economy." *American Political Science Review.* Vol. 86, No. 3: 597–611.

Mansbridge, Jane. 2003. "Rethinking Representation." *American Political Science Review.* Vol. 97, No. 4: 515–28.

Manza, Jeff, and Fay Lomax Cook. 2002. "The Impact of Public Opinion on Public Policy: The State of the Debate." In J. Manza, F. L. Cook, and B. I. Page, eds., *Navigating Public Opinion: Polls, Policy, and the Future of American Democracy.* Oxford, UK: Oxford University Press. 17–32.

Matthews, Donald R., and James A. Stimson. 1975. *Yeas and Nays: Normal Decision Making in the U.S. House of Representatives.* New York: Wiley.

Mayhew, David R. 1974. *Congress: The Electoral Connection.* New Haven, CT: Yale University Press.

McCarty, Nolan M., and Keith T. Poole. 1995. "Veto Power and Legislation: An Empirical Analysis of Executive and Legislative Bargaining from 1961 to 1986." *Journal of Law, Economics, and Organization.* Vol. 11, No. 2: 282–312.

Meernik, James, and Michael Ault. 2001. "Public Opinion and Support for U.S. President's Foreign Policies." *American Politics Research.* Vol. 29, No. 4: 352–73.

Miller, Warren E., and Donald E. Stokes. 1963. "Constitutency Influence in Congress." *American Political Science Review.* Vol. 57: 45–56.

Mondak, Jeffrey. 1993. "Source Cues and Policy Approval: The Cognitive Dynamics of Public Support for the Reagan Agenda." *American Journal of Political Science.* Vol. 37, No. 1: 186–212.

Monroe, Kristen R. 1978. "Economic Influences on Presidential Popularity." *Public Opinion Quarterly.* Vol. 42 (Autumn): 360–69.

Monroe, Kristen R. 1979. "Inflation and Presidential Popularity." *Presidential Studies Quarterly.* Vol. 9 (Summer): 334–40.

Mueller, John. 1970. "Presidential Popularity from Truman to Johnson." *American Political Science Review.* Vol. 65, No. 1: 18–34.

Mueller, John. 1973. *War, Presidents, and Public Opinion.* New York: Wiley.

Neustadt, Richard E. 1960. *Presidential Power and the Modern Presidents: The Politics of Leadership.* New York: Free Press.

Newey, W. K., and K. D. West. 1987. "A Simple Positive Semi-Definite, Heteroscedasticity and Autocorrelation Consistent Covariance Matrix." *Econometrica.* Vol. 55, No. 3: 703–8.

Norpoth, Helmut. 1996. "Presidents and the Prospective Voter." *Journal of Politics.* Vol. 58, No. 3: 776–92.

O'Connor, Karen, and Larry J. Sabato. 1993. *American Government: Roots and Reform.* New York: Macmillan. O'Connor

Obama, Barack. 2004. *The Audacity of Hope.* American Rhetoric Online Speech Bank. http://www.americanrhetoric.com/speeches/convention2004/barackobama2004dnc.htm.

Oberg, Barbara B., ed. 2006. *The Papers of Thomas Jefferson.* Vol. 33. Princeton, NJ: Princeton University Press.

Ornstein, Norman, and Thomas Mann, eds. 2000. *The Permanent Campaign and Its Future.* Washington, DC: American Enterprise Institute and the Brookings Institution.

Ostrom, Charles W., Jr., and Brian Job. 1986. "The President and the Political Use of Force." *American Political Science Review.* Vol. 80, No. 2: 541–66.

Ostrom, Charles W., Jr., and Dennis M. Simon. 1985. "Promise and Performance: A Dynamic Model of Presidential Popularity." *American Political Science Review.* Vol. 79, No. 2: 334–58.

Ostrom, Charles W., Jr., and Dennis M. Simon. 1989. "The Man in the Teflon Suit: The Environmental Connection, Political Drama, and Popular Support in the Reagan Presidency." *Public Opinion Quarterly.* Vol. 53, No. 3: 353–87.

Page, Benjamin I., and Robert Y. Shapiro. 1985. "Presidential Leadership through Public Opinion." In G. C. I. Edwards, S. A. Shull, and N. C. Thomas, eds., *The Presidency and Public Policy Making.* Pittsburgh, PA: University of Pittsburgh Press. 22–36.

Page, Benjamin I., and Robert Y. Shapiro. 1992. *The Rational Public: Fifty Years of Trends in American's Policy Preferences.* Chicago: University of Chicago Press.

Page, Benjamin I., Robert Y. Shapiro, and Glenn R. Dempsey. 1987. "What Moves Public Opinion?" *American Political Science Review.* Vol. 81, No. 1: 23–43.

Paicopolos, Ernie. 2008. "Fox News Poll: Americans Bail on the Bailout." In Fox Movietone News: Fox News. http://www.foxnews.com/story/0,2933,436041,00.html.

Patterson, Thomas E. 1990. *The American Democracy.* New York: McGraw Hill.

Pennock, J. Roland, and John Chapman, eds. 1968. *Representation.* New York: Atherton Press.

Peterson, Marc A. 1990. *Legislating Together: The White House and Capitol Hill from Eisenhower to Reagan.* Cambridge, MA: Harvard University Press.

Pew Research Center. 2008. "Economic Bailout: Public Remains Closely Divided Overall, but Partisan Support Shifts." Pew Research Center for the People and the Press. http://pewresearch.org/pubs/985/economic-bailout.

Phillips, P. C. B. 1995. "Fully Modified Least Squares and Vector Autoregression." *Econometrica.* Vol. 63, No. 5: 1023–78.

Phillips, Peter C. B. 1992. "Simultaneous Equation Bias in Level VAR Estimation." *Econometric Theory.* Vol. 8 (June): 307.

Pika, Joseph A., John Anthony Maltese, and Norman C. Thomas. 2006. *The Politics of the Presidency.* Revised 6th ed. Washington, DC: Congressional Quarterly Press.

Pious, Richard M. 1996. *The Presidency.* Boston: Allyn and Bacon.

Pitkin, Hanna Fenichel. 1967. *The Concept of Representation.* Los Angeles: University of California Press.

Plant, Mark. 1984. "An Empirical Analysis of Welfare Dependence." *American Economic Review.* Vol. 74, No. 3: 393–408.

Poole, Keith T. 1998. "Recovering a Basic Space from a Set of Issue Scales." *American Journal of Political Science.* Vol. 42 (July): 954–93.

Poole, Keith T., and Howard Rosenthal. 1991. "Patterns of Congressional Voting." *American Journal of Political Science.* Vol. 35, No. 1: 228–78.

Public Papers of the Presidents. 1981. Washington, DC: U.S. Government Printing Office.

Public Papers of the Presidents. 1996. Washington, DC: U.S. Government Printing Office.

Public Papers of the Presidents. 2000. Washington, DC: U.S. Government Printing Office.

Public Papers of the Presidents. 2004. Washington, DC: U.S. Government Printing Office.

Ragsdale, Lyn. 1984. "The Politics of Presidential Speechmaking, 1949–1980." *American Political Science Review.* Vol. 78, No. 4: 971–84.

Ragsdale, Lyn. 1987. "Presidential Speechmaking and the Public Audience: Individual Presidents and Group Attitudes." *Journal of Politics.* Vol. 49, No. 3: 704–36.

Richardson, J. D. 1907. "Compilation of Messages and Papers of the Presidents." Gutenberg Project. http:Gutenberg.us/PG/titl1.htm eBooks-No. 10893.

Riker, William H., and Peter Ordeshook. 1973. *An Introduction to Positive Political Theory.* Englewood Cliffs, NJ: Prentice–Hall.

Ritter, Kurt, and David Henry. 1992. *Ronald Reagan: The Great Communicator.* Greenwood, CT: Greenwood Press.

Rivers, Douglas, and Nancy Rose. 1985. "Passing the President's Program: Public Opinion and Presidential Influence in Congress." *American Journal of Political Science.* Vol. 29, No. 2: 183–96.

Roosevelt, Theodore. 1913. *The Autobiography of Theodore Roosevelt.* Centennial edition. New York: Scribner's.

Rosen, Corey M. 1973. "A Test of Presidential Leadership of Public Opinion: The Split Ballot Technique." *Polity.* Vol. 6, No. 2: 282–90.

Rozell, Mark J. 2003. "Presidential Image-Makers on the Limits of Spin Control." In J. E. Cohen and D. Nice, eds., *The Presidency: Classic and Contemporary Readings.* Boston: McGraw–Hill. 105–126.

Schwartz, Nancy. 1988. *The Blue Guitar: Political Representation and Community.* Chicago: University of Chicago Press.

Schwartz, Randal L., Erik Olson, and Tom Christiansen. 1997. *Learning Perl on Win32 Systems.* Cambridge, MA: O'Reilly.

Sharp, James Roger. 1993. *American Politics in the Early Republic.* New Haven, CT: Yale University Press.

Sigelman, Lee. 1979. "Presidential Popularity and Presidential Elections." *Public Opinion Quarterly.* Vol. 43: 532–34.

Sigelman, Lee. 1980a. "Gauging the Public Response to Presidential Leadership." *Presidential Studies Quarterly.* Vol. 10, No. 3: 427–33.

Sigelman, Lee. 1980b. "The Commander in Chief and the Public: Mass Response to Johnson's March 31, 1968 Bombing Halt Speech." *Journal of Political and Military Sociology* Vol. 8 (Spring):1–14.

Sigelman, Lee, and Carol K. Sigelman. 1981. "Presidential Leadership of Public Opinion: From 'Benevolent Leader' to 'Kiss of Death.'" *Experimental Study of Politics.* Vol. 7, No. 1: 1–22.

Silvestri, Vito N. 2000. *Becoming JFK: A Profile in Communication.* Westport, CT: Praeger.

Simon, Dennis M., and Charles W. Ostrom. 1985. "The President and Public Support: A Strategic Perspective." In I. George C. Edwards, S. A. Shull, and N. C. Thomas, eds., *The Presidency and Public Policy Making.* Pittsburgh, PA: University of Pittsburgh Press. 50–70.

Simon, Dennis M., and Charles W. Ostrom. 1989. "The Impact of Televised Speeches and Foreign Travel on Presidential Approval." *Public Opinion Quarterly.* Vol. 53, No. 1: 58–82.

Sims, Christopher A. 1980. "Macroeconomics and Reality." *Econometrica.* Vol. 48 (January): 1–48.

Sims, Christopher A., and T. Zha. 1999. "Error Bands for Impulse Responses." *Econometrica.* Vol. 67, No. 5: 1113–56.

Stevens, Ann Huff. 1994. "The Dynamics of Poverty Spells: Updating Bane and Ellwood." *American Economic Review.* Vol. 84, No. 2: 34–37.

Stimson, James A. 1976. "Public Support for American Presidents: A Cyclical Model." *Public Opinion Quarterly.* Vol. 40 (Spring): 1–21.

Stimson, James A. 1976–77. "On Disillusionment with the Expectations/Disillusion Theory: A Rejoinder." *Public Opinion Quarterly.* Vol. 40 (Winter): 541–43.

Stimson, James A. 1991. *Public Opinion in America: Moods, Cycles, and Swings.* Boulder, CO: Westview Press.

Stimson, James A. 1999. *Public Opinion in America: Moods, Cycles, and Swings.* 2nd ed. Boulder, CO: Westview Press.

Stimson, James A. 2004. *Tides of Consent: How Public Opinion Shapes American Politics.* New York: Cambridge University Press.

Stimson, James A., Michael B. MacKuen, and Robert S. Erikson. 1995. "Dynamic Representation." *American Political Science Review.* Vol. 89 (September): 543–65.

Tenpas, Katherine Dunn. 2000. "The American Presidency: Surviving and Thriving amidst the Permanent Campaign." In N. Ornstein and T. Mann, eds., *The Permanent Campaign and Its Future.* Washington, DC: American Enterprise Institute Press and The Brookings Institution. 108–133.

Thomas, Dan B., and Lee Sigelman. 1985. "Presidential Identification and Policy Leadership: Experimental Evidence in the Reagan Case." In I. George C. Edwards, S. A. Shull, and N. C. Thomas, eds., *The Presidency and Public Policy Making.* Pittsburgh, PA: University of Pittsburgh Press. 37–49.

Tulis, Jeffrey. 1987. *The Rhetorical Presidency.* Princeton, NJ: Princeton University Press.

U.S. Treasury Department, ed.. 2008. "Statement by Secretary Henry M. Paulson, Jr. on Actions to Protect U.S. Economy." Washington, DC: U.S. Government Printing Office.

Waterman, Richard W, Hank C. Jenkins-Smith, and Carol L. Silva. 1999. "The Expectations Gap Thesis: Public Attitudes toward an Incumbent President." *Journal of Politics.* Vol. 61, No. 4: 944–66.

Wayne, Stephen J. 1982. "Great Expectations: What People Want from Presidents." In T. E. Cronin, ed., *Rethinking the Presidency.* Boston: Little, Brown. 185–199.

Weekly Compilation of Presidential Documents. 2008. Washington, DC: U.S. Government Printing Office.

Western Standard Publishing Company. 2000. *American Reference Library* [CD-Rom]. Western Standard Publishing Company 2000. Available from http://www.OriginalSources.com. Many dates required multiple accesses over many months.

White, Halbert. 1980. "A Heteroskedasticity-Consistent Covariance Matrix Estimator and a Direct Test for Heteroskedasticity." *Econometrica.* Vol. 48, No. 4: 817–30.

Wildavsky, Aaron. 1966. "The Two Presidencies." *Trans-Action.* Vol. 4 (December): 7–14.

Wildavsky, Aaron. 1984. *The Politics of the Budgetary Process.* 4th ed. Boston: Little, Brown.

Wilson, Woodrow. 1908. *Constitutional Government in the United States.* New York: Columbia University Press.

Wittman, Donald. 1983. "Candidate Motivation: A Synthesis of Alternatives." *American Political Science Review.* Vol. 77 (No. 1): 142–57.

Wlezien, Christopher. 1995. "The Public as a Thermostat: Dynamics of Preferences for Spending." *American Journal of Political Science.* Vol. 39, No. 4: 981–1000.

Wlezien, Christopher. 1996. "Dynamics of Representation: The Case of U.S. Spending on Defense." *British Journal of Political Science.* Vol. 26, No. 1: 81–103.

Wood, B. Dan. 2000. "Weak Theories and Parameter Instability: Using Flexible Least Squares to Take Time-Varying Relationships Seriously." *American Journal of Political Science.* Vol. 44, No. 3: 603–18.

Wood, B. Dan. 2007. *The Politics of Economic Leadership.* Princeton, NJ: Princeton University Press.

Wood, B. Dan, and Angela Hinton Andersson. 1998. "The Dynamics of Senatorial Representation." *Journal of Politics.* Vol. 60, No. 3: 705–36.

Wood, B. Dan, and Stephen Huss. 2008. "Explaining Attention to Civil Rights Issues." Presented at the Southern Political Science Association Convention. New Orleans.

Wood, B. Dan, and Han Soo Lee. 2009. "Explaining Presidential Liberalism: Pandering, Partisanship, or Pragmatism." *Journal of Politics.* Forthcoming.

Wood, B. Dan, and Jeffrey S. Peake. 1998. "The Dynamics of Foreign Policy Agenda Setting." *American Political Science Review.* Vol. 92, No. 1: 173–84.

Zaller, John R. 1992. *The Nature and Origins of Mass Opinion.* Boston: Cambridge University Press.

Zaller, John R. 2003. "Coming to Grips with V.O. Key's Concept of Latent Opinion." In M. MacKuen and G. Rabinowitz, eds., *Electoral Democracy.* Ann Arbor, MI: University of Michigan Press. 311–336.

Zupan, Mark A. 1992. "Measuring the Ideological Preferences of U.S. Presidents: A Proposed (Extremely Simple) Method." *Public Choice.* Vol. 73, No. 2: 351–61.

Index

Note to index: An *f* after a page number denotes a figure on that page. An *n* following a page number denotes a note on that page. A *t* following a page number denotes a table on that page.